Migration and Ethnicity in Middle-Range Societies

Migration and Ethnicity in Middle-Range Societies

A View from the Southwest

Tammy Stone

THE UNIVERSITY OF UTAH PRESS

Salt Lake City

The Defiance House Man colophon is a registered trademark
of the University of Utah Press. It is based on a four-foot-tall
Ancient Puebloan pictograph (late PIII) near Glen Canyon, Utah.

19 18 17 16 15   1 2 3 4 5

Library of Congress Cataloging-in-Publication Data

Stone, Tammy, 1961-
  Migration and ethnicity in middle range societies : a view from the Southwest /
Tammy Stone.
     pages cm
  Includes bibliographical references and index.
  ISBN 978-1-60781-401-6 (hardback) -- ISBN 978-1-60781-402-3 (paper)
  1. Paleo-Indians--Southwest, New--Migrations. 2. Point of Pines Site (Ariz.)
3. Ancestral Pueblo culture. 4. Mogollon culture. 5. Archaeology--Southwest,
New. I. Title.
  E78.S7S84 2015
  979'.01--dc23

                                                          2014043445

Printed and bound by Sheridan Books, Inc., Ann Arbor, Michigan.

For Doc Haury, scholar and teacher

Contents

Figures

Tables

Acknowledgments

I've worked on the material from the Point of Pines Region for more than 10 years, and this volume is the culmination of that research. A project this big, lasting this long cannot be carried out to a successful end without the help of numerous people. First and foremost are the excavators who collected the data. Point of Pines Pueblo was excavated by the University of Arizona archaeological field school under the direction of Dr. Emil Haury from 1946 to 1960. Over 325 students, instructors, and staff participated in the field school during those 14 years (see Haury 1989 for a complete list).

The artifacts and field records from the field school are housed at the Arizona State Museum at the University of Arizona. Mike Jacobs has been of invaluable help when examining the artifacts from the survey and various excavated sites in the region. He has never failed to provide support and encouragement on the various publications coming from this research. This particular volume is based heavily on the archived field notes and room excavation forms from Point of Pines Pueblo itself. Alan Ferg aided me in collecting data from the archived field notes that allowed the architectural analysis to occur. Finally, Jannelle Weakly aided me in searching the archives for the field photographs that are included here.

For their unflagging support, encouragement, editorial comments, and excellent suggestions on the organization of this volume I wish to thank Rich Wilshusen and Susan Dublin. Additional editorial comments came from Barb Roth. Dr. Harriet Coussons patiently edited the manuscript before it went out for review. Thanks to her painstaking work, the end project is considerably more polished and readable. Thanks also go to Reba Rauch of the University of Utah Press, who patiently and enthusiastically guided me through the publication process, and Alexis Mills for the final copyediting. Finally, thanks to my husband, Carroll Reichen, who has had to listen to years of ruminations, conjectures, and analyses on migration and ethnic interaction in middle-range societies in general and Point of Pines Pueblo in particular.

CHAPTER 1

One Hundred Years of Discussion on Migration and Identity

A Global View

Over the last hundred years, interest among archaeologists in migration in prehistory in general and in middle-range societies in particular has seen many ups and downs. The reason for this variability in its popularity as a research question within the archaeological community is manyfold and is tied to broader shifts in paradigmatic stances in the field, as well as changes in the importance of contemporary migrations, immigration, and invasions in world, regional, and local politics (Adams et al. 1978; Cabana 2011; Chapman 1997; Chapman and Hamerow 1997; Härke 1998; Trigger 1989). Despite the considerable amount of ink spilled decrying past models that accompany the shifts in popularity of migration as an arena of archaeological exploration, the differing views have had more in common than their rhetoric implies until relatively recently. In large part, this commonality is due to considerable continuity in concepts and assumptions in two areas. The first is the formation of identity in general and ethnicity in particular, which are integrally tied to our understanding of the impact of migration on both migrant and host populations. Issues of identity have increasingly become the subject of intense theoretical examination. A seismic shift in the way archaeologists think about ethnicity has occurred recently as the fluid and dynamic nature of identity formation is increasingly studied through the interplay of agency and structure (Archer 2000; Giddens 1991). This shift in our understanding

of identity formation is only now being felt in the area of migration studies. The second relatively recent shift is a movement away from the view of material culture as solely a reflection of culture or behavior (sometimes several times removed) to a realization that material culture and the landscape are actively engaged in social interaction (Cobb 2005; Gamble 2007; Thomas 1996; Tilley 1994). This engagement results in a data set (architecture) that can be examined to understand migration and host-migrant interaction in a more nuanced and dynamic manner.

This book examines migration and host-migrant interaction with these new perspectives in mind and uses a detailed architectural analysis to better understand a particular case study in the American Southwest, the Point of Pines Pueblo located in the Mogollon Highlands of east-central Arizona. The presence of a migrant enclave at Point of Pines Pueblo was recognized more than half a century ago (Haury 1958). Unfortunately, a detailed examination of the pueblo was never conducted. This volume uses the field notes from the original excavation housed in the archives of the Arizona State Museum at the University of Arizona in a detailed study of migration and ethnic interaction from the perspective of both the Kayenta migrants and their Mogollon hosts at Point of Pines Pueblo. As such, this study facilitates our understanding not only of this particular community but of the larger issue of Kayenta migration in the American

TABLE 1.1. Underlying assumptions in schools of thought within ethnography and archaeology

Perspective 1 (includes processual perspectives)	Perspective 2 (includes post-processual perspectives)
Deduction	Induction
Evolutionary models	Historically based models
Generalizing (macro-scale) models	Particularizing (micro-scale) models
Concentration on commonalities between groups	Concentration on differences between groups
Concentration on long term change	Concentration on synchronic organization
Environmental emphasis	Ideological emphasis
Analogies based on organisms/systems	Analogies based on language/meaning

Note: cf. Service 1985:289; Tilley 1994:8.

Southwest. The importance of this study, however, extends far beyond the Southwest. As I demonstrate at the end of this chapter, migration occurred in middle-range societies throughout prehistory: it is a truly global phenomenon. The results of these migration events demonstrate considerable variability in host-migrant interaction due to differing initial conditions in terms of population density, community organization, and the asymmetrical power relations present in both the host and migrant populations. Added to this is the dynamic manner in which individuals and families within communities form alliances and competitive relationships. Because middle-range societies lack centralized decision making and institutionalized ranking in terms of status, each decision is an instance in which power relationships, status, and alliances are negotiated, challenged, and/or reified. The resulting communities are characterized by heterogeneous mosaics that must balance a variety of different interest groups rather than a homogenous integrated unit whose behavior can be predicted in a linear manner.

The processes of migration and identity formation are not the province of a single location or moment in time. Rather, they occur in middle-range societies throughout the world and have long histories of scholarly study. An understanding of this history of scholarly work and current theoretical views regarding identity and community are crucial for our understanding of any individual case.

Setting the Stage: Paradigmatic Shifts in Archaeology

Paradigmatic shifts in both ethnography and archaeology have long been subsumed within a broader tension of two sides of a basic question on the appropriate manner in which to conduct research in the social as well as natural and physical sciences. Specifically, this tension centers on the question of whether it is most appropriate to begin with the theory and hypothesis followed by data collection (deduction), or whether the collection of data should occur first, to be followed by the construction of theories to explain evident patterns (induction). The debate over the primacy of theory versus data in anthropology dates back to the 1800s and has resulted in two different categories of explanation of culture that can, at some level, still be seen today (Service 1985; Tilley 1994; Trigger 1989). In his landmark history of the first century (1860 to 1960) of theoretical debates in ethnography, Service (1985) characterized these two families of theoretical approaches based on enduring assumptions (cf. Trigger 1989). Tilley (1994) has more recently found similar differences within the debate in archaeology between processualists and post-processualists (see Table 1.1 for abstraction of both schemes). It is against this backdrop and historical context that much of the debate over migration has occurred for the last 100 years.

Within the shifts of dominance between these perspectives, the use of migration as an explanation for either the organization of a group or alterations in it at any one time also has seen changes in popularity. Interestingly, however, migration has been used by scholars in both perspectives and has found popularity in some areas of the world as an explanation of archaeological remains regardless of the theoretical perspective that is dominant at the time. For example, during the 1970s, Perspective 1, in the guise of "new" (processual) archaeology, dominated research in both North America and Europe. Although migration largely fell out of favor in the United States and England during this time, it remained an important and frequently invoked model in France, Germany, and Scandinavia (Chapman 1997; Härke 1998). Differences in the recent histories, particularly associated with World War II, and contemporary political issues regarding conquest, refugees, and migrant workers from former colonial holdings have been cited as a contributing factor for this variability. More recently, the role of ethnic/national identities in the breakup of the Soviet Union and Yugoslavia, as well as large-scale migration due to economic shifts in an increasingly globalized world, has led scholars throughout the world to examine issues of ethnicity and identity formation anew (Burmeister 2000; Härke 1998). This new interest in identity/ethnicity has led to a resurgence of interest in migration, and in particular the issue of culture contact and host-migrant interaction, for scholars from both perspectives. To understand the current views of both migration and identity/ethnicity and to create a model in which these issues can be studied, a historical context of migration models within archaeology is necessary.

Migration Models Proposed by Culture Historians

In the first half of the twentieth century, the culture history approach to archaeology dominated both North America and Europe (Trigger 1989). In North America, much of the early work was spurred by students of Franz Boas as both an attempt to collect information on indigenous peoples before they disappeared (including their histories) and to collect data within the histor-

ically based model (Perspective 2) of historical particularism as a reaction to the unilineal evolutionary models of the late 1800s. In Europe, Perspective 2 also dominated at this time with a concentration on understanding how different ethnic groups/nationalities came to be distributed in the way they were. Early on, this work was hindered by an absence of absolute dating methods. The result was a long period of concentration on the principles of stratigraphy and seriation, along with elaborate taxonomic schemes defining different artifact classes, as well as clusters of artifacts, house types, and site types that could be used as trait lists to define a block of time within a location (e.g., Ford 1938; McKern 1939; Willey and Phillips 1958). Based on trait lists and the phases and components they identified, basic historical sequences within regions were defined. Similarities in historical sequences within adjacent areas were used to characterize culture areas. Differences between areas were seen largely as the result of dissimilar historical trajectories within specific regions. The assumption of the direct link of the trait lists to culture allowed culture historians to make inferences regarding past societies based on artifacts that were believed to be a direct reflection of the activities of peoples in the past. In turn, cultures were seen as bounded, homogenous, and unchanging in nature (Bernardini 2011a; Cabana 2011; Chapman and Hamerow 1997; Cobb 2005). For example, Rouse (1986) linked archaeological remains to culture in the following way: "prehistoric archaeologists work primarily with cultural remains, that is, with artifacts and other kinds of materials deposited by human beings. Each deposit is termed an *assemblage*. The inhabitants of an area who have laid down similar assemblages may be said to comprise a culturally homogenous population or *people*" (30, emphasis in original).

Once the basic outline of the time-space systematics of an area had been defined, it became obvious that not only were there differences from one area to the next, but that changes occurred in the trait lists from one time period to the next within an area. Because the trait lists were seen as the archaeological manifestation of the group ethos (in which ethnicity, language, culture, and behavior were locked together), a change in any aspect of the trait list represented a change in what constituted the group and its culture (Adams et al. 1978; Anthony 1990; Bernardini 2011a; Burmeister 2000; Cabana 2011). Because cultures were seen as homogenous and fairly static, introduction of new traits had to originate outside the area and be introduced either through diffusion or migration. These processes could be distinguished based on the number of traits that differed from one time to the next: the intrusion of one or a small number of traits was termed a "trait-unit intrusion" and proposed to be the result of diffusion. Conversely, the change in a large number of traits was seen as evidence of a "site-unit intrusion" and represented the migration of a new group into the region (Rouse 1958; Willey et al. 1955).

Although not all culture historians assumed that the only source of new traits in an area was either diffusion or migration, the use of migration as an explanatory model for change reached its height at this time. Two major syntheses illustrate this point. In Europe, V. Gordon Childe (1950) used migration to explain most of the major changes that occurred in European prehistory from the rise of agriculture to metallurgy (see also Adams et al. 1978; Anthony 1990; Gamble 2007; Thomas 1996; Trigger 1989). Among the many volumes he wrote in his career, this focus was most obvious in *Prehistoric Migrations in Europe* (Childe 1950). A similar approach was used by Harold Gladwin (1957) in his synthesis of the American Southwest. Gladwin explained the introduction of agriculture and domestic architecture as well as brown and red polished ceramics as the result of a migration from the east coast of Mexico. He termed this "the Red migration," after the red polished ceramics he associated with these peoples. He proposed that migrants had penetrated the entire region, resulting in the change from foraging to horticulture, though the effects of this migration were differentially felt based on distance from the original homeland of the migrants:

when the Red migration was entering the Southwest [it] was already populated by Foragers, Cave Dwellers, Basket Makers, and Farmers, with density increasing from south to north. It is therefore obvious that as they moved north from the Mexican Border, the proportion of immigrants to the resident population varied in each village. In the south…the incoming Reds clearly outnumbered the resident Foragers, but as they worked their way up to the Plateau and began meeting more and more Basket Makers, their proportional representation declined, until by the time they finally reached the San Juan, it is rather surprising that there were enough of them left to leave any trace of their presence. (Gladwin 1957:95)

Gladwin proposed a second period of migration, this time from the north toward the south, to explain the appearance of painted black-on-white and polychrome pottery as well as changes in domestic architecture and burial patterns in about AD 1000 in the Tonto Basin of Arizona. The mixture of the local population and these northern migrants resulted in a new cultural group in the Southwest known as the Salado. Two hundred years later, Salado migrants moved out of the Tonto Basin to the south and east, where they overwhelmed the local populations, as was evident by the appearance of their polychrome ceramics: "there was enough of their typical pottery to be able to say that if this was the result of 'trade,' it was the Salado potters themselves, not the just their pots, that were traded" (Gladwin 1957:291).

In both the work of Childe and Gladwin the assumption is that the trait list (or assemblage, as Rouse put it), or in the case of Gladwin's Salado migration the pottery alone, equals the people. Beyond this generalizing assumption, migration was seen as an inductively based explanation for patterning in the archaeological remains of particular cultures rather than a cause of broader patterns in human history/prehistory. As a result, migration models were subject to criticisms from the proponents of Perspective 1 when it again rose in popularity in the 1960s and 1970s. The resurgence of scholars more aligned with Perspective 1, tied to processualism, resulted in fewer studies that evoked migration as an explanation for culture change with one notable exception: the work of Irving Rouse (1986). Rouse's monograph attempted not only to place migration within a generalizing theoretical framework but also to provide specific test implications that distinguished it from local innovation that could be investigated in the archaeological record. He then applied this model to four case studies. The lasting impact of Rouse's study, which is still widely cited even today, is probably twofold. The first is that he provided specific test implications that could be used as a starting point for rigorous empirical study of migration within a processual, deductive methodology when migration again rose in popularity as an explanatory model in the 1990s. The second factor is that his four case studies dealt with the migration of peoples into previously uninhabited locations (Polynesia, Japan, the Caribbean, and the northern Canadian border) so that the issues of ethnic interaction and changes in the artifact assemblage did not have to be discussed or explained beyond recognition of the need to adapt to new environmental constraints. For the most part, however, the rise of processualism as the dominant theoretical model in both North America and England during the 1960s and 1970s resulted in a dearth of migration studies.

Processualism and a Retreat from and Return to Migration

In 1978, Adams, Van Gerven, and Levy published "The Retreat from Migrationism," in which they systematically discount models of migration that had been proposed for a number of areas around the world by providing data showing indigenous development in each case. This study was interpreted by many as representing a rejection of migration as an explanatory model in archaeology, though the authors never explicitly called for this to occur. Rather, studies on migration dwindled in the archaeological record (with the notable exception of Rouse 1986) as the empha-

sis of study shifted away from understanding particular cultural trajectories and toward generalizing, causal models that could be used to explain human behavior on a more global scale (Adams et al. 1978; Cabana 2011; Chapman and Hamerow 1997; Trigger 1989). Models invoking migration as an explanation of culture change for specific cases (even in the case of Rouse 1986) fell short in this task because they tended to be descriptive of change rather than offering causal explanations for why the migrations occurred when they did and why they did not occur at other times. Lewis Binford, in a series of landmark articles that began in the early 1960s, argued that if archaeology was to contribute anything to the broader field of anthropology, it should concentrate on the area in which archaeologists, with their long time frames and global perspective, can contribute the most: understanding cultural evolution and the use of culture to mediate the interaction between humans and their environments (Binford 1962, 1965, 1968, 1972; see Clark 1952 for a similar argument in Europe). To accomplish this, we must understand that, contrary to the assumptions of culture historians, not all aspects of material culture are equally important. Binford argued that we should concentrate in particular on those aspects of material culture that articulate directly with the environment. In other words, culture is made up of several subsystems that change at different rates and that affect other aspects of the cultural system to varying degrees, with those articulating with the environment being the most important. By understanding these articulations, and how changes in these aspects of the cultural system occur, we will understand how cultures in general change. Cordell and Plog (1979) go one step further and argue that culture change results from internal innovations created as a reaction by the group to population/resource imbalances. These innovations may differ from culture group to culture group, and even between communities within the same region, thus resulting in the diversity we see within the archaeological record. Additionally, lack of change could be explained by a lack of local population/resource imbalances. In other words, cultures tend toward homeostasis with their environments and change only when they have to due to some external perturbation.

Despite rejection of migration by early processualists, there is in fact nothing that prohibits it from being examined as a causal model (Chapman and Hamerow 1997), specifically one that contributes to population/resource imbalances through an influx of additional people to an area. When viewed as a causal model rather than an ad hoc explanation, migration fits well within the processual mode. Increasing awareness of migration studies in geography and ethnography in the 1980s, combined with information from oral histories of indigenous peoples (Anthony 1990; Bernardini 2005, 2011a; Cobb 2005; Härke 1998; Naranjo 1995, 2008; Whiteley 2002) have made it abundantly clear that migration does occur; as a result, migration again became a focus of study in archaeology in the 1990s, this time from within the processual model. The focus, however, shifted from the culture historian's perspective of "migration explains the change in the material culture" to an examination of the reasons that migration occurred (i.e., the why). These causal explanations are generally classified under the heading of push-pull models (Anthony 1990; Burmeister 2000; Cabana 2011; Cameron 1995; Stone and Lipe 2011). These models fit well within the processual paradigm, even when dealing only with specific cases, because of the assumption of extensive information networks and economic rationality. More specifically, push-pull models are based on three assumptions. First, in keeping with the generalized acceptance of the principle of homeostasis, it is assumed that people will not leave their homeland unless there is a compelling reason to do so (the push), often stated in terms of population/resource imbalances. Second, it is assumed that individuals do not wander aimlessly across the landscape. Rather, they go to places that they know something about either due to trade connections or the firsthand knowledge of individuals who have moved to the new locations and returned (the pull). Third, individuals and families will make decisions about whether or

not to move based on the economic conditions of their homeland and the information they have on their destination in terms of the availability of resources that serve as a pull to these new locations. The weighing of the pushes of the homeland and pulls of the new locations are such that the move is more likely to occur when the pulls of the potential new home are more attractive than the existing homeland given the existence of pushes in terms of a cost-benefit ratio.

Along with the analysis of pushes and pulls for any given migration came the realization that the number of people who migrate can vary considerably from individual marriage partners or migrant workers, to families, to large segments of communities (Anthony 1990; Bernardini 2011a; Burmeister 2000; Stone 2003; Stone and Lipe 2011). The size of the group that migrates is dependent on several factors, including the amount of information present, the distance of the proposed migration, and the ease of movement from one area to the next.

Unfortunately, however, these new models concentrate heavily on the motivations of the migrants and largely ignore the impact on and reaction of the host communities. Why would a host community allow migrants to enter their area? Additionally, what is the nature of the interaction between the host and migrant communities? Increasing numbers of studies are demonstrating that the relationships between migrants and hosts are highly varied (Barth 2007; Beekman and Christensen 2003, 2011; Cobb 2005; Gamble 2007; Stone 2003; Stone and Lipe 2011; Thurston 2009), resulting in the maintenance of ethnic enclaves in some cases and complete assimilation in others. One of the reasons current migration studies have had difficulty dealing with the variability of interactions after migration, despite their ability to account for the variability prior to and during the event, is related to assumptions that have deep histories stretching back to the beliefs of the culture historians of almost 100 years ago. Specifically, until relatively recently, there has been insufficient appreciation of the highly fluid and varied nature of identity. This is accompanied by a view of ethnic groups as highly bounded and tied to tradition

(Bernardini 2011a; Cabana 2011; Cobb 2005). Further, there has been an implicit, largely unexamined assumption that material culture and modifications to the landscape *reflect* behavior rather than being actively *engaged* and *manipulated* as part of human interaction (Gamble 2007; Thomas 1996). These assumptions have hindered our ability to fully understand identity formation in general and ethnic interaction in particular, and thus the nature of host-migrant interactions and their influence on the variability of the outcome of migrations. The use of practice theory (Archer 2000; Giddens 1991) is beginning to challenge these assumptions and has resulted in greater appreciation of both the variability present in culture contact resulting from migration and the complexity of identity formation.

Models of Identity Based in Concepts of Agency and the Active Engagement of Material Culture

Increasingly, archaeologists who study small group interaction (including but not exclusively the interaction between migrants and host populations) in middle-range societies have concentrated on the heterogeneous and dynamic nature of communities in which these interactions occur (Alt 2006; Kolb and Sneed 1997; Yaeger and Canuto 2000). Specifically, it is increasingly apparent that individuals and aggregates of individuals at a variety of scales in these communities frequently move back and forth between cooperative and competitive relationships with others for a variety of reasons (Cobb 2005; Kohler and Van West 1997; Stone 1999, 2005a) resulting in the formation of small group alliances within the overarching structure of communities. Sometimes these alliances are highly transitory, but at other times they are more enduring. Additionally, the axes of identity along which alliances may form (kin, religious sodality, political status, age, gender) vary as different aspects of individual or family identity are emphasized or suppressed given the particular issue of concern being negotiated and the historical context of past experiences. The result is a constant negotiation and reconstitution of the small group alliances made by individuals

against a backdrop of the larger social structure and its historical context. Ultimately, communities are heterogeneous affairs full of individuals, families, and small groups with differing views of the social and political structures in which they live their everyday lives and differing personal goals for which they strive (Isbell 2000; Pauketat 2008; Robb 1998; Shortman and Urban 1998; Stone 2005a, 2008). This heterogeneity is increased when communities include migrant groups from distant areas, which provide an additional axis of negotiation and small group alliances.

To understand the complex and dynamic nature of heterogeneous communities, it is important to understand that the structure in which individuals, families, and small groups live their everyday lives is neither static nor perceived by all members of the community in the same way. Rather, large communities are, as Pauketat (2008) and Alt (2006) suggest, a mosaic of different small groups and substructures that are brought together into a larger composite. Individuals, families, and small groups within communities interact with and perceive aspects of the mosaic and the composite differently because of their different personal histories, status, gender, age, and membership in kin groups, religious sodalities, and ethnic groups (Shortman and Urban 1998; Stone 1999, 2005a). The individual perceptions of actors (and groups of actors) result in differing personal goals which may range from increasing status and access to resources at one end of the spectrum to ensuring personal situations do not deteriorate at the other. Added to this variability, perfect knowledge of community structure and the goals of its other members are not possible. Individuals and families must act on the information they have, incomplete as it may be (Stone 2008). Differences in knowledge and perceptions of structure, as well as sometimes conflicting personal goals, produce social settings filled with tension and contradiction, and against which alliances and participation in small groups within communities are negotiated.

Further, community structures sit within a historical context in which the related themes of history, meaning of place and the multiple ways in which social memory is constructed, negotiated, and reconstituted through purposeful action at multiple scales are defined, experienced, and interpreted (Creese 2012; Johnson 2012; Thomas 1996; Tilley 1994). More specifically, individuals live and interact within a historical context (their own and their society's) in which past decisions impact both the actual and perceived choices of the present and future, as well as rights to resources (material, social, and ritual) within a complex social structure that is constantly renegotiated (e.g., Barth 2007; Beck et al. 2007; Bernardini 2011a; Cameron and Duff 2008; Pauketat 2000, 2001a, 2001b, 2008; Yaeger and Canuto 2000). Additionally, transformative events radically alter organizational structures and future trajectories of social interaction. The perception of these events and the reaction to them by individuals, families, and small groups is simultaneously impacted by existing social memory and used to negotiate new histories through its manipulation. Social memory is tied to history and historically situated structures which are created and re-created through repeated action; it is used to establish and give permanency to social constructs and relations, and to de-emphasize tensions and contradictions (Basso 1996; Nielsen 1995; Van Dyke 2004; Van Dyke and Alcock 2003a, 2003b). Manipulation of social memory also can be used to alter history by emphasizing some aspects of past interactions and alliances while de-emphasizing others. It can, in some instances, deny history and the rights associated with it to individuals or small groups, effectively writing them out of a community's history.

This view of community dynamics is operationalized with the aid of two assumptions. The first is that material culture is not merely a reflection of human behavior. Rather, individuals and groups consciously make decisions about the material culture they create and surround themselves with for a variety of reasons. In short, material culture is not merely epiphenomenal but actively created, used, engaged, and changed for social reasons. It is imbued with meaning and used by individuals and groups in the course of their interactions with others to aid in the negotiation of structure and the reinforcement of their positions within society (Bailey 1990; Chenoweth 2009; Gamble 2007; Locock 1994; Robb 1998; Wells 1998). The second assumption centers on concepts of space and the role of architecture (as a form of material culture) in creating and defining space. Specifically, space is imbued with social meaning as well as history (Basso 1996; Feld and Basso 1996; Smith 2003; Thomas 1996). Furthermore, particular events "transform spaces" (Beck et al. 2007:835; see also Pauketat 2008) and, in doing so, "history." Thus architecture and changes in it can be used in purposeful social action to negotiate and create new histories and social memories. These affect alliances and small group formation among community inhabitants, resulting in a diversity of community structures in general, and host-migrant interactions in particular. These issues must be incorporated into migration studies if we are to understand the various ways in which hosts and migrants interact and how new members are absorbed into host communities. The result can range from total assimilation to the maintenance of bounded enclaves. Only by understanding these broader issues of community dynamics and alliance formation can we understand this variability.

Case Studies of Migration in Middle-Range Societies in Prehistory

Migration and the resulting interaction of individuals and groups with very different identities are far from unusual either today or in the past. Migration was, in fact, a very common event in middle-range societies in prehistory (Cobb 2005) and worldwide in its scope. The nature of the interaction between host and migrants varied considerably. The reasons for this variability are multifold and related to, among other factors, the demographic profile (i.e., size/density, gender, and age distribution) of the migrant and host populations as well as both the fluidity and the social/political organization of both groups (Stone 2003). A brief overview of four case studies from around the world demonstrates this diversity.

Migrating Pastoralists in the Middle East:
The Case of the Canaan Highlands

Settlement in the Early Iron Age in the Canaan Highlands of the Levant has recently been the subject of intensive study (Levy et al. 1999; Levy and Holl 2002). Based on extensive surveys and excavation of both domestic structures and cemeteries it is apparent that at least two different nomadic and seminomadic pastoral groups occupied the region in the thirteenth through eleventh centuries BC, entering the highlands from the north, east, and west. Although initial population densities for each group were low and mobility relatively high, interaction between the groups intensified through time. Specifically, pressure due to encroachment from more settled groups surrounding the highlands led to diminished territories and circumscription of pasture lands. By the end of the Early Iron Age, settled villages increased in frequency. These villages are remarkably consistent in house construction and layout, indicating a merging of concepts of domestic use of space despite the heterogeneous nature of the groups that formed them. Excavations in associated cemeteries confirm the coalescence of the two groups. Levy and Holl (2002:113) suggest "[t]he fluidity of pastoral socioeconomic systems allows for an easier absorption of newcomers and displaced groups" and the merging of diverse cultural practices resulting in the ethnogenesis of a new group in which traditions were blended rather than one group dominating the other or continuing emphasis on differentiation. This creation of a new identity out of a synthesis of multiple groups can be contrasted with situations in which the interaction of migrants and hosts results in the dominance of one group over the other in some areas but the continuation of the traditions of another group in other areas of the social, political, and economic organization of villages and regions.

Norse Migration to the
Outer Hebrides of Scotland

Recent survey and excavation on the Island of Uist (Sharples and Parker Pearson 1999), on the western coast of Scotland, has demonstrated a well-established land use pattern of farming and dairying settlements and homesteads on the agricultural soils of the western coast of the island beginning in the Middle Iron Age (100 BC–AD 300) that continues through the Late Iron Age (AD 300–AD 800). Settlements vary considerably in size but consist of mound clusters which excavation reveals to be multi-structure house compounds surrounding a central yard. The eastern side of the island contains several deep sea lochs. Use of this side of the island for permanent habitation sites does not appear to have occurred. Finally, in the center of the island are several brochs, which are dry stone towers, built on high ground that likely housed elite members of the island (Parker Pearson et al. 1996).

The Norse period began in the AD 800s and is signified by abandonment of the brochs, changes in ceramic decoration and forms, and the introduction of Norse style combs, bronze pins, copper buckles, and some aspects of house construction. Conversely, there also is remarkable continuity with earlier periods with respect to settlement patterns on the western coast and the layout of house compounds. The eastern sea lochs, which in some ways resemble fjords of their homelands and provide excellent fishing grounds, were not used on Uist by the Norse. With the exception of the discontinuation of the brochs (indicating a disruption to the elite segment of the population), there is no evidence of dislocation of the population. Rather, Sharples and Parker Pearson (1999:58) argue that the indigenous (host) population reacted to the influx of Norse migrants by continuing "an ancient tradition of building but according to new rules of style because they decided it would benefit them to do so. The attractions of becoming a Viking [for the host population] may have been considerable." The result was a blending of aspects of both groups but a political and social dominance by the Norse migrants. Settlement pattern and house compound organization of the host population continued while at the same time material culture, political organization and construction technology associated with the migrants were brought to the fore.

Northern Iroquois of New York and Ontario

A somewhat more controversial example of migration, in which the migrants displaced the indigenous population, involves the Northern Iroquois of New York and Ontario (Snow 1995, 1996). Although some scholars continue to propose a model of in situ development (Crawford and Smith 1996), Snow has marshaled a variety of data sources (both ethnographic and archaeological) to argue for a migration of Iroquois groups from central Pennsylvania to northern New York and southern Ontario at ca. AD 900 that displaced the foraging groups in the area. Ethnographically, Northern Iroquois groups can be distinguished from their Algonquian neighbors not only by their linguistic differences but by the use of multifamily longhouses containing matrilineal kin groups that followed matrilocal postmarital residence patterns and were heavily dependent on maize agriculture. Prior to AD 900, areas east of Lake Ontario were occupied by broad-based hunting, foraging, and fishing groups using the Point Peninsula ceramic complex, which is characterized by elongated, coil-and-scrape vessels with parabolic shaped bases. Sites consisted of small, temporary camps located in highly productive patches of wild resources. At AD 900 there is a dramatic shift in both settlement patterns and economics as villages of large, multifamily habitation structures (i.e., longhouses), new ceramic construction techniques (molded ceramics with rounded bases), and maize agriculture appear in the archaeological record. Sites were located on hilltops or adjacent to rivers or lakes. Based on the "major discontinuity in site location, settlement size, and house form" (Snow 1995:73), and similarity to material in central Pennsylvania and the ethnographic distribution of ethnically Iroquoian groups, Snow (1995:74) hypothesized "[d]isplacement of small non-Iroquoian hunter-gather populations" by Iroquoian migrants in the region.

Western Mogollon Highlands of the American Southwest

The final case study is the western Mogollon Highlands of the American Southwest, which witnessed the migration of a variety of Puebloan groups from the north into the region starting in the late AD 1100s. Migrations into the area resulted in a variety of host-migrant interactions related to differing population densities, social/political organizations of the host communities, and the demographic profile of the migrants (Stone 2003). The best documented of these migrations (to date) occurred in the Grasshopper Plateau region of Arizona (Reid 1989; Reid and Whittlesey 1982, 1999) and involved a relatively small group of migrants, demographically dominated by women from a variety of locations (Ezzo and Price 2002; Lowell 2007). Migrants have been identified in the burial assemblage at Grasshopper Pueblo by differences in cranial deformation patterns tied to cradle boarding and clear-cut differences in strontium isotope ratios in tooth enamel (Price et al. 1994). Additional evidence of migrants who were raised with different learning frameworks can be found in the introduction of new paint formulas and tempering/clay recipes in the ceramics (Zedeño 1994; Zedeño and Triadan 2000) as well as differences in building technologies and the arrangement of space within domestic structures (Riggs 2001). The migrants did not, however, actively signal a separate ethnic identity in their material culture and, based on grave good distribution, were fully integrated into the economic and political structure of the community (Ezzo 1993; Reid and Whittlesey 1999). The reasons for this lack of ethnic signaling and apparent integration into the Grasshopper community are related to the fact that the migrants entered the area during a time of increased conflict on the Grasshopper Plateau, as evident in the switch from the use of the atlatl to bow-and-arrow and the burning of small sites (Lowell 2007). Some communities welcomed the newcomers, and the result was increasing aggregation in a defensive location.

To the west of Grasshopper Pueblo is the Point of Pines region (Figure 1.1), where a very different pattern is evident. Point of Pines Pueblo was occupied from AD 1250 to 1400, and at its height the site consisted of approximately 800 masonry rooms organized into a series of massed room blocks. Excavation was conducted at the pueblo and several other sites in the area between 1947 and 1963 by the University of

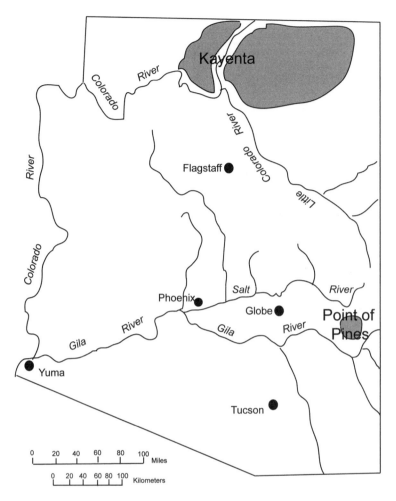

FIGURE 1.1. Locations of the Kayenta and Point of Pines regions.

Arizona archaeological field school under the direction of Emil Haury (1989). Of the pueblo's estimated 800 rooms, 130 were excavated, revealing 204 floors. Early in the excavation process, Haury (1958, 1989; see also Lindsay 1987; Stone 2003) identified a series of pithouses as well as a room block at the center of the site that appeared to be different from others in the pueblo. He suggested this room block represented an enclave of migrants from the Kayenta area to the north. Two-story construction and burning at abandonment contrasted with one-story construction and lack of burning elsewhere in the site. Associated with the room block was a D-shaped kiva and 76 burials that were interred in a flexed or semiflexed position (Rodrigues

2008). A rectangular Great Kiva and several small kivas were associated with other one-story room blocks at the site, as well as inhumations that were extended and cremations. In addition to architectural and ritual differences between the migrants and host population, Kayenta and Maverick Mountain (Kayenta designs on local ceramics) ceramics were found in the two-story room block and D-shaped kiva (Haury 1958; Lindsay 1987; Stone 2003; Zedeño 2002), as were varieties of corn and squash found in the Kayenta region but not elsewhere in the Point of Pines region (Bohrer 1973; Haury 1958). The two-story room block was occupied for the first 50 years of village occupation; in 1300 it was burned. The remainder of the village continued to be occupied for another 100 years. Subsequent occupation in areas of the migrant room block resembled architectural construction elsewhere in the community.

Point of Pines Pueblo witnessed the presence of a large group of migrants not only possessing a different ethnic identity, but one that actively signaled their ethnic "otherness" through construction and maintenance of a cluster of houses, a ritual structure and different burial patterns. The enclave was evident at the founding of the site in 1250, but after the burning of their houses the migrants largely left the area, possibly joining other groups leaving the Kayenta region and moving south of the Point of Pines region, into the southern Basin and Range region of Arizona. Those few migrants who may have remained at Point of Pines no longer expressed their ethnic "otherness" through domestic or ritual architecture or through ceramic decoration. Indigenous Mogollon inhabitants continued to occupy the pueblo until 1400. This history of Kayenta migration, Kayenta/Mogollon interaction and Mogollon aggregated community life is painted in broad strokes. A detailed and nuanced under-

standing of the choices individuals, families, and small groups made about identity, the alliances that were formed within the broader community, and how these interactions were played out through concepts of place, ethnicity, history, and social memory is the focus of the case study presented in this volume.

Before examining the architectural evidence for alliance formation, ethnic interaction, and the creation, destruction, and re-creation of social memory within the structural mosaic at Point of Pines Pueblo, discussion of previous models of Kayenta migration that characterize communities like Point of Pines Pueblo as part of a larger diaspora is called for. Unfortunately, this model is not supported by the data (as demonstrated in Chapter 2). A new model using concepts of agency-structure interaction and the importance of place in general and the transformative nature of architecture in particular to better understand migration and host-migrant interaction in middle-range societies is presented in Chapter 3. The model is then tested in subsequent chapters.

Kayenta Migrations
in the American Southwest

A Proposed Diaspora

We have long known about Kayenta migrations south into the Mogollon Highlands and southern reaches of the Basin and Range region of Arizona from both archaeological data and Hopi oral history (Bernardini 2005, 2008; Di Peso 1958; Gerald 1975; Haury 1958, 1989; Lindsay 1987). Based on the most recent synthesis of demographic data from the Kayenta region (Dean 2002) these migrations began well before final abandonment of the area. Specifically, data from both the Kayenta region (Dean 2002) and the Mogollon Highlands (Rodrigues 2008) indicate the migrations began during the Transition phase (AD 1150–1250) and continued at varying levels of intensity through the end of the Tsegi phase (AD 1300), at which time the Kayenta region was completely abandoned. In a recent series of publications (Clark and Reed 2011; Lyons 2013; Lyons and Clark 2012; Lyons et al. 2008; Lyons and Lindsay 2006; Mills 2011) diasporas have been used to explain the migration and active signaling of ethnic boundaries to varying degrees by Kayenta groups in southern Arizona (Figure 2.1). In-depth discussion of exactly how a model developed to explain transnational migration of groups in response to colonial pressure (and in the postcolonial world the process of globalization) is applicable to middle-range societies in general and the prehistoric Southwest in particular merits examination. As Robin Cohen (1997) notes, the use of the concept of diaspora by ethnographers,

sociologists, and geographers in the modern and postmodern world, where the model originates, is severely under-theorized. Kim Butler (2001), in particular, has argued that the proliferation of the use of the term *diaspora* has resulted in an ill-defined concept that is in danger of losing all *explanatory* value in discussions of contemporary groups. It behooves us, therefore, to examine the concept in depth and distinguish between different types of social actions like migration, ethnic interaction, and diaspora before moving forward with this line of reasoning. This action allows us to move beyond description of prehistoric movement across the landscape to an explanation and nuanced understanding of social action and agential choice by people in the past.

What Is a Diaspora?

Current theories about diasporas originate with ethnographers, geographers, and historians and specifically reference how diasporic communities operate in a colonial and globalized world. Part of this explanation is explicit reference to their continental and transcontinental scope (Esman 2009; Sheffer 2003). Archaeological applications also have tied diasporic behavior to state-level societies, in particular Stein's (2002) work with Uruk, and Owen's (2005) work with Tiwanaku (though note Lilley's [2007] work with the Lapatia in the Bismark Islands for contrast). Given this, is it appropriate to apply this model to middle-range societies like the those in the

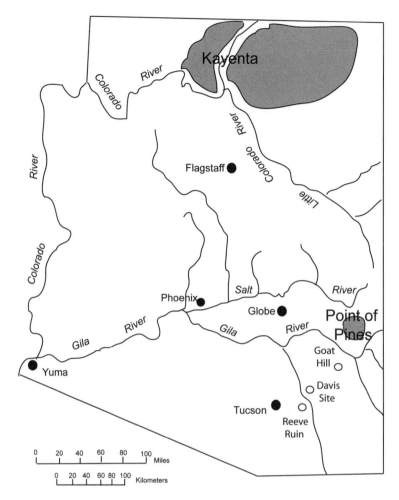

FIGURE 2.1. Known Kayenta enclaves in the Mogollon Highlands and southern Basin and Range region of Arizona.

prehistoric Southwest? Can the model of a diaspora be modified to encompass middle-range societies, or do we need to think about this in a completely different way?

As a first step, we need to think about what a diaspora is, and in the process of doing this keep in mind Butler's (2001) caution that expansion of the diaspora concept to all migrations waters it down so much as to make it meaningless (see also Cohen 1997 and Sheffer 2003). In other words, we must remember that not all migration and ethnic interaction is the result of diasporic behavior. Additionally, to make a diasporic model explanatory of the patterns we see in the archaeological record (rather than merely de-

scriptive), we must move beyond identification of the presence of migrants and start to think about social choices and the nature of interactions between groups at a variety of scales. A first step in this process is a working model of diasporic behavior.

Well-studied diasporas of the historic era indicate they exist for a multitude of reasons, including forced dispersions due to warfare, ethnic cleansing, and slavery. Alternatively, dispersions can be voluntary, the most common being for the purpose of colonizing other areas, pursuing economic benefits (such as establishing a trading outpost), or moving away temporarily to escape economic difficulty at home. Regardless of the

TABLE 2.1. Archaeological implications for a Kayenta diaspora

Characteristic	Archaeological Implication
Transnational in scope with multiple enclaves	Kayenta material should be found in multiple locations of the Mogollon Highlands and southern Basin and Range region of Arizona.
Multiple ethnic enclaves that are alienated from the host community	Migrants form communities and/or barrios within communities where they actively express their ethnic "otherness" through community layout, domestic and ritual architecture, mortuary practice, and ceramic decoration. There should not be evidence of migrants assimilating into their host communities.
Enclaves are maintained for multiple generations	Enclaves should be evident in the same location, or in close proximity, for multiple generations.
Image of homeland and "ideology of return"	Continued economic or ritual interaction with the Kayenta region by the enclaves until AD 1300 when Kayenta region is abandoned.
Communication between enclaves	Economic and ritual interaction between the enclaves.

Note: See also Owen 2005.

reasons for the dispersion of peoples from their homelands, most researchers (Butler 2001; Clifford 1994; Cohen 1997; Mavroudi 2007; Sheffer 2003; Stock 2010) agree that five characteristics combine to distinguish diasporas from other types of migrations and ethnic interaction.

First, on a purely descriptive level, diasporas are transnational, with multiple enclaves in which ethnic otherness is not only present but actively signaled. In other words, groups move into multiple locations where the host communities differ culturally, politically, and economically from themselves. Second, the migrants come together to form ethnically distinct communities for several generations within the host territory. These two aspects are perhaps the easiest to distinguish archaeologically. The remaining three characteristics, however, are not only necessary but are at the very heart of distinguishing diasporas from other types of migrations and ethnic interaction. It is, in fact, these last three characteristics that move the diasporic model from the realm of description to explanation. These characteristics are the result of conscious and purposeful choices about how to interact with others and how to conceive of self. The third characteristic is that diasporic communities remain alienated from their host communities, resisting all attempts to assimilate. They see themselves, and are viewed by their hosts, not only as a category of "other" but purposefully sepa-

rate. They are temporary residents, even if their residency lasts for hundreds of years. The reason for the continued maintenance of an idea of separateness is the fourth crucial characteristic; it is the ideology of return to their homeland. This ideology results in cultural practices in which the homeland is "imagined, recreated, longed for, [and] remembered" (Stock 2010:24) and in the case of voluntary diasporas, interacted with. Fifth, because diasporas are cultural and political actions as well as geographic movements, communication between enclaves in different locations is maintained in an attempt to keep the ideology of the homeland, and even the dream of eventual return to the homeland, alive. When the homeland still exists and is inhabited, communication with those remaining in the homeland occurs. These last three characteristics do not mean all enclaves look exactly alike; a certain amount of adaptation to local conditions is necessary. *Purposive* social, political and economic action, however, is required in the maintenance of otherness, communication between enclaves, and in the ideology of return.

Bruce Owen (2005) has successfully applied a diasporic model to better understand the establishment of colonial economic outposts by the Tiwanaku state in the Middle Horizon in the south-central Andes. We can modify the archaeological test implications he specifies for use with a middle-range society to determine if a diasporic model helps us to understand Kayenta migration in the prehistoric American Southwest (Table 2.1). Specifically, we should see evidence of multiple locations in which migrants from the Kayenta area are not only present but take social action to avoid assimilation with their host community, resulting in active and highly visible signaling of their ethnic "otherness" for multiple generations. This social action should be evident through multiple lines of data including community layout, architecture (particularly ritual), mortuary practices and ceramic decoration (Stone 2003). Additionally, for migrations that occurred prior to final abandonment of the homeland there should be evidence of continued contact with the Kayenta homeland through trade, shared ritual and stylistic patterning indicative of interaction. Finally, there must be evidence of interaction between the enclaves through trade and sharing of ritual and stylistic design.

Did a Kayenta Diaspora Exist?

Evidence of migrants from the Kayenta region in communities to the south of their homeland are numerous; however, active expression of ethnic otherness through burials, ritual structures and architecture is lacking at many of these locations. For example, the Safford and Aravaipa Valleys (Neuzil 2008) and the Roosevelt Basin (Clark 2001; Stark et al. 1998) lack evidence of active expression of ethnic otherness, and migrants are identified only through the more subtle expressions of learning frameworks in areas of manufacture that are not visible to others. We do know of at least four sites (Figure 2.1) where Kayenta enclaves existed and actively signaled their cultural differences from the surrounding population. Point of Pines Pueblo (AD 1250–1400) is the largest (800 rooms) and includes a room block of Kayenta migrants for part of its occupation (AD 1250–1300) (Haury 1958, 1989; Lindsay 1987; Stone 2003). The other three sites are Kayenta communities that actively signaled their ethnic differences relative to other communities in the local area: Goat Hill, dated from AD 1275–1325 (Woodson 1999), and Reeve Ruin and the Davis site, both dated AD 1350–1400 (Di Peso 1958;

Gerald 1975). Because Point of Pines has not previously been reported in detail and is the subject of the remainder of this volume, I concentrate on the other three sites here. These three sites are ideal to examine because they were founded by some of the early migrants out of the Kayenta region and one was occupied prior to the final abandonment of the Kayenta homeland.

At each of these three sites, architectural evidence indicates an active attempt to maintain separateness from indigenous communities and signal "otherness" in terms of their ethnic identity through the use of Kayenta style community spatial organization and differences in ritual behavior, as seen in the use of kivas and burial practices (Figure 2.2). In terms of community layout, each of these sites resembles the plaza-oriented sites commonly used during the Transition phase in the Kayenta region (Dean 1996, 2002) in which a central plaza is surrounded by a combination of masonry rooms and an enclosing wall. At each of these locations, however, the maintenance of separate ethnic identities occurs in only one phase. Although each of these phases is technically longer than a generation, short duration of this social action should give us pause given the test implications discussed above.

Connections with the Homeland

Continued interaction and communication with the homeland is potentially evident in two forms of data: trade and ritual connections. In terms of trade, most emphasis has been placed on ceramics, in particular the presence of Tsegi wares and perforated plates. The amount of imported ceramics at each of these sites is somewhat limited. Trade wares reported for Goat Hill, the Davis site, and Reeve Ruin (Di Peso 1958; Gerald 1975; Woodson 1999) represent predominately trade connections to the south, as well as widely distributed Salado Polychromes, but not ceramics originating in the Kayenta region.

Lyons and Lindsay (2006) have studied the distribution of perforated plates and Maverick Mountain painted ceramics throughout the Southwest. Perforated plates originated in the Kayenta region around AD 600 and continued to be used in that area until abandonment. Based

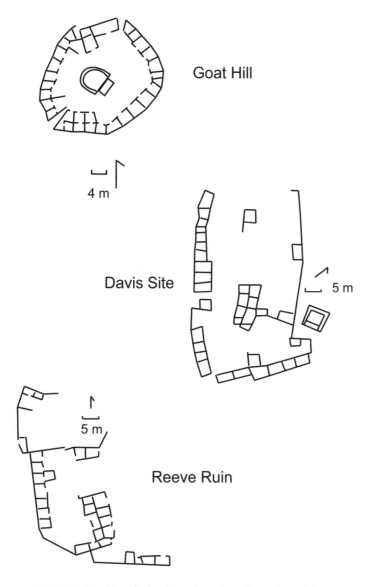

FIGURE 2.2. Sites identified as Kayenta enclaves in southern Arizona.

on use-wear, they are believed to have been involved in ceramic manufacture, serving as a base mold in the initial construction of vessel forms. After AD 1250, perforated plates are also found in a variety of locations in the Mogollon Highlands and the southern Basin and Range region, particularly in the lower Salt River basin of southern Arizona and New Mexico, including the three enclaves noted above. Compositional analysis indicates local production of the plates where they were found rather than trade with the Kayenta region.

A similar pattern is evident with Maverick Mountain Black-on-Red and Maverick Mountain Polychrome. Maverick Mountain ceramics were made with local clays but Kayenta style designs (Lyons and Lindsay 2006; Zedeño 2002). Maverick Mountain ceramics were first identified at Point of Pines Pueblo (Haury 1958; Lindsay 1987) and have subsequently been identified at a number of sites in the southern Basin and Range region of Arizona, including Goat Hill (Woodson 1999). Interestingly, however, neither Kayenta trade wares nor Maverick Mountain ceramics are mentioned in the site reports for the Davis site or Reeve Ruin (Di Peso 1958; Gerald 1975). Equally interesting, Lyons and Lindsay (2006) report the presence of both perforated plates and Maverick Mountain ceramics along the San Pedro River where architecture and ritual evidence of ethnic enclaves is lacking. In short, Maverick Mountain ceramics and perforated plates are present at sites that appear to represent Kayenta enclaves, but they are made of local clays, and there is no evidence of continued economic interaction with the Kayenta homeland despite their contemporaneity with sites in the Kayenta region. Further, the presence of perforated plates and Maverick Mountain ceramics at sites lacking evidence of active signaling of Kayenta identity hints more at widespread sharing of ideas regarding ceramic production and decoration than diasporic behavior.

Ritual connection with the homeland can be examined through both mortuary behavior and ritual architecture. Mortuary behavior during the Transition and Tsegi phases in the Kayenta region is consistently characterized by flexed to semiflexed inhumations (Ambler et al. 1964; Anderson 1980; Beals et al. 1945; Hobler 1974). Flexed inhumations are found at Point of Pines Pueblo and have been used to identify the burials of migrants at the site. Osteological analysis (Rodrigues 2008) indicates the migrants did not differ significantly in terms of grave goods or skeletal trauma from the indigenous population. No burials were recovered from Goat Hill (Woodson 1999) but those from the Davis site (Gerald 1975) are semiflexed, and Reeve Ruin (Di Peso 1958) contains both cremations and semiflexed inhumations.

Ritual structures are informative as well. There is considerable variability in kiva style in the Kayenta region in terms of shape and internal features (Stone 2013). However, almost all Kayenta kivas are semi-subterranean and have a hearth, deflector, and ventilator shaft com-plex. Beyond these near universal components there is considerable variability in size, shape, and presence or absence of floor features. Kivas are present at all three southern Arizona sites examined here, as well as Point of Pines Pueblo (Haury 1989), though considerable variability is present. The kivas at Goat Hill and Point of Pines are semi-subterranean (as expected of Kayenta kivas) and D-shaped (which is present but rare in the Kayenta region, representing less than 6 percent of the excavated kivas from the Transition and Tsegi phases). The kiva at the Davis site is also semi-subterranean, though square in shape. Additionally, the kivas at all three sites contain the hearth, deflector, ventilator shaft complex common in the Kayenta area, as well as a variety of other features including *sipapus*, benches, wall recesses, loom anchor holes, and foot drums. The kiva at Reeve Ruin is aboveground and built into a room in the structure. It contains a bench but no other features. In a recent study of 69 kivas from the Transition and Tsegi phases in the Kayenta region, only one aboveground kiva was identified in a rockshelter, and only one (though not the same kiva) lacked the hearth, deflector, and ventilator shaft complex (Stone 2013). These results (in terms of both mortuary patterns and ritual structure) indicate the continuation of some aspects of Kayenta ritual concepts at the enclaves though show only minimal continuity in others. Neither the mortuary patterns nor kiva structures, however, provide evidence of sustained contact with the Kayenta homeland by migrants at the two earliest sites—a key aspect of the diaspora model.

Communication between Enclaves

Communication between enclaves is present in diasporas and can be examined here in terms of lithic exchange between the enclaves and shared ceramic style. Specifically, Clark and Reed (2011) have recently suggested obsidian exchange may represent evidence of interaction between enclaves that non-Kayenta communities in the area do not have access to, or if they do, it is in a much reduced amount. Published data from the Aravaipa Valley, however, does not support this contention. Neuzil's (2008) study of the Aravaipa area indicates the probable presence of Kayenta migrants but lacks evidence of ethnic enclaves. Her analysis of obsidian (Neuzil 2008:72, Table 5.5) suggests a significant chi-square result but notes the results are suspect due to cells with expected values of less than 5, which lowers the power of the statistical test and can result in inaccurate results (Reynolds 1984). When the data are collapsed to a 2 × 2 table (presence/absence of perforated plates associated with migrants vs. obsidian from Mule Creek vs. other sources) the chi-square score leads to rejection of the null hypothesis of independence of the two variables at the .05 alpha level ($x^2 = 5.731$; df = 1; $n = 192$) but the Cramer's V measure of association (V = .0298) indicates the association is so weak it is negligible.

Much of the most recent studies arguing for the diaspora model have concentrated on the production and distribution of Roosevelt Red Wares, also known as Salado Polychromes. Roosevelt Red Ware is a widespread ceramic tradition in southern Arizona and New Mexico postdating AD 1300. It is one of several glaze ware and polychrome traditions that developed at this time (Cordell and Habicht-Mauche 2012). These glaze ware traditions co-occur with major reorganizations of the entire Southwest, including migrations, abandonments, aggregation in new areas, and ethnogenesis (Ortman and Cameron 2011). The first major, comprehensive stylistic analysis of Roosevelt Red Ware (Crown 1994) notes that it shares stylistic elements with several other ceramic traditions and suggests these shared styles were part of a widespread religious ideology known as the Southwest Cult that united peoples of different cultural traditions together during a period of social upheaval and transformation. More recently, Lyons and Clark (Lyons 2013; Lyons and Clark 2012) have argued that Salado Polychrome represents not a joining together of different groups but an effort to maintain cultural and ethnic "otherness" among diasporic groups originating in the Kayenta region through use of Roosevelt Red Wares in inter-enclave feasting and ritual. They provide several lines of data to support this conjecture.

First, they argue that "in all of the places where Roosevelt Red Ware appeared, it represented the introduction of a radically different paint technology and a new firing technology. Indeed, among the mountains, there was no locally produced decorated pottery (except for painted corrugated) until the arrival of the immigrants" (Lyons and Clark 2012:31). Second, they argue the design patterns present on Roosevelt Red Wares share stylistic patterns with Tsegi and Maverick Mountain ceramics and were made in a limited number of locations and possible exchange between production locations (see also Triadan 2013). Finally, Lyons (2013:183) argues that Roosevelt Red Ware bowls postdating 1350 have increasingly large orifice diameters (averaging 35 cm) reinforcing the idea of their use in feasts.

There are, however, several problems with this line of argument. First, it is not accurate that the Mountain Mogollon lacked a locally decorated pottery tradition. In addition to painted ceramics obtained through trade with their neighbors to the south (Mimbres Black-on-White tradition) and the north (Cibola White Ware and White Mountain Red Ware traditions) over a long period of time predating Kayenta migrations, decorated ceramics were also locally made. Much of the decorated ceramic tradition in the Mogollon Highlands centered on methods of texturing and polishing, and sophisticated control of firing conditions resulting in smudged wares, but there were painted decorations as well. The painted traditions occurred on corrugated vessels (McDonald Corrugated) and non-corrugated vessels in the form of Starkweather Smudge and Tularosa White-on-Red (Rinaldo and Bluhm 1956), as well as Forestdale Black-on-Red and Corduroy Black-on-White (Ferg 1980). These painted styles predate migrations into the highlands by several hundred years and are characterized by chevrons, diamond and square spirals, interlocking frets, zig-zags, and line designs with attached triangles that grew out of the widespread Mimbres Boldface Black-on-White tradition.

Second, the earliest evidence of Roosevelt Red Ware production is not actually associated with Kayenta migrants. Crown (1994) notes the two earliest dated occurrences of Roosevelt Red Ware are Point of Pines Pueblo and Grasshopper Pueblo. Although Kayenta and Maverick Mountain wares are found at Point of Pines Pueblo, Roosevelt Red Wares are actually fairly rare (Haury 1976). For example, of the 178 whole vessels recorded on room floors in the field notes, only the five used by Crown in her study are Roosevelt Red Ware (2.8%). Additionally, of the 7505 sherds from painted wares recorded on floors of excavated rooms in the field notes, only 635 (8.5% of painted wares) are Roosevelt Red Ware; when plain, red-slipped, and textured wares are included, the percentage is even lower (1.4% of recorded sherds). (Plain, red, and corrugated shreds were frequently listed as "many" rather than as a count in the field notes, so the percentage is lower still.)

The Grasshopper Plateau, on the other hand, is a major center of production for Roosevelt Red Ware, and the earliest examples are found at the site of Choodistas dated to AD 1263–1290 (Crown 1994; Montgomery and Reid 1990). Roosevelt Red Wares quickly become the dominant painted ware on the Grasshopper Plateau. Choodistas is an ideal locality to examine the development of Roosevelt Red Wares because of its well dated sequence of dendrochronological dates and the presence of more than 300 whole vessels on room floors under burned roof fall. The site was abandoned after burning, and the inhabitants moved to the newly aggregated community of Grasshopper Pueblo. The presence of migrants in the Grasshopper region are evident at both Choodistas and Grasshopper Pueblo based on the introduction of new ceramic technologies and differences in house organization and construction, cradle boarding, mortuary practices, and strontium isotope analysis on tooth enamel (Price et al. 1994; Reid 1989; Reid and Whittlesey 1999; Riggs 2001; Zedeño 1994; Zedeño and Triadan 2000).

Choodistas and Grasshopper Pueblo present a robust test for the Kayenta diaspora model in which Roosevelt Red Wares are made by Kayenta migrants as a visible ethnic marker and used by those migrants in ritual feasting that served to tie the disparate migrant enclaves together. Lowell's

(2007) careful demographic analysis indicates a gender imbalance in the migrant population at Grasshopper Pueblo, with women representing 64 percent of the migrants from the early phase and 67 percent from the late phase. This gender imbalance is in line with those expected for a local population accepting war refugees (which are more frequently women). The lack of trauma in the women migrants suggest they were refugees welcomed into the community rather than war captives. Further, Ezzo and Price (2002) compared the strontium isotope results from the migrants at Grasshopper Pueblo to other regions of the Southwest and found matches to several other regions (including the Tonto Basin, the Payson area, Walnut Creek, and the Chevelon region), but not the Kayenta region.

Finally, a stylistic comparison does not support an exclusively Kayenta base for Roosevelt Red Wares. Although there are several similarities between Kayenta designs and those found on Roosevelt Red Wares (Lyons 2013), Crown's (1994) analysis indicates additional stylistic ties, including the masked figures, cloud terraces, and parrots of Mimbres Classic ceramics to the southeast, decorative layouts common on Hohokam ceramics from the Phoenix Basin to the south (Whittlesey and Reid 2012) and interlocking solid and hatched forms common to Cibola White Ware and White Mountain Red Wares to the northeast (Crown 1994; Carlson 1970). Given the demographic and stylistic data, Crown's (1994) model of a pan-Southwestern religious ideology that united disparate peoples during a turbulent time through trade and shared stylistic patterns appears more parsimonious than the use of Roosevelt Red Ware in feasting rituals used to link enclaves of the a Kayenta diaspora.

Migration, Landscapes, and Identity in the Broader Context

In conclusion, diasporic behavior is a conscious social action tied to negotiations of identity and social power (Butler 2001) that goes beyond the presence of migrants and even ethnic enclaves. Combined, active ethnic signaling, connections with the homeland, and interaction between enclaves are the elements that separate diasporic behavior from other kinds of migrations and ethnic interactions. Data from locations containing Kayenta migrants does not, at present, support a diasporic model. Specifically, the data supporting continuing ties to a homeland and interaction between enclaves of Kayenta migrants in the American Southwest is minimal at best. More specifically, some indication of architectural and ritual continuity between the Kayenta homeland and the enclaves exists, but there is no evidence of the maintenance of economic ties. Additionally, the rise of Roosevelt Red Wares, as seen in the data from Choodistas and Grasshopper Pueblo, do not occur in a region with a Kayenta enclave. The stylistic patterns present in Roosevelt Red Wares bear similarity to numerous ceramic traditions in the Southwest, and these same stylistic patterns are found in other glaze ware traditions of the time (Cordell and Habicht-Mauche 2012) indicating a widespread ideology, as suggested by Crown (1994), rather than the control of production by one group. Further, a diasporic model does not explain why in addition to the ethnic enclaves discussed here we have numerous incidents of Kayenta migrants "blending in" and declining to participate in social action signifying "otherness." A more useful approach to understanding the relationships between Kayenta migrants and their host communities and regional neighbors may be to concentrate on the nature of the multiple migrations out of the Kayenta region, starting as early as AD 1150 and continuing until abandonment in 1300, and the interaction between the migrants and their host communities. In the past I have argued that these migrations had very diverse demographic profiles, and in-

dividuals, families, and groups adapted to highly variable social geographies upon their arrival in their new homes (Stone 2003; Stone and Lipe 2011). The result is local variations in social adaptation and the negotiation of identity that require considerably more study.

As noted in Chapter 1, migration and host-migrant interaction is actually a global phenomenon among middle-range societies. This broader perspective clearly demonstrates that the past, like identity itself, is not simple. It is complex and contested; like people and their identity it does not fit into clear, non-overlapping types. For example, in the American Southwest, the Hopi are not the only group whose oral traditions discuss southern migrations; a concept of the gathering of the clans from multiple locations is a common theme. Further, the Zuñi talk of movement across the same landscape as the Hopi in their oral history, and the Zuñi identify places like Reeve Ruin and the Davis site as part of their migration histories (Colwell-Chanthaphonh and Ferguson 2006). The point here is not to contest specific ancestral claims to specific sites but rather to point to the complicated nature of migration as a social action and the resulting interactions and dynamic nature of identity formation. Both Hopi and Zuñi oral histories recognize this complexity (Bernardini 2005, 2011b; Colwell-Chanthaphonh and Ferguson 2006; Dongoske et al. 1997; Welch and Ferguson 2013), and we should attempt to view the past with this in mind. An alternative model that attempts to embrace this complexity is presented in Chapter 3. This model is then tested in subsequent chapters.

A Model of Migration and
Ethnic Interaction in Middle-Range Societies

The previous chapter provided a brief overview of changes in migration theory for middle-range societies over the last 100 years and demonstrated its worldwide relevance. A more focused approach, concentrating on how current migration theory and our understanding of identity formation in general and ethnicity in particular occur, is presented here. To facilitate discussion of this model, the American Southwest is used as an example. As in other areas of the world, migrations of indigenous peoples are known to have occurred throughout the Southwest, both in historic and prehistoric times. Migrations are not only an adaptation to an arid landscape and periodic droughts, but also a crucial aspect of history. They are actions that not only occurred in the past, but remain a part of who the people are and how they are part of the landscape today (Basso 1996; Ferguson et al. 2009; Fowles 2010; Naranjo 1995). I begin this discussion with an overview of how migration occurs, followed by an examination of the nature of migrant-host (and equally important host-migrant) interactions and how architecture can help us to view these processes through time.

As noted in Chapter 1, our models of migration have become increasingly sophisticated, but old assumptions remain that must be overcome. For example, some (e.g., Bernardini 2005) have recently argued that an emphasis on location and territoriality of migration to the exclusion of other dimensions is tied to an intellectual legacy of the culture area approach that was popular in the first half of the twentieth century. This focus has greatly hindered our ability to fully understand the process of migration and its meaning in identity formation, particularly with reference to ethnicity. The result is a view of migration as a single, unusual action for which one set of pushes and pulls can be defined and for which a uniform set of reactions between migrants and hosts in their new homes can be predicted. However, as our brief overview of case studies in Chapter 1 reveals, this model is not supported by the data. This approach glosses over the variability of migration experiences and has difficulty dealing with migrant-host interaction within the context of dynamic communities, identity, history, and social memory. What is needed is a more nuanced view that examines migration as a dynamic process within the interplay of structure and agency, demography and space, combined with an understanding of varying personal goals, alliance formation, and engagement of material culture and space.

Multiple Scales of Migration

In terms of understanding a single migration, examining multiple dimensions simultaneously, as well as their interplay, is vital to understanding the migrants' decision-making process. Differing initial conditions will most likely result in very different social interactions both during the migration and with the host group(s) in the destination. As such, we should not expect to see a single migration signature in the archaeological record, but very diverse patterns resulting from differing negotiations of identity and status within newly forming structural mosaics and particular historical contexts (Stone 2003; Stone and Lipe 2011). Minimally, three scales (temporal, spatial, and social) need to be considered. In beginning this discussion, it is important to emphasize that each of these scales is continuous rather than dichotomous, resulting in a three-dimensional matrix within which individual migration events can be conceived and understood (Figure 3.1). By analyzing the continuous nature of these multiple scales, an appreciation of the process can be gained.

On the temporal scale, we can see a range of abandonments/migrations, including those that occur seasonally by pastoral agriculturalists such as the Tarahumara (Hard and Merrill 1992) and Puebloan horticulturalists on the Rio Grande who move between main villages and outlying farmsteads in an effort to balance scheduling conflicts of the agricultural and ritual cycles (Preucel 1990). Although most archaeologists probably do not include these "seasonal circulations" as migration, they are, in fact, at one end of a scale which has abandonment of a region lasting for multiple generations at the other end. By keeping the entire scale in mind when discussing migration, our understanding of the complexity of the process and the interplay of the temporal scale with the others is considerably enhanced. For instance, by understanding the full temporal scale involved in abandonment and migration, we are able to view abandonment of field houses, farmsteads, and villages within a drainage system (e.g., Varien 1999) at one end of a continuum. Also encompassed in this same continuum are abandonments of several decades followed by reoccupation of drainages (e.g., Nelson and Anyon 1996) or entire regions (e.g., Duff and Wilshusen 2000; Wilshusen and Ortman 1999). The entire continuum represents a transformation of use (as suggested by Nelson 1999 and Nelson and Hegmon 2001) through time rather than a discarding of loci and severing of ties. Additionally, our view of the process

is transformed from one in which migration is a last, desperate reaction to deteriorating conditions to one in which it is one among many options individuals and groups have in actively negotiating their relationships with the landscape and with each other.

Similar variability is evident on the spatial scale, ranging from very short movements within a local area (Cameron 1999a; Herr and Clark 1997; Varien 1999) to movements from one region to another (Cameron 1995). The decision-making process with regard to the spatial scale in individual cases is usually discussed in terms of "pushes" in the original home that encourage the migration and "pulls" to the destination area. The nature of pushes and means of gaining information about the pulls vary considerably with the distance traveled and through time. Specifically, with increased temporal and spatial distance, the ability to continue to return to the former residence for rituals and resource extraction decreases. Additionally, as distance increases, the mechanisms available to gain information about the pulls of potential destinations switch from overlapping kin, ritual and socially close relations to more socially distant personal contacts (like trade partners). The nature of the information may also change with distance because contact is less frequent with individuals in more socially and geographically distant areas. For example, the nature of the cooperative alliances between geographically close individuals with multiple overlapping ties is different from those between individuals of greater social and geographical distance, and are increasingly restricted to the economic realm. If ethnic as well as geographic boundaries are crossed, differences between the individuals involved may become even greater. Therefore, alliances and the decreased frequency of interaction may have considerable impact on the quality and quantity of information and thus the nature of the pulls in the decision-making process regarding migration.

The result of these differences in the transmission of information, and decision-making based on that information, is tied directly to our third dimension of variation: the social scale.

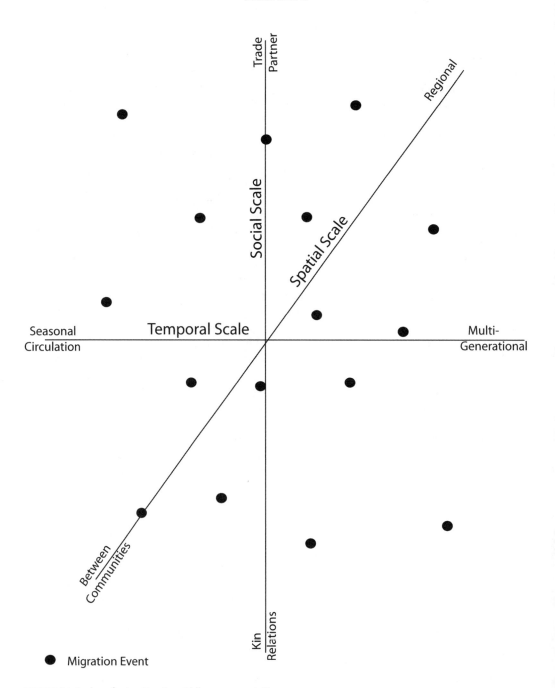

FIGURE 3.1. Scales of migration in middle-range societies.

This scale is concerned with differences and similarities in cultural concepts and societal structures, and thus the nature of the community mosaic in which host-migrant interactions first occur. It also operates to set the historical context in which subsequent alliances are negotiated. In the southwestern United States, both oral histories (Naranjo 1995, 2008; Whiteley 2002) and ethnographically documented migrations among the Hopi (Levy 1992; Titiev 1944) and Tewa (Dozier 1966) occurred in large, supra-family groups. Conversely, we also have historic reports of families in the Southwest moving between villages that are sometimes linguistically and ethnically different (Ellis 1979; Naranjo 1995, 2008). Finally, the quality of information and the perception of the economic, social, and political structure of the destination area may shift as ties with individuals (like trade partners) change or new ties develop with individuals and groups that migrated at an earlier time in a chain migration sequence. In this situation, early migrants may "pave the way for subsequent migrations by sending information to members of their family or village" (Kok 2010:217) and thereby ease their integration into the economic structure of the destination area (see also Marshall and Foster 2002). Clearly, the process by which decisions about migration occur and the size of the groups that ultimately participate is complex and multiscalar.

The position taken here is that rather than approaching migration strictly from an agency-up or structure-down perspective, we need to look at multiple levels simultaneously. Individuals are not passive drones acting solely under the rules of a social structure; rather, they independently gather and evaluate information in the course of making decisions, even though this process occurs within a family and community structure (Archer 2000; Kok 2010). Although personal goals and decisions may differ considerably from individual to individual based on age, gender, kin relations, ritual affiliation, ethnicity, and place within the power structure, these decisions are not made in isolation. Individuals live their everyday lives within social, economic, and kinship structures that are integral to decision-making processes. Also, there is abundant evidence that the size of migrating groups varies considerably, ranging from single individuals (marriage exchange) to large groups (Stone 2003). To understand the actions that occur and the varying social scales involved, a multi-scalar approach that tacks between individuals, families, small groups, and communities can aid in understanding the migration process in general and any one event in particular. In ad-

dition, our understanding of the interplay of the social, temporal, and spatial scales over which migration occurs is crucial for understanding the negotiations of identity and status that inevitably result.

Migrant-Host Interactions and the Role of Ethnic Identity

Once a migration has been identified, the conversation generally moves on to the social changes that occur in the new mosaic communities regardless of whether the process is a large-scale social transformation involving movement over a short distance by socially close individuals (i.e., the process of aggregation) or a long-distance migration involving alliances with socially distant contacts that last for multiple years. Whatever the scale, the end result of migration is a set of complex and highly varied interactions between the individuals involved. Recently, there has been considerable debate among archaeologists on the process of long-term migration over long distances in the Southwest (Clark 2001; Herr and Clark 1997; Lyons 2003; Reid 1997; Stone 2003; Stone and Lipe 2011). Almost all of the historically recorded migrations in the region involve individuals and groups moving from one community to another or within an already occupied region (Cameron 1999a; Dozier 1954, 1966; Herr and Clark 1997; Naranjo 1995, 2008). The nature of the interactions between the host and migrant populations in these ethnographic cases varies considerably from complete assimilation to the maintenance of separate ethnic enclaves and occasionally conflict. There is evidence for similar variability in prehistoric times (Cameron 1995; Cordell 1995; Herr 2001; Mills 1998; Reid 1997; Reid and Whittlesey 1999; Stone 2003; Stone and Lipe 2011; Walsh 1997). The initial conditions of interaction appear to be critical in this process, and the nature of the resulting relationship is greatly affected by slight differences in any one of the following factors (Clark 2001; Duff 1998; Lyons et al. 2008; Stone 2003; Stone and Lipe 2011): size and social structure of the migrating group; distance of the move; reason for abandoning the previous home region; the history of contact between the two groups prior to cohabitation; the host group's social structure, settlement pattern (dispersed vs. aggregated) and population density; and availability of land and flexibility of the host group's land tenure system. The key to understanding the variability in the possible outcomes of migrant-host interaction when people come from distant regions is tied to shifting our view of identity and ethnicity from a static typology to a dynamic social category that is situationally expressed and/or suppressed. The expression of one aspect of the multiple identities all individuals possess (such as ethnicity) is part of an ongoing negotiation of relationships between individuals, families and small groups. As such, it channels interaction and, in turn, is subject to change and redefinition (Chenoweth 2009; Meskell 2002).

As with any axis of identity, the importance of ethnicity and ethnic signaling is not universal, and its expression differs considerably given the individuals involved, their personal goals, the social structure in which they live their everyday lives, and the historical context in which that structure is embedded. Following migration events, differences may be de-emphasized or even eliminated for some groups yet magnified for others within newly formed communities. In some instances, migrants may choose, and are allowed by their hosts, to "blend in," but in other cases they may "stand out" as ethnic enclaves (Stone and Lipe 2011). Additionally, within a single community, aspects of identity that were unimportant in the past may form rallying points of social action in the future. Alternatively, aspects of identities like ethnicity may cease to be important and disappear or be subsumed into new concepts of self as the structural mosaics of the community shift through time (Hornborg 2005; Khan 2007; Stone and Lipe 2011). To understand this community mosaic and the small group dynamics that occur within it, we must again look at individual and family decision making.

Ethnicity is one of many socially constructed identities. As with any socially constructed identity, it is not expressed in every interaction. That is, it can be emphasized or de-emphasized situationally in interactions between individuals and groups as they strive to achieve their personal goals. Personal goals differ among individuals due to the social, political, and economic constraints that exist within the larger social structures of their everyday lives. Personal roles and status are negotiated daily within these historically constructed boundaries. The expression of one or more of an individual's identities is tied to these negotiations and the pursuit of personal goals. When viewed as just one of several socially constructed identities that individuals simultaneously use, the fluid and dynamic nature of ethnic interaction can be appreciated and pulled into larger discussions of community. In other words, ethnic differences and their expression are another axis along which alliances can be formed within heterogeneous communities. Alternatively, individuals may choose to suppress ethnic differences, participating in power negotiations and alliance formations that cut across ethnic boundaries in favor of other axes of cooperation and competition. Finally, individuals and groups may emphasize their ethnic differences at some periods in the history of the community and de-emphasize them at others. In the early years at Point of Pines Pueblo, migrants entered the area and chose to "stand out" as an ethnic enclave. We must ask ourselves why, in such cases, ethnicity became a dominant axis of identity for this segment of the community, thus adding an additional piece to the structural mosaic of the community that individuals, families and small groups must negotiate in daily life. Agential action at any scale (individual, family, ethnic enclave) does not occur in isolation but in reference to structure, and to understand these processes we must tack between the two.

When migrants enter an area that is densely populated and characterized by existing aggregated communities in middle-range societies they must negotiate their positions relative to the existing structural mosaic that defines access to status, ceremonial participation, and land tenure in terms of existing kin relations and sodality membership (Beck et al. 2007; Cameron and Duff 2008; Lyons et al. 2008; Pauketat 2001b). The very act of long-distance migration, however, disrupts migrants' kin and sodality ties (Bernardini 2008; González-Ruibal 2005; Kok 2010; Shortman and Urban 1998). They are disassociated from their previous homes, social networks, and cultural constructs during the process of migration; they are removed from society and enter a state of liminality (Alt 2006; Cobb and Butler 2006). As such, they must be integrated into new social networks and cultural contexts upon reaching their destination. However, unlike the states of liminality associated with ceremonial rites of passage, the communities that migrants are integrated into exist in different cultural and historical contexts than the ones they left. If a sufficiently large migrant group exists in the host community, individuals and families of the newcomers may attempt to establish themselves within the structural mosaic of the host community through strategic actions that encompass the larger ethnic group. This is achieved by manipulating concepts of affinity, agnates, and fictive kin that refer back to at least some aspects of the cultural and historical contexts they left behind. Conceptually, kinship and ethnicity are overlapping and share numerous characteristics and synergies, including common histories, group founders whose lineal relationships are assumed rather than demonstrated, and reinforcement of future ties through marriage alliances and enculturation within the household. The mechanics of putting these strategic actions into place can be conceptualized by drawing on the idea of "house societies" originally proposed by Claude Lévi-Strauss (1979, 1984). In trying to understand a number of ethnographic groups in both western North America and Island Southeast Asia that lack unilineal kinship systems, Lévi-Strauss seized on *emic* concepts of the "house" as a physical manifestation and locus of identity and status for groups of people tied together through the extension of kinship beyond the realm of biological relationships. This conceptualization allows the group to be "perpetuated [through time] by transmission of its name, wealth and titles through a real or fictitious descent line which is recognized as legitimate as long as the continuity can be expressed in the language of descent

or [marriage] alliance or, most often, of both" (Lévi-Strauss 1984:152; see also 1979:174).

The concept of house societies has been profitably used by ethnographers working in Island Southeast Asia and the Northwest Coast of North America, as well as archaeologist working in Iron Age Europe and Mesoamerica (Carsten and Hugh-Jones 1995; Gillespie 2000a, 2000b, 2000c; González-Ruibal 2005; Waterson 1995). Houses, and the social units formed by their members (households), are long-lived social entities organized for a variety of reasons that function both in the moment and, due to biological reproduction and their role in the enculturation of children, through time (Gillespie 2000c). As such, house membership is used by individuals in some societies as yet another axis of identity that may rise to preeminence in periods of social change (Waterson 1995). The concept of house and house membership is not, however, limited to nuclear or even extended families; it may be expanded to include other households to form broader social segments when other axes of identity are disrupted, as occurs during long-distance migrations. For example, Bernardini (2008) has suggested that the house society concept is helpful in understanding the maintenance of ritual and control of particular rituals by specific clans featured in Hopi oral histories of clan migrations. Specifically, the core house of lineages and clans is responsible for the preservation of ceremonies and the esoteric knowledge they encompass, even though their performance may be in the hands of ritual sodalities whose membership cuts across lineages and clans. Membership in the core house carries with it the responsibility of maintaining the ceremony and associated paraphernalia in the present and ensuring its continued existence in the future. As a result, membership in and maintenance of the house becomes a major source of identity. Members are the holders and protectors of ceremony, esoteric knowledge and ritual paraphernalia, and they undertake strategic social actions (such as marriage alliances) to ensure continuation of the house.

During the periods of disruption and transition that characterize migration and the resulting changes in the nature of interaction between migrants and hosts of different cultural/ethnic traditions, house membership can rise to the fore and serve as a tangible and concrete axis of identity. This, in turn, creates historical depth that produces a landscape full of "dense webs of signification... [that] serve as basic cognitive models used to structure, think and experience the world" (Carsten and Hugh-Jones 1995:3). In other words, houses anchor individuals in a particular place and time and provide both meaning and structure that locate them in the future with reference to the past (Gillespie 2000a, 2000c; González-Ruibal 2005; Waterson 1995). In addition to providing a sense of belonging, membership in a house with links to the past and views to the future also can open avenues for access to social status, political power, and material resources. As noted above, the concept of house is not limited to the scale of a single nuclear or even extended family. The organizing ideas of "house societies" can be extended to larger groups such as ethnic enclaves through an extension of concepts of kinship and historical connectedness. As such, multiple houses can strategically bind themselves together within a larger community, resulting in an ethnic enclave that "stands out" as separate. Architecture is used in these circumstances not only to house the social unit but to create "rootedness" and the "idea of perpetuity" (González-Ruibal 2005:160; see also Gillespie 2000a, 2000c). In essence, individual houses or clusters of them in an enclave give meaning to place and a sense of permanency and history to the migrants (Basso 1996; Feld and Basso 1996). They can be used to rewrite history to provide a timelessness and a permanence within a community (Nielsen 1995; Van Dyke 2004; Van Dyke and Alcock 2003a) by creating a social memory that is reinforced through visual architectural cues and daily movement through the community.

Host-Migrant Interactions

Although this heading may seem redundant, it is not, for it shifts our focus to another perspective. All too often, migration and postmigration interactions are viewed only from the perspective of the migrants and migrant action; the previous section was written from that perspective. Not only must we ask why migrants choose to blend in or stand out, but we must also ask why the host population allows them to integrate or segregate. To gain a more complete and nuanced understanding, it is equally important to examine the perspective and agential action of the host population within large, multiethnic communities. To understand long-term community dynamics, we must examine the motivation for social alliances within the indigenous population in terms of their position/reaction to the migrants, their preexisting social dynamics, and the creation, negotiation, selective editing, and re-creation of history and how it is reinforced through social memory. This is particularly relevant to a community like Point of Pines Pueblo, where occupation of the site continued for another 100 years after abandonment of the Kayenta enclave.

In recent years, archaeologists have begun to move away from the view of large communities in middle-range societies as autonomous, self-contained, well-integrated units to an understanding of them as heterogeneous, dynamic, and sometimes volatile social collectives (Isbell 2000; McGuire and Saitta 1996; O'Gorman 2010; Stone 1999, 2008; Stone and Howell 1994; Yaeger and Canuto 2000). The benefits of participation in large communities have been well documented in terms of increased competitive advantage over other groups for preferential use rights to material resources, marriage arrangements, ceremonial participation and information (Adler et al. 1996; Duff and Wilshusen 2000; Wilshusen and Ortman 1999). The joining together and integration of diverse individuals and families into a lasting structural mosaic is not an easy task, however, and village fissioning is always a threat. As the scale of the community increases, competition between individuals and families within the community for economic, political, and ritual resources increases, and factional tendencies come to the fore. The resulting tensions are played out in the political arena as alliances form and break down depending on the particular issue at hand. Charismatic individuals may arise in these situations and attempt to solidify their positions within the community, forming more lasting alliances by tapping into shared aspects of identity including age, gender, kin, and sodality. One of the most effective arenas to solidify alliances in middle-range societies is ritual (Rothenbuhler 1998; Stone 1999, 2005a). Ritual is an important arena because of its ties to the supernatural and the packed nature of its messages, which go beyond specific acts or images. Ideals of behavior in terms of the ways individuals relate and organize are played out in the ritual realm with references to the past as well as projections into the future. These ideals are sanctified by connections to the supernatural.

Because of the diversity of individuals, their personal goals, and divergent pasts, there is never complete agreement on these ideals within aggregated communities, however. Minimally, there are always at least two factions in large communities, though there may be more. One faction is happy with the status quo, while the other has a different view of the situation, one that challenges the status quo (Stone 2005a; Stone and Howell 1994). The result is competing interest groups. Because of these two views, the status quo is never, in fact, static, and the structural mosaic within which individuals live their everyday lives is continually negotiated, sometimes being reified with only minor adjustments, at other times being reinvented, and at still other times resulting in the community breaking apart. Communities that persist for long periods of time do so because they develop means of recognizing and balancing differing loyalties and boundaries between small groups and the needs of the broader collective of the community. An effective mechanism for achieving this balance may be counterintuitive in that it entails increasing the axes of identity for individuals and families through the formation of multiple sodalities, thus increasing the heterogeneity of the community mosaic. Increasing the number of axes that individuals may call upon to form crosscutting alliances also enlarges the number of overlapping networks in which an individual can potentially participate and expands the ties to other individuals and small groups. The

result is a tightly entwined social and political mesh in which each individual has a unique position tied to his/her participation in varying sodalities and multiple scales of kin groups, but in which everyone has some position and in which individual networks overlap, creating larger social structures. At different points of time, different axes of identity and networks of alliances may come to the fore while others are de-emphasized. However, these other axes and networks are never completely eliminated and help form dense webs of connectedness within a community.

In the case of Point of Pines Pueblo, the Kayenta migrants entered an area with large, aggregated communities where a complex and heterogeneous structural mosaic of social mechanisms was already in place to balance existing tensions between the formation of factions and community integration (Stone 2003). This can produce two possible outcomes. The host population, or segments within it, may insist on assimilation of the migrants within the existing structure, thus maintaining the status quo. Alternatively, the host community, or a segment within it, may challenge the status quo by welcoming a new and different axis of identity and potential network of alliance formation in the community. Which alternative occurs may shift through time, resulting in tolerance and even celebration of ethnic otherness at some times but discouraging or even forbidding it at others. For example, McGuire and Saitta (1996:211) argue that founding segments of a community may "benefit materially, socially, and ideologically by attracting others. The [founding segment] would maintain their primary status, but give new arrivals good land and an important position in the ritual calendar." McGuire and Saitta's study is concerned with the process of aggregation rather than host-migrant interaction, but we can extend their argument for our purposes. In other words, the position of a segment of the host community that wishes to challenge the status quo may improve by welcoming a potential group of new allies into the community and rewarding the migrants' alliance and support on some issues by encouraging their choice to emphasize their ethnic otherness, thus creating a new status quo that incorporates additional diversity.

The ability of a segment of the host community to take this type of action is dependent on the conditions present at a particular time and place. As conditions change, segments of the new multiethnic community may again challenge a status quo in which ethnic otherness is allowed. McGuire and Saitta (1996) argue that material, social, and ritual "thresholds" exist that may change the view of the host community to newcomers. Specifically, they argue that as preferential use rights to resources such as agricultural lands exceed those available and the ceremonial calendar becomes increasingly crowded, newcomers will no longer be as welcome. In times of scarcity, the newest arrivals may be pressured to leave. The types of ethnic and ritual differences seen at Point of Pines Pueblo would add an extra source of potential conflict and an additional aspect of ritual thresholds discussed by McGuire and Saitta. Ritual is so powerful in ethnic interaction not only because it lays out ideals of behavior, relationships, and organization, but also because of its potential to separate members of the community along multiple lines, including categories of audience versus performer but also between those who have been initiated and possess the esoteric knowledge to fully understand the ceremony and those that do not (Dozier 1966; McGuire 1986; Stone 2003). For example, a major source of conflict between hosts and migrants among ethnographic groups in the American Southwest occurs in the ritual realm. The performance of ceremonies may be exclusive to only one ethnic group or create conflicts in the ritual calendar between the groups. The most thoroughly documented of these occurs at the Tewa pueblo of Hano (Dozier 1954, 1966; Stanislawski 1979), founded by Tewas who migrated from the Rio Grande in the 1700s to First Mesa on the Colorado Plateau, adjacent to the Hopi pueblos (though see Ellis 1979 for an example from Laguna Pueblo). At Hano, the Tewa residents participate in Hopi ceremonies on First Mesa, but each group excludes members of the other from some ceremonies. Another source of tension between the two groups is the

scheduling of katchina dances, in particular Hano's use of the Tewa ceremonial cycle in which katchina dances occur after the Hopi Niman ceremony, when Hopi believe the katchinas leave the mesa and return to their homes in the mountains.

Point of Pines Pueblo was not the first aggregated community in the region, nor is the Kayenta enclave present at the pueblo the only evidence of migrants (though it is the earliest and only enclave). Additionally, the pueblo continued to be used after the destruction of the enclave in AD 1300 for another 100 years. Analysis of ethnic interaction from the perspective of both the migrants and the indigenous population is crucial. Further, it is important to extend our analysis to include changes in the organizational constructs of the existing community before, during, and after the enclave's existence. The crucial importance of house and ritual in the organization of this community calls for an investigation of how daily life was structured and social memory created, negotiated, destroyed, and re-created through architectural construction, abandonment, and remodeling.

Viewing Community Interaction through Architecture

An understanding of complex relationships within aggregated communities and between hosts and migrants can be gained through an examination of architecture. Specifically, space in general and architecture in particular is not only imbued with social meaning but manipulated as part of the negotiation of social relations (Bailey 1990; Beck et al. 2007; Gillespie 2000a; González-Ruibal 2005; Hendon 2000; Locock 1994; Nanoglou 2011; Smith 2003; Tilley 1994; Waterson 2000; Wilson 2010). That is, the construction and transformation of architecture are powerful forces in the creation, negotiation, and reification of history and the rights of groups within a community. Architecture gives meaning and permanence to locations; it situates social action and relationships and anchors them in place and time. Domestic and ritual architecture is such an important factor in the creation of political landscapes and local history through the manipulation of social memory because it is the locus of enculturation (Bailey 1990; Blanton 1994; Lawrence and Low 1990; Scott 1994; Wilk 1990), community integration (Adler and Wilshusen 1990; Stone 2002a), small group formation and political action (Gilman and Stone 2013; Ferguson 1996; Nielsen 1995; Saunders 1990; Stone 1999, 2000, 2013), as well as the symbolic representation of the cosmos (Cameron 1996; Kus and Raharijaona 1990, 2000; Moore 1986; Ortiz 1969; Shafer 1995).

Furthermore, architectural structures physically organize space by partitioning off some areas and opening up others. They separate the private from the public and constrain who has access to events occurring within their walls. They direct movement through and around, thus impacting daily life, interaction and bodily experience of the world. Individuals not only move through space and architecture, they experience it in their daily lives. It has an impact on how they move as well as what they see and interpret (Byrd 1994; Carsten and Hugh-Jones 1995; Ferguson 1996; Gamble 2007; Hillier and Hanson 1984; Johnson 2012; Kent 1990; Kuijt 2000; Nielsen 1995; Tilley 1994; Wilson 2010). Because of its ability to structure movement and to organize and segregate interaction, architecture can be used to negotiate new social and political orders or to reinforce an existing one, and to reify these within social memory. Social memory, however, is not static. It is contested and negotiated; it is created, denied, and re-created (Jones 2007; Silliman 2001, 2009; Wilson 2010). In other words, social memory is inherently political and is used in defining relationships (both competitive and cooperative), identity, and access to material and nonmaterial resources. In much the same way, architecture is not static and is a social undertaking. Modifications and additions to existing architecture are not only tied to the social orders they create, negotiate, and/or reify because of the action of individuals and households. They also carry with them the sanction of at least part of the community. Architecture and social memory are thus mutually reflective and reflexive. But it goes beyond this, for architecture is consciously created and manipulated as well as subcon-

sciously experienced and interpreted (Creese 2012; Johnson 2012; Thomas 1996).

Social memory is constructed through the reinforcement of social categories (kin, gender, ethnicity, and age) that are emphasized or negotiated within society with architectural cues provided in the organization of space and architecture's effect on movement through space. Architecture defines public versus private space, giving it the ability to exclude or include, and it has a powerful symbolic role in reinforcing history, giving meaning to place and the relationships that occur there (Creese 2012; Hendon 2000; Johnson 2012; Kus and Raharijaona 1990, 2000; Moore 1986; Nanoglou 2011; Rapoport 1990; Wilson 2010). Changes in these cues are integrally tied to changes in relationships that are important enough to the inhabitants that they invest resources and labor to construct new buildings or remodel old ones. These investments are either sanctioned by the community or disallowed, the latter resulting in heightened tensions between the house and other members of the community. Community sanctioning of the house can be seen not only in construction but in the ritual sphere. Many societies have house blessing ceremonies (Joyce 2000) such as those used by the Btammaliba of Africa (Blier 1987), the Toraja of Indonesia (Waterson 2000), and the Zuñi of the American Southwest (Bunzell 1932; Green 1979). At blessing ceremonies, houses and their members are recognized and sanctioned by the larger community, and the connections between houses and the community (and the cosmos) are recognized. In short, houses are concrete manifestations of concepts of both cosmic and social order (Kus and Raharijaona 1990, 2000) at multiple scales and are thus a point of negotiation between the agential actions of the house and the structure of the community. Tangible symbols of the dialogue between house and community are visible and can be manipulated in the construction and remodeling of houses.

The ongoing negotiations between communities, houses, and small groups (enclaves) within communities can also be seen in ritual space tied to segments of the community. Both

Nielsen (1995) and Van Dyke (2004) have argued that public space can be used to reinforce group solidarity and legitimize authority through the creation of social memory. The act of constructing ritual architecture and its visual impact are used to create social memory that is tied to place and to the historical context of the community (or portions of it), thus reinforcing the status quo of the structural mosaic of the community and the identities housed in it (Jones 2007; Pauketat and Alt 2003; Van Dyke 2004). But as noted by Rodman (1992), perception and interpretation of place and architecture are not monolithic (see also Smith 2003; Van Dyke and Alcock 2003a; Wilson 2010). Just as personal goals differ from individual to individual within a community, so does the interpretation of social memory, and thus the perception of place and architecture.

Therefore, the decision-making process involved in architectural design and its role in negotiating alliances and rights by members of houses are multifaceted. Aside from the constraints of climate, resource availability, technology, and labor that direct architectural design and construction, social factors at numerous scales (individual, family, small group, community) are crucial in the design process and in subsequent remodeling (Bailey 1990; Beck et al. 2007; Blier 1987; Duncan 1981; Locock 1994; Rodman 1992; Saunders 1990). The multidimensional social nature of this design and construction process also results in multiple perceptions and interpretations of the process, which can be both a source and result of contradiction and tension. Equally important, treatment of abandoned structures (leaving them unused, scavenged, remodeled, or razed, and rebuilt on a different footprint) is part of an ongoing social dialogue and negotiation of rights and social relations between community members (Creel and Anyon 2003; Gillespie 2000a; González-Ruibal 2005; Lightfoot 1993; Shafer 1995; Walker 2002; Waterson 2000). Though a theme for many, Bailey's (1990) call for an architectural biography to understand processes of identity and the negotiation of social relationships is particularly eloquent.

I suggest that the actions of a house are best read in terms of a biography. By this I mean that the house is an active participant in society just as a human member of society is. The house plays a variety of roles in the creation and maintenance of social reality.... Thus, one may speak of the life-cycle of a house: a house is born, it lives, it dies, it is buried or cremated, and its spirit is remembered after its death. (Bailey 1990:28)

Intrinsic to this approach is the recognition that neither social orders nor architecture are static. The degree of change that occurs in the remodeling is related to the degree of changes that occurred in the negotiation of social relations. For example, Bailey (1990), Gillespie (2000a), Waterson (2000), and Wilson (2010) argue that remodeling within the same footprint of a building (reusing existing foundations) indicates a degree of continuity and a desire to maintain claims to rights and privileges based on past social structures and personal histories. In these instances, remodeling may relate to changing composition and size of a household over generations (Cameron 1996; Reynolds 1981) or to changes in household status (Wilk 1990). Conversely, leveling a previous building site, creating a new foundation in a different orientation and a new structure symbolically reinforces a complete break with past social relationships (Bailey 1990; Wilson 2010). It not only prevents scavenging by previous inhabitants, it removes evidence of their existence (and therefore rights). Not only does it rewrite the history of social relationships, *it writes those relationships out of the community's architectural history.*

Ethnic Interaction
at Point of Pines Pueblo

To illustrate these points, a detailed analysis of the architecture at Point of Pines Pueblo was undertaken. As already mentioned, the pueblo contained not only an indigenous population but an enclave of Kayenta migrants. The Kayenta region of the Colorado Plateau witnessed considerable variability in territorial size and

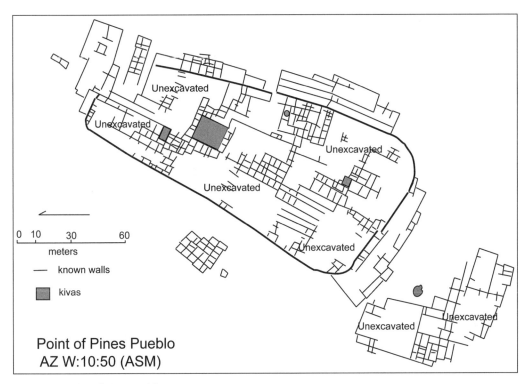

FIGURE 3.2. Point of Pines Pueblo.

settlement pattern through time. Migration out of the area occurred at various times. One of the places where the migrants relocated was the Point of Pines region of what is today the San Carlos Apache Reservation in the highlands of east-central Arizona. Although there is evidence for the presence of migrants in the region prior to the founding of Point of Pines Pueblo itself, active signaling of ethnic difference is not evident elsewhere (Figure 3.2).

Point of Pines Pueblo (AD 1250–1400) has long stirred the imagination of scholars interested in migration in middle-range societies. It is a large pueblo (800 rooms) in which the inhabitants created, negotiated, and re-created relationships through agential actions within a heterogeneous structure. A major axis of this negotiation for at least part of the occupation of the pueblo was ethnicity. Specifically, a migrant group from the Kayenta region to the north inhabited a room block within the pueblo for the first 50 years of its 150-year occupation.

The nature of the interaction between the two groups within the pueblo has been the subject of academic speculation since the early reports of the presence of an enclave by Haury (1958) and the large number of archaeologists who received their initial field training in the region between 1947 and 1963 at the University of Arizona archaeological field school (Haury 1989). Although other sites in the region have been the subject of theses, dissertations, and field monographs, an in-depth analysis of Point of Pines Pueblo itself was never produced. The nature of identity formation, ethnic interaction, and community dynamics at Point of Pines Pueblo is used in this volume to provide a window into these processes in middle-range societies. To gain a nuanced understanding of these shifting alliances and the manipulation of social memory and history that both migrants and host populations undertook, a biography, or history, of the pueblo is needed. The medium through which we examine these social actions and create this biography is architecture. By understanding how, when, and where structures were constructed and remodeled within the pueblo, as well as how they were abandoned and treated after abandonment, insight can be gained on the negotiation of alliances along varying axes of identity, and how history and social memory were created, negotiated, manipulated, destroyed, and re-created.

In creating a biography of Point of Pines Pueblo, several variables are particularly important. First, because individuals and groups make decisions about the future based on their perceptions of current interactions, their own personal history, and their society's history, it is necessary to have a firm grasp of the prehistories of both the Kayenta and Point of Pines regions. Important aspects of these histories include the nature of social, political, and ritual organization. These characteristics can be discussed in terms of mobility across the landscape, settlement pattern, household organization, and ritual structures. The historical context also must focus on contact between the two areas prior to the formation of the enclave at Point of Pines Pueblo in terms of either small-scale migration (at the level of the individual or family) or trade contacts. These interactions demonstrate both the continuous nature of migration and the information sources members of the migrant enclave had prior to their movement south.

Once the historical context is established, emphasis shifts to the nature of the migrant-host and, conversely, host-migrant interactions following the migrant group's arrival at the pueblo. It is important to determine if core households were established by both the migrants and the indigenous Mogollon peoples that served as central houses in which esoteric knowledge, ritual ceremonies, and identities were maintained and passed down to the next generation. These core houses were the axes around which the two ethnic groups orbited and should be evident both during the establishment of the pueblo and con-

tinued occupation through time. Differences in ethnic identity of the inhabitants of the core houses are evident in both their subconscious and conscious actions. Subconscious actions are housed in the learning frameworks of the one group that may not be evident to the other, such as building techniques including footings and wall construction that are then covered with plaster. Conscious actions, on the other hand, are those purposefully undertaken to reinforce identities and affiliations with house and ethnicity. They engage material culture and space; they bound it and influence movement, and thus the manner in which that space is experienced. Some of these engagements are directed at the ethnic group (size, shape, and internal organization of ritual and domestic structures) and others are directed at the community as a whole (size and shape of public spaces, placement of structures, size and number of stories of room blocks, enclosing walls). Finally, changes in the community through time tell the story of community dynamics and shifting alliances. This is evident not only in changes in the construction of public spaces (large communal structures and plazas as well as the presence of a compound wall surrounding the community) but also in how abandoned structures were treated. Were residents allowed access to their former homes? Were houses remodeled within the same footprint, or were new houses placed over old ones in new footprints? These issues are addressed for Point of Pines Pueblo in the following chapters as an illustration of how migration and resulting ethnic interaction occur between migrants and hosts in middle-range societies. Although the data is specific to one community, it is illustrative of processes that occurred throughout prehistory on a global scale. Similar social actions occurred, though with different results, in the Canaan Highlands, the Outer Hebrides, northern New York/southern Ontario, and countless other locations around the world.

The Historical Context
of the Kayenta Migration to
Point of Pines Pueblo

As noted in Chapter 3, migration is not a singular event but a process of movement across the landscape that engages it and its inhabitants in a variety of ways at multiple scales. To understand any individual instance of movement, it must be placed within this broader context. Before we can understand why individuals make the decisions they make in terms of migration and identity expression at a particular time and place, and how these decisions are operationalized, we must understand the historical context of people's everyday lives (Pauketat 2001b). Past engagements with the landscape and its inhabitants affect both the perception of events and possible paths along which individuals and groups may proceed in their relationships with others. It is therefore important to have a solid foundation in the culture histories of the homelands of both the migrants and the host communities as part of our creation of the biography of the Point of Pines community. Similarly, our interpretations of the past are impacted by the work that has occurred in the regions we study, for we operate within a historical context as well. Because archaeological knowledge builds upon the work of earlier times, a review of previous research in both the Kayenta and Point of Pines areas (see Figure 1.1) is necessary before we can begin our analysis. Once this background is established, specific architectural engagements at Point of Pines Pueblo can be investigated.

Archaeological Research in the Kayenta Region

The Kayenta region in north-central Arizona is generally viewed as a coherent region of interacting settlements based on the internal consistency of its ceramics and exchange networks that differ considerably from the Mesa Verde region to the northeast and the Chaco region to the east/southeast (Dean 1996). Movement across the landscape within the Kayenta region was a common phenomenon prehistorically, resulting in considerable variability in the size of the area through time. At its greatest geographic extent during Pueblo II (PII) times, it was bounded on the north by the portion of the San Juan River located in Utah and on the west by the Colorado River with considerable evidence of occupation on the southern edge of the Colorado River in the Glen Canyon region. The southern and eastern edges of Black Mesa defined the remainder of the region. The core area of the Kayenta region was occupied fairly consistently from ca. AD 600 until its abandonment in AD 1300. This core area is located in a series of canyons and plateaus clustered around the modern town of Kayenta, including Long House Valley, Tsegi Canyon, the Shonto Plateau, the Kayenta Valley, and the Klethla Valley (Figure 4.1).

Archaeological work in the area has a long history. During the first half of the twentieth century much effort was concentrated on some

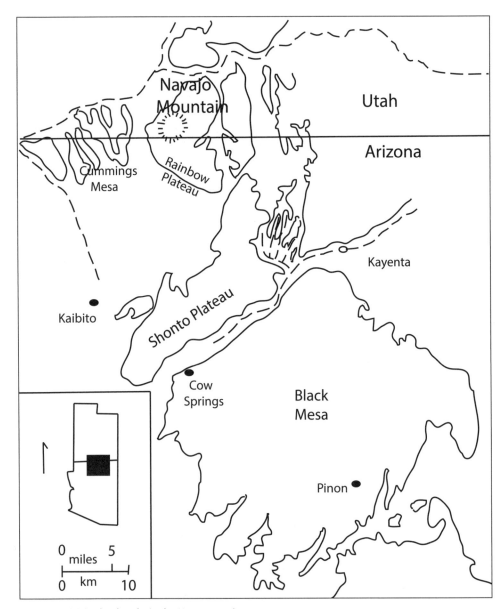

FIGURE 4.1. Major landmarks in the Kayenta region.

of the more spectacular geographical landmarks such as Rainbow Bridge (Beals et al. 1945; Morss 1931). The area was visited by many of the founding fathers of Southwestern archaeology (Cummings 1945; Guernsey 1931; Kidder and Guernsey 1919; Morss 1931). Much of our current knowledge of the area is based on a series of large cultural resource management (CRM) projects (Table 4.1) starting with the Museum of North-

ern Arizona's work throughout the region in the 1960s and 1970s (Adams et al. 1961; Ambler 1985, 1994; Ambler et al. 1964; Ambler and Olson 1977; Dean et al. 1978; Geib et al. 1985; Hobler 1964, 1974; Lindsay et al. 1968; Neely and Olson 1977; Stein 1984; Ward 1975) followed by the University of Utah's work south of Glen Canyon in the vicinity of the Coombs site (Jennings 1998; Lister 1959; Lister et al. 1960; Lister and Lister 1961),

TABLE 4.1. Excavation site reports from major CRM projects in the Kayenta region

Project Location	Reference
Individual Sites	
Betatakin	Anderson 1971; Dean 1970
Coombs Site	Jennings 1998; Lister 1959; Lister et al. 1960; Lister and Lister 1961
Kiet Siel	Anderson 1971; Dean 1970, 2000
Inscription House	Ward 1975
Neskahi Village	Hobler 1964, 1974
Pottery Pueblo	Stein 1984
Standing Fall House	Klesert 1982
Larger Projects	
Black Mesa	Andrews et al. 1982; Christenson and Perry 1985; Gumerman 1970; Gumerman et al. 1972; Klesert 1978; Klesert and Powell 1979; Linford 1982; Nichols and Smiley 1984; Powell 1984; Powell et al. 1980; Powell and Smiley 2002; Smiley et al. 1983; Swarthout et al. 1986
Chilchinbito	Bond et al. 1977
Cow Springs	Ambler and Olson 1977
Cummings Mesa	Ambler et al. 1964
Klethla Valley	Anderson 1980
Lee Canyon	Whittlesey 1992
Long House Valley	Dean 1990; Dean et al. 1978; Effland 1979; Haas and Creamer 1993; Harrill 1982
Lower Glen Canyon	Adams et al. 1961; Long 1966
Monument Valley	Neely and Olson 1977
Navajo Mountain and surrounding areas	Ambler 1985; Geib 2011; Geib et al. 1985; Lindsay et al. 1968
Shonto Plateau	Schroedl 1989
Tsegi Canyon	Christensen 2003; Dean 1969

and the long-lived Black Mesa Archaeological project (see Powell and Smiley 2002 for an overview). This work was supplemented with smaller salvage and highway archaeology projects until fairly recently (Anderson 1980; Bliss 1960; Bond et al. 1977; Geib 2011; Schroedl 1989; Swarthout et al. 1986; Whittlesey 1992).

Based on these studies it is clear there was a long-lived prehistoric tradition in the area with occupation from Basketmaker II (BM II) through PIII times that was distinct from those in other areas of the Colorado Plateau. Synthesis of this material shows considerable variability in site location through time, site layout, and domestic and communal architecture, including the continued use of semi-subterranean pithouses as domestic structures alongside aboveground pueblos through PIII times (Dean 1996, 2002; Haas 1986, 1989; Hobler 1964, 1974; Lindsay 1969; Powell and Smiley 2002; Stone 2014).

Intensive analysis has concentrated on the region's political, economic, and social organizations as they relate to two areas. The first issue concerns human adaptation to a region characterized by environmental variability in terms of both long- and short-term drought cycles that affected settlement patterns and resulted in demographic shifts (Dean et al. 1985; Gumerman 1988; Gumerman and Dean 1989). Much of this work has become the basis for agent-based modeling of adaptation to complex environmental conditions throughout the world (see, for example, Berry et al. 2002; Gumerman and Gell-Mann 1994; Kohler and Gumerman 2000; Kohler and Van der Leeuw 2007). The second focus of work has concentrated on the economic, social, and political organization of the late PIII (Tsegi phase) occupation of the Tsegi Valley and Long House Canyon. These projects have sought information relating to the organization of individual communities, particularly Betatakin and Kiet Siel (Christensen 2003; Dean 1969, 1970, 2000) and, more broadly, regional organization in terms of warfare (Haas 1986, 1989; Haas and Creamer 1993).

In more recent years, a number of studies in the Kayenta region have attempted to better understand the oral history of the Hopi people on the southern edge of Black Mesa (First, Second, and Third Mesas) by linking prehistoric remains to Hopi oral traditions regarding both migration histories and the role of the clan in ritual organization (Bernardini 2008, 2011b). Hopi oral history talks about the earliest migrants to the Hopi mesas, the Motisinom, as originating in the Black Mesa/Kayenta area. These groups were characterized by small, dispersed communities dominated by matrilocal postmarital residence and matriclan kinship organization centered on avunculocal relationships (mother's brother to ego) in their political and ritual organization. Small kivas in PII and PIII villages in the Kayenta region served as loci for both the performance of clan ceremonies and a place for the men of the clan who lived in their wives' villages to congregate in their natal homesteads away "from the prying eyes of in-married husbands of other descent groups" (Bernardini 2011a:218; see also Ware 2002). The result is considerable variability in kiva construction and internal features as each clan created ritual space for its own purposes (Stone 2013). Hopi oral history also talks about some clans (the Nùutungkwisinow) migrating over considerable areas of Arizona before finally arriving at the Hopi mesas where they live today (Bernardini 2011b; Lyons 2003). While on these migrations, clans were charged

with maintaining their clan ceremonies, which are still practiced today. Clan histories also describe contacting and living among many other groups during these migrations (Bernardini 2008). In other words, movement across the landscape and engagement with that landscape and the peoples who lived there is a crucial aspect of Hopi oral tradition, of what it means to be Hopi today.

The nearly century's worth of research conducted in the Kayenta region has resulted in a considerable database from which to construct a culture history. Recent summaries of Kayenta culture history by Dean (1996, 2002), Haas (1986, 1989; Haas and Creamer 1993), and Geib (2011) propose considerable movement of people across the landscape within the Kayenta region surrounding a core area of canyons in the Laguna Creek drainage south of the San Juan River in northeastern Arizona, which was consistently inhabited. The area was occupied as early as Paleoindian times, and architecture is evident in the form of small pithouses at the beginning of Basketmaker II (BM II) times. The summary of occupation in the region from BM II through the end of PI is presented in Table 4.2. A more detailed discussion of the periods relevant to this study (PII and PIII) is presented below. This information is a synthesis of several recent studies (Dean 1996, 2002; Geib 2011; Haas and Creamer 1993).

Pueblo II (AD 950/1000–1150)
The greatest geographic extent of Kayenta settlement in the region occurred during PII (AD 950/1000–1150) times, when Kayenta communities could be found on the interior of Black Mesa to the south of the core and extending north to Monument Valley and the southern reaches of Glen Canyon. This period is characterized by a transition in the ceramic assemblage (Geib 2011) with the appearance of Sosi Black-on-White and Dogoszhi Black-on-White by the middle of the period. Tsegi Orange wares are present by the end of the period.

Domestic structures included semi-subterranean pithouses, surface masonry and

TABLE 4.2. Summary of the Kayenta region culture history from Basketmaker II through Pueblo I times

Period	Date	Description
BM II	1000 BC–AD 500	Mixed hunter-gatherer/horticultural subsistence system with increasing population levels and decreasing mobility through the period. Sites include rockshelters and small pithouse villages on mesa tops.
BM III	AD 500–850	Mixed hunter-gatherer/horticultural subsistence continues. There is an increase in frequency of villages with sites found both on mesa tops and along drainages.
PI	AD 850–950/1000	Masonry and jacal storerooms are present at some pithouse village sites. Villages remain small and are found in a variety of geographical locations.

jacal rooms, and ramadas. Milling rooms containing multiple sets of manos and metates for the grinding of corn are common and were found in a variety of structure types: pit structures, masonry rooms, ramadas (Dean 1996; Haas 1986). Villages were widely spread across the landscape and generally fairly small (less than 10 rooms/structures), though occasionally larger sites (30 rooms) were present. Masonry room blocks were organized in classic "unit pueblo" style with a trash mound and kiva in front of a row of masonry and jacal rooms used for storage and generalized living activities.

Transition Phase (AD 1150–1250)

Dean (1996, 2002) refers to the Early PIII period between AD 1150–1250 as the Transition phase because of the considerable transformations that occurred in settlement pattern, village layout and apparent regional organization. The ceramic assemblages are dominated by Flagstaff Black-on-White, Tusayan Black-on-White and Tsegi Orange wares (Geib 2011). The settlement pattern at the beginning of the Transition phase is a continuation of the PII period pattern with widespread distribution of highly dispersed, small communities. By the end of the Transition phase, however, much of the outlying areas, like Black Mesa and Monument Valley, were abandoned, and larger sites began to appear, clustered together in denser concentrations separated by unused areas of the landscape. Interestingly, Dean (2002) argues that although the population in these locations increases, it does not do so enough to account for all of the population that lived in the outlying areas. Some migration

out of the Kayenta area probably occurred at this time. It should be noted that flexed burials that appear similar to the mortuary patterns used in the Kayenta area first appear in the Point of Pines region in small numbers at the beginning of this phase (Rodrigues 2008). The Kayenta enclave at Point of Pines Pueblo was established by the end of the Kayenta Transition phase (see below).

Environmental reconstructions indicate a decrease in annual precipitation and an increase in periodic droughts of varying severity after AD 1150 (Dean 2002; Haas 1989), both of which probably contributed to abandonment of outlying areas during the Transition phase. Villages in the occupied area were larger than in the previous period but remained highly variable in terms of domestic and ritual architecture, as well as site layout (Dean 1996, 2002; Stone 2013, 2014). Semi-subterranean pithouses, jacal structures, and masonry rooms are found by themselves and in combination in settlements that start to conform to definite patterns of site layout. Four habitation site types are generally recognized (Dean 1996). First are pithouse villages, consisting of varying numbers of pit structures, often with a kiva and milling room. These sites have considerable variability in how structures are arranged relative to each other. This can be contrasted with front-facing unit pueblos and plaza pueblos, which consist of masonry room blocks and sometimes rows of pit structures with enclosing walls that contain defined plazas and one or more kivas. Finally, Dean (1996) notes the presence of "ad hoc" sites in which community structure is in some way constrained by topographic features on the landscape, most frequently rockshelters. The size of these sites increased during the Transition phase, though they were still generally smaller than 50 rooms.

Tsegi Phase (AD 1250–1300)

The Tsegi phase (AD 1250–1300) is characterized by both Kayenta Black-on-White and Kiet Siel and Kayenta Polychrome ceramics. By the beginning of the Tsegi phase, outlying areas had been completely abandoned, and community clusters were found on the upper reaches of drainages in the core area, including Long House Valley, Tsegi Canyon, the southern Shonto Plateau, the Kayenta and Klethla Valleys, and Cummings and Segazlin Mesas (Dean 1996). Haas (1989) argues for some indications of hierarchical arrangement of settlements within valleys and canyons in terms of both site size and type. Intersettlement communication within the community clusters was facilitated with line-of-sight placements between them (Dean 1996; Haas and Creamer 1993). Within sites, 10 different types of domestic rooms/structures are evident (Dean 1996) including generalized living rooms (both aboveground masonry room blocks and semi-subterranean pithouses), two types of storage facilities (masonry store rooms and granaries), milling rooms, three types of extramural spaces (plazas, galleries, courtyards), and three types of ceremonial spaces (kivas, kiva annexes, and towers). Varying combinations of these structure types are organized into plaza pueblos, pithouse villages and ad hoc communities similar to the previous period. Additionally, courtyard pueblos lacking formal plazas appeared. Rooms were organized around courtyards, and sometimes along long linear galleries. All of these site types varied in size, with some of the plaza and courtyard pueblos located near permanent water sources having more than 100 rooms with multiple kivas.

Subsistence stress continued throughout the Tsegi phase, and water control features (most commonly reservoirs) appear in some settlements (Haas 1989). Storage increased dramatically in others (more than 60 percent at Kiet Siel) (Dean 2006) to mitigate impacts of decreased precipitation. Final abandonment of the region began in AD 1290 and was complete by AD 1300.

Post-AD 1300

By the end of the thirteenth century, the traditional Kayenta heartland had been abandoned, and its former inhabitants had migrated to at least two different locations. Some Kayenta groups coalesced with closely related and archaeologically similar Tusayan groups in Ancestral Hopi villages. The Kayenta region is recognized by Hopi oral tradition as an ancestral homeland (Bernardini 2011b). Other groups moved to a variety of locations to the south before returning to the Hopi mesas (Dean 1996; Clark 2001; Bernardini 2008, 2011b). Known locations of the southern migrations include the Mogollon Mountains, including the Point of Pines region (Dean 1996; Haury 1958; Lindsay 1987; Lyons 2003) and locations farther south in the Tonto Basin of southern Arizona (Bernardini 2011b; Clark 2001; Dean 1996; Lindsay 1987; Woodson 1999). The emphasis of this study is the migration to the Point of Pines region and the interactions that occurred there. Dendrochronological dates demonstrate early construction of a masonry room block by Kayenta migrants at Point of Pines Pueblo by at least 1250.

Archaeological Research in the Point of Pines Region

The Point of Pines region is located on the San Carlos Apache Reservation in the highly dissected mountains of east-central Arizona (Figure 4.2). Ecologically, the region consists of mixed forest/prairie biomes ranging in elevation from 6000 to 8000 feet above sea level (Haury 1989; Reid and Whittlesey 2010). The region is bounded geographically by the Nantack Ridge and Cienega Creek to the south and the Black River to the north. Sawmill Creek forms the western boundary and Eagle Creek the eastern. The area is dominated by three major drainage systems, and the result is a relatively well-watered area within the arid Southwest. In the north is the Black River and its major tributaries, Squaw and Clover Creeks and Stove Canyon. Willow Creek and its tributaries of Point of Pines

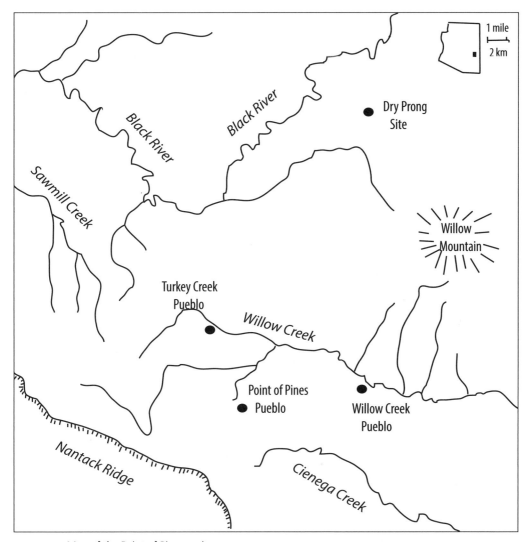

FIGURE 4.2. Map of the Point of Pines region.

and Turkey Creeks dominate the south-central portion of the region.

From 1946 to 1960 the Point of Pines region was the location of the University of Arizona archaeological field school under the direction of Emil W. Haury (and in the final years Raymond Thomson). The field school had several goals (Gifford and Morris 1985; Haury 1989; Mills 2005; Reid and Whittlesey 2010), the first being the training of students in hands-on methods of survey, excavation, and analysis, as well as the decision-making processes involved in a large archaeological project. This was particularly important for students in the university's newly established PhD program in anthropology, of which Haury was department chair, but the project had a much broader impact. More than 300 students enrolled in the field school during its 14 years of operation (Gifford and Morris 1985; Haury 1989). Although many of these students, particularly those that served as field supervisors, were enrolled at the University of Arizona, 57 other universities and colleges were represented. Additionally, the project twice hosted the Pecos Conference (1948 and 1951), in which the concept of the Mogollon as a culture area distinct from Anasazi to the north and Hohokam to the southwest was a major topic of discussion. The second goal of the field school centered on addressing the continuing controversy over the validity of the concept of the Mogollon culture area.

Haury first visited the sparsely populated mountains of central Arizona and New Mexico in 1931 as part of a reconnaissance survey he conducted with Russell Hasting for the Gila Pueblo. The general goal of this survey was to establish the boundaries of the red-on-buff (Hohokam) culture area currently under investigation by Harold Gladwin. As Reid and Whittlesey (2010) point out, what they found had far greater consequences. During this survey, they visited the Forestdale Valley and identified pithouse settlements (including Bluff and Bear Village) and pueblo villages (including Tla Kii, Forestdale, and Tundastusa) as well as sites in the Pine Lawn/Reserve and Upper Gila areas. All three areas would become important in Haury's development of the Mogollon concept (Haury 1936, 1940).

The Forestdale Valley was the location of the University of Arizona archaeological field school from 1939 to 1941. Data from the Bluff site and Bear Village proved vital in defining the early phases in the northern reaches of what he would come to define as the Mogollon culture area (Haury 1940; Reid and Whittlesey 2010). Haury's publications on excavations from the Pine Lawn/Reserve, Upper Gila River and Forestdale Valley regions defining the Mogollon set off a firestorm of controversy (Reid and Whittlesey 2010) in which the work at Point of Pines would play an important role. In 1945 Haury received funding from the Wenner-Gren Foundation. He and Edwin Sayles conducted a six-week reconnaissance survey of the Point of Pines region (Haury 1945, 1989) that revealed the presence of a large number of archaeological sites dating from the Archaic through protohistoric Apache periods. These sites had seen little disturbance by modern construction, and many contained large quantities of brown ware ceramics indicating Mogollon occupation. The survey revealed the perfect location for establishing a long-term ar-

chaeological field project with a permanent base that could be returned to year after year and at which his dual goals (education of students and further investigation of the Mogollon culture area) could be pursued.

Because of the focus on training students in archaeological methods, surveys were undertaken and several different types of sites were excavated to give students the full range of skills they would need in their careers (Haury 1989). In addition to excavating Point of Pines Pueblo, students did extensive work at Turkey Creek Pueblo, several pithouse villages, and the Archaic period Cienega Creek site. More limited testing of varying levels of intensity occurred at other sites ranging from agricultural features to rockshelters and small masonry pueblos (see Haury 1989 for a summary of the excavations and the resulting theses, dissertations, and publications). A series of reconnaissance surveys (both on horseback and on foot) in the vicinity of known sites and along prominent drainages were also conducted. The surveys resulted in preliminary site descriptions and locations, site maps, and collections of diagnostic artifacts from 170 sites during the years of the field school (Stone 2002b). The result is a well-established culture history defining changes in architecture and settlement patterns. Unfortunately, no radiocarbon dates currently exist for these sites, and dendrochronology dates (Bannister and Robinson 1971; Lowell 1991; Parker 1967; Smiley 1949) are largely restricted to only two phases (Tularosa and Maverick Mountain). Therefore, the sites were dated on the basis of ceramic cross dating using imported painted wares from the Zuñi region to the north. Since these sites were excavated, the ceramic chronologies have been refined considerably and the dates at both the very beginning (Circle Prairie phase) and the very end (Point of Pines phase) of the sequence have been updated to reflect these new cross dates. The methodology used to accomplish this is detailed in a series of reports on file at the Arizona State Museum Archives (Stone 2002b, 2006).

Like most of the mountain regions of central Arizona and central New Mexico, the Point of Pines region was abandoned ca. AD 1400 and not reinhabited until the arrival of Apache groups at least 100 years later (Asch 1961). Rinaldo (1964) argued that inhabitants from the Mogollon Highlands migrated north to the Zuñi River and joined with groups who lived there, and with whom they had long had trade relations as evident by the importation of Zuñi ceramics. Zuñi oral history (Bunzell 1932; Ferguson and Hart 1985) includes discussions of the migration of the Zuñi through both other worlds and across the landscape of this world before they came to their current home. Occupation of the Mogollon Highlands by Ancestral Zuñi people and their coalescence with long-time inhabitants of the Zuñi River and its tributaries prior to the arrival of the Spanish is also an important theme in Zuñi oral history. The Zuñi claim the Mogollon Highlands as part of their traditional use area (Ferguson and Hart 1985; see also Gregory and Wilcox 2007). Examination of nonmetric traits from burials at the protohistoric/historic Zuñi village of Hawikuh demonstrates the presence of a genetically diverse population, suggesting that groups from more distant locations had immigrated shortly before and/or during the site's occupation (Howell and Kintigh 1996).

Based on the archaeological remains identified in the Point of Pines region, prehistoric occupation occurred between 2000 BC and AD 1400. Architectural remains in the form of pithouse villages were built starting around AD 400–600. The chronology has been divided into nine phases beginning with the appearance of the first pithouse villages and ending when the area was abandoned in AD 1400. Habitation sites from each phase were excavated as part of the field school exploration of the area. Data from this work led to construction of the culture history of the region. The full sequence of this culture history—combining both the survey and excavation data and the updating of phase dates with recent cross dating—is presented below.

Circle Prairie Phase (???–AD 600)

Two sites dating to the Circle Prairie phase have been identified in the Point of Pines region. The first is a rockshelter located on the south face of Nantack Ridge that was not excavated. The

second is Crooked Ridge Village (AZ W:10:15 [ASM]) (Haury 1989; Wheat 1954; see also Stone 2002a, 2002b, 2005b), which serves as the type site for this phase. It was excavated in 1948 and 1949 and consists of a pithouse village on an isolated ridge. When initially identified on the survey, it was estimated to have approximately 100 pithouses, of which 23 domestic and two ritual pit structures were excavated. The habitation structures are square to slightly round with informal or clay-lined hearths and east-facing ramp entrances. They average 21 m² and about half have annexes or antechambers. Substantial roof structures were supported with two to 12 primary posts and numerous secondary posts. The two ritual structures were identified principally by their size (81.2 and 112.3 m²) and the presence of floor grooves that when covered with boards could be used as foot drums. Wheat (1954) originally assigned a date of AD 400–600 to the site based on a ceramic assemblage dominated by plain and red-slipped wares, and the almost total absence of textured, corrugated, and painted wares. Based on more recent dating of ceramic types at other sites, the ending date appears reasonable given the lack of textured wares, which were common in the 700s. The beginning date cannot be confirmed due to the absence of chronometric dates in the region but appears similar to the dates of early pithouse villages with plain and red ware assemblages elsewhere in the Mogollon region.

Stove Canyon Phase (AD 600–900)

Sixteen sites dated to the Stove Canyon phase were identified on survey. These sites are concentrated in Stove Canyon and along the tributaries of Point of Pines, Willow and Turkey Creeks. Site types range from rockshelters and lithic/sherd scatters to small villages. Two of the villages that were extensively excavated became the type sites for the Stove Canyon phase (Haury 1989; Neely 1974). The Stove Canyon site (AZ W:9:10 [ASM]) consists of 17 pithouses and two ritual structures. The Lunt site (AZ W:9:83 [ASM]) consists of 14 pithouses. Both sites are located on south-facing hillsides adjacent to streams and were excavated in 1960. Stove Canyon phase habitation structures are similar to Circle Prairie sites in shape but slightly larger. Stove Canyon site domestic structures average 21 m² while Lunt site domestic structures average 30 m², though they lack the annexes and antechambers of earlier structures. The number of primary and secondary posts, lack of storage pits, and the use of east-facing ramp entrances is similar to the previous phase. The main difference in features is an increased formalization of hearth form, with clay-lined circular hearths predominating.

Of the two ritual structures identified at the Stove Canyon site, one resembles a Hohokam ball court (Johnson 1961; Neely 1974), and the other is a 62 m² rectangular kiva that has floor grooves for foot drums (Neely 1974; Stone 2002a). These sites were assigned a later date than Crooked Ridge Village due to the addition of ceramics in the Alma Textured series to the plain and red wares found at Crooked Ridge Village. Corrugated wares were still rare, as were painted wares. The addition of the textured wares but paucity of the corrugated and painted intrusive ceramics led Neely (1974) to assign a date of AD 600–900 to the Stove Canyon phase, an assignment supported by current ceramic cross dating.

Nantack Phase (AD 900–1000)

Surveys in the region identified 41 sites dated to the Nantack phase found on tributaries of all the region's major drainages, especially those at higher elevations. Nantack Village (AZ W:10:111 [ASM]), the type site for the phase (Breternitz 1959), was excavated in 1954 and 1955. Like the Lunt and Stove Canyon sites, it is a small pithouse village (10 domestic structures and 2 ritual structures) located on a small ridge between two drainages. The pithouses resemble those of the previous two phases, being square and averaging 21 m² with zero to eight primary post supports, numerous secondary postholes, few pits, and east-facing ramp entrances (Breternitz 1959; Stone 2005b). Hearths continue to increase in formalization with stone-lined versions joining the clay-lined hearths of earlier sites. Lowell (1999) has suggested that the switch to stone-lined hearths indicates an increased use of domesticated crops that required long, slow cooking. The stone-lined hearths allow pots to be supported above a low fire and facilitate the frequent addition of fuel during the cooking process.

The two ritual structures are large (152.8 and 60 m²) and contain floor grooves that when covered with boards could have served as foot drums (Breternitz 1959; Stone 2002a). In the ceramic assemblage, neck-banded jars and Reserve Corrugated vessels are present, along with plain, red-slipped, and textured wares. Painted intrusive ceramics are more common, with most originating to the southeast (Mangas and Mimbres Black-on-White, Encinas and Nantack Red-on-Brown) and southwest (Sacaton Red-on-Buff). The date of the intrusive wares and lack of Tularosa Corrugated ceramics resulted in Breternitz's assignment of AD 900–1000 to this phase, which is supported by current ceramic cross dating.

It should be noted that although the type site for this phase is a pithouse village, 34 aboveground masonry sites containing ceramics suggesting a Nantack phase date were identified during reconnaissance surveys (Stone 2002b). All of these sites are small and appear to represent the beginnings of the pithouse to pueblo transition in the region.

Reserve Phase (AD 1000–1150)

A large number of sites (61) dated to the Reserve phase were identified by the reconnaissance surveys. The pithouse to pueblo transition that began during the Nantack phase continued during the Reserve phase, when aboveground masonry pueblos dominate. Most masonry sites are relatively small with fewer than 25 rooms. Additionally, sites dated to this period are found in a greater diversity of locations. Tributaries in higher elevations continued to be used, but sites are also found at lower elevations along the major creeks themselves.

The Dry Prong site (AZ W:6:5 [ASM]) is the type site for the Reserve phase (Haury 1989; Olson 1960). Excavated in 1959, it contains a large (204 m²), rectangular Great Kiva with benches and foot drums (Stone 2002a). Eighteen habitation rooms also are present: two as isolated rooms, two in a room block, and the remaining 14 in a single room block (Olson 1960). The relatively large size of the Great Kiva relative to the small number of habitation rooms suggests this site may have hosted other small communities for ritual performances. The site's date of AD 1000–1150 was assigned based on the presence of both Reserve and Tularosa corrugated ceramics as well as plain, red-slipped, textured, and painted wares imported from the Mimbres area to the southeast (Encinas and Nantack Red-on-Brown and Mimbres Black-on-White). The most common painted ware, however, is Reserve Black-on-White, imported from the Zuñi area to the north.

Tularosa Phase (AD 1150–1250)

Although the survey data indicate that small pueblos (fewer than 20 rooms) continued to be common (Stone 2002b), during the Tularosa phase very large, aggregated sites appeared. Two of these were extensively excavated: Turkey Creek Pueblo (AZ W:9:123 [ASM]) with over 300 rooms (Johnson 1965; Lowell 1988, 1991) and Point of Pines Pueblo (AZ W:10:50 [ASM]) with an estimated 800 rooms (Haury 1989) were founded during the Tularosa phase.

Turkey Creek Pueblo, generally considered the type site for the Tularosa phase, overlays an earlier pithouse village (Lowell 1991). It started as four room blocks that grew through accretion. At its largest, the pueblo consisted of a single large, massed room block with two plazas and a single Great Kiva (192 m^2). The plazas and Great Kiva were incorporated within the room block, resulting in limited access to these spaces by individuals who were not members of the community (Stone 2000). The room block includes both habitation and storage rooms that were joined together to form multiroom household suites (Lowell 1991). These suites were linked into four larger architectural groupings during their initial construction. Supra-household groupings can be identified by long, continuous walls used by several house suites, suggesting they were built during the same building sequence. The supra-household groupings that were built at the same

time eventually were joined to other supra-household groupings as the village continued to grow and additional rooms were added to the existing structure.

Thirteen dendrochronological samples were recovered from Turkey Creek Pueblo, with the dates clustering between AD 1217 and 1240 (Bannister and Robinson 1971; Lowell 1991). Reserve Black-on-White and Tularosa Black-on-White from the Zuñi region to the north dominate the intrusive ceramics recovered from the site, confirming a late 1100s/early 1200s date. Based on the patterning of trash deposition in the rooms, Lowell (1991) suggests the site was abandoned slowly over several years. Based on surface ceramics, it appears Point of Pines Pueblo was founded toward the end of the Tularosa phase (Stone 2002b) while Turkey Creek Pueblo was still occupied. Lowell (1991) suggests that as Turkey Creek Pueblo was abandoned, its inhabitants may have moved to the newly formed Point of Pines Pueblo.

In an analysis of all of the inhumations recovered in the Point of Pines Region ($n = 518$), Rodrigues (2008) identified the presence of migrants in the region based on the variability in mortuary rituals. Specifically, the vast majority of inhumations excavated in the Point of Pines region were buried in an extended position. Conversely, 76 individuals were buried in flexed body positions similar to those identified in the Kayenta region. Twenty-two of these were recovered at sites dated to the Tularosa phase. Specifically, 20 migrant burials were recovered from Turkey Creek Pueblo and two from W:10:56, a small masonry site with limited testing. Both males and females are present in the migrant sample, as are all ages. As noted above, recent demographic reconstructions for the Kayenta area by Dean (2002) indicate that migration out of the area began as early as 1150, which corresponds well with the appearance of flexed burials at these sites. Despite the apparent presence of migrants at Turkey Creek Pueblo and W:10:56, however, there is no evidence in the architecture, ceramics or other ritual activity that the migrants attempted to signal their ethnic otherness at this time (Lowell 1991).

Pinedale/Maverick Mountain
Phase (AD 1265–1300)

The reconnaissance surveys identified 67 sites that contained ceramics indicative of a Pinedale phase occupation. Most sites dated to this time period are relatively small (fewer than 24 rooms but occasionally as large as 60) and are located on all of the major creeks and tributaries, though a particularly high density of settlements (relative to other drainages) is found along the main channels of Turkey, Point of Pines, and Willow Creeks. In addition to small sites, the survey identified the 300-room Willow Creek Pueblo (Asch 1961) and the much larger Point of Pines Pueblo.

Haury (1989) suggests that Point of Pines Pueblo may have been occupied as early as the Reserve phase, though ceramic and dendrochronological data suggest a more likely starting date in the mid-Tularosa phase (Bannister and Robinson 1971; Parker 1967; Stone 2002b). Its founding overlaps the occupation at Turkey Creek Pueblo, as noted above. Portions of the site were excavated during each season that the field school operated in the Point of Pines area. Haury estimated the site contained approximately 800 rooms. Based on preliminary surface indications, these rooms were clustered into several room blocks that surrounded a number of plazas, one of which was tested. In addition to the plaza, excavators identified a Great Kiva (264 m^2) with two separate floors (Haury 1989; Gerald 1957; Stone 2002a), several smaller round and square kivas (Stone 2002a), and a D-shaped kiva (Haury 1958, 1989). The D-shaped kiva and a cluster of burned rooms in the center of the site, along with a series of pithouses postdating AD 1250 adjacent to the site (Stone 2005b; Wendorf 1950) suggested to Haury (1958) that a migrant group joined the Point of Pines community well after it was established, constructed an ethnic enclave, and remained until it was burned (however, as Chapter 5 demonstrates, the enclave was present at the beginning of construction at the site based on stratigraphic profiles and ceramic cross dates). Dendrochronological samples (Bannister and Robinson 1971; Parker 1967) from the masonry room block

indicate a date of AD 1265–1300 for occupation of most the enclave. Based on the presence of Tsegi Polychrome ceramics in the burned room block as well as Maverick Mountain Polychrome (Tesgi Polychrome designs made on local clays [Zedeño 2002]), Haury (1958, 1989) suggested the Kayenta region was the likely homeland of the migrants (see also Lindsay 1987). Similarity in burial treatment of 54 individuals at the site to those in Kayenta lends further support to it as a homeland (Rodrigues 2008).

Haury (1958, 1989) designated the occupation of the burned room block at Point of Pines Pueblo the Maverick Mountain phase. The remainder of the site was dated to the Pinedale phase. Haury originally suggested the Pinedale phase should be extended to 1350; however, due to the dramatic social changes that occurred at the end of the Maverick Mountain phase, a closing date of 1300 seems more appropriate.

Canyon Creek (1300–1350) and
Point of Pine Phases (AD 1350–1400)

Point of Pines Pueblo and the remainder of the region continued to be occupied after the Pinedale/Maverick Mountain phase. In the region's original chronology, the dates for the Canyon Creek phase were AD 1300–1400 and the Point of Pines phase AD 1400–1450. However, with more accurate dating of the intrusive ceramics on which these phases are based, a terminal date for both Point of Pines Pueblo and the region as a whole appears to be closer to AD 1400. The ceramic assemblage of the last phases of occupation is dominated by Pinedale Polychrome and Fourmile Polychrome, with limited amounts of Gila Polychrome also present. Later types are not found in the region (Stone 2002b). The last 100 years of occupation are split between these two phases, with Gila Polychrome being diagnostic of the last phase.

The Canyon Creek phase is characterized by continued occupation of the two large, aggregated sites present during the Pinedale phase and three smaller sites in the southeastern portion of the region. Conversely, during the Point of Pines phase, the population occupied smaller sites, usually consisting of 30 to 50 rooms spread

TABLE 4.3. Excavation reports of sites in the Point of Pines region (other than Point of Pines Pueblo) examined by the University of Arizona archaeological field school

Site	Reference
AZ W:6:5 (ASM), Dry Prong site	Olson 1960
AZ W:9:10 (ASM), Stove Canyon site	Neely 1974
AZ W:9:83 (ASM), Lunt site	Johnson 1961; Neely 1974
AZ W:9:123 (ASM), Turkey Creek Pueblo	Cook 1961; Johnson 1965; Lowell 1986, 1988, 1991; W. Stein 1962
AZ W:10:15 (ASM), Crooked Ridge Village	Wheat 1952
AZ W:10:37 (ASM)	Olson 1959
AZ W:10:47 (ASM	Di Peso 1950; Smiley 1952; Wasley 1952
AZ W:10:48 (ASM)	Smiley 1952; Wasley 1952
AZ W:10:51 (ASM)	Wendorf 1950
AZ W:10:52 (ASM)	Smiley 1952; Wasley 1952
AZ W:10:56 (ASM)	Olson 1959
AZ W:10:57 (ASM)	Olson 1959
AZ W:10:65 (ASM)	Olson 1959
AZ W:10:105 (ASM), Willow Creek Pueblo	Asch 1961
AZ W:10:111 (ASM), Nantack Village	Breternitz 1957, 1959
AZ W:10:112 (ASM), Cienega Creek site	Haury 1957
Cliff dwellings	Gifford 1957, 1960
Agricultural features	Woodbury 1961
Burials at a regional level	Rodrigues 2008
Ground stone at a regional level	Adams 1994
Water resources and climate	Thompson 2000; Wheat 1952

throughout the region (Morris 1957; Wasley 1952; Wendorf 1950), many of which have been archaeologically tested. These sites were open, with multiple accesses to informal plazas. Many lacked ritual structures. In many ways, these late sites are similar to layouts of the Reserve period sites such as Dry Prong (Stone 2000). The area was completely abandoned in AD 1400 and not reoccupied until Apache groups arrived in the 1500s (Asch 1961).

History of Research at Point of Pines Pueblo

Excavations and testing of varying levels of intensity were undertaken by the University of Arizona archaeological field school at 29 sites in the Point of Pines region between 1947 and 1960 (Haury 1989). Site reports were produced for most of these excavations in the form of master's theses and doctoral dissertations, as well as articles published in *Kiva*, *American Antiquity*,

and other publications (Table 4.3). Additionally, several synthetic studies of the Point of Pines region as a whole have been undertaken dealing with ceramics (Breternitz et al. 1957), ground stone (Adams 1994), skeletal trauma evident in burials (Rodrigues 2008), water features (Wheat 1952), agricultural features (Woodbury 1961), geomorphology (Heindl 1955; Thompson 2000), and architecture (Smiley 1952; Stone 2000, 2002a, 2003, 2005b, 2009). Finally, Charles Di Peso (1950) published an article on three sandstone slabs with painted figures recovered in a room at W:10:47, a small Point of Pines phase site. These stones contain masked figures that are stylistically similar to those from the Zuñi, Hopi, and Showlow areas of Arizona and the Pecos Pueblo area of New Mexico.

Analyses of the remains of Point of Pines Pueblo itself have been relatively restricted to date. Several works have been published regarding the field school experience at Point of Pines

(Gifford and Morris 1985; Haury 1989; Mills 2005), as well as the role the region played in defining the Mogollon culture area (Reid and Whittlesey 2010) and the importance of migration in the Southwest (Haury 1958; Lindsay 1987; Stone 2003; Stone and Lipe 2011). Despite the absence of a study of the pueblo as a whole, in-depth analyses of limited portions of the pueblo do exist. For example, Kenneth Bennett conducted a preliminary analysis of the burials at the site for his dissertation (1967), which was later published (Bennett 1973). Charles Merbs (1967) and William Robinson and Roderick Sprague (1965) undertook additional studies of the burials (see also Robinson 1958, 1959; Rodrigues 2008).

Reports of some of the architectural remains also exist. The Great Kiva at the site was described by Virginia Gerald in her master's thesis (1957). Room blocks apparently inhabited at the end of the site's occupation were the subject of Elizabeth Morris's master's thesis (1957) and part of William Wasley's master's thesis (1952). Additionally, studies of the climate and environment have been conducted. Walter Stein (1962, 1963) and Vorsila Bohrer (1973) studied the fauna and flora recovered from the site. A site report of the excavations at AZ W:10:51 (ASM), which is directly adjacent to Point of Pines Pueblo, was published by Fred Wendorf (1950). AZ W:10:51 (ASM) is within 20 m of Point of Pines Pueblo and is considered part of the same community for the purpose of this study.

Although a comprehensive report on Point of Pines Pueblo was not produced as part of the original excavations, the field notes, excavation forms, and maps from the site are curated in the archives of the Arizona State Museum at the University of Arizona in Tucson. Based on the field notes, a synthesis of the chronology and detailed analysis of the building sequences at Point of Pines Pueblo are presented in Chapter 5.

CHAPTER 5

Construction and Abandonment
at Point of Pines Pueblo

Individuals engage with space, transforming it into a socially meaningful place, through architecture. Because of its ability to bound space and direct bodily movement through the community, architecture has a major impact on how a settlement is perceived and experienced by individuals and groups in their everyday lives. Further, people manipulate architecture in both conscious and subconscious ways as they negotiate status, form alliances, raise their children, and express their ethnicity. Before we can begin to reconstruct the complexities of community dynamics at Point of Pines Pueblo through an analysis of architecture, however, we must have a firm grasp on the site's architectural chronology. As such, this chapter concentrates on the sequence of construction and abandonment of various portions of the site. Comparative analyses of domestic and ritual structures constructed by the Mogollon host communities and Kayenta newcomers at Point of Pines Pueblo, as well as changes through time in house suite arrangement and ritual structures, are presented in Chapter 6. Further modification to the pueblo—in which history was written, destroyed, and rewritten by changes in its architecture after the destruction of the Kayenta enclave—is presented in Chapter 7.

The chronology of construction and abandonment presented here was determined by examining both floor and subfloor deposits (sterile deposits, sheet trash, architectural re-

mains). Chronometric dates were assigned to construction phases using ceramic cross dating from artifacts recovered from the floor and subfloor deposits, as well as dendrochronological dates when possible. This information was combined with wall bonding/abutting patterns to determine which walls were constructed first and which were added later (Crown 1991; Lowell 1991).

Equally important to community growth in understanding community dynamics is abandonment. It must be remembered that abandonment is not a presence/absence state but a social process tied to decision making by individuals and groups at a variety of social scales (Cameron 1999a; Nelson 1999; Nelson and Hegmon 2001; Rothschild and Dublin 1994; Varien 1999). For example, random patterns of room abandonment throughout the pueblo are likely related to changes in house membership, whereas abandonment of entire portions of the community while the remainder continued to be occupied is part of a larger social dynamic. Additionally, connection with architectural structures by house members does not stop when a family moves (Bailey 1990; Cameron 1999a; Lekson and Cameron 1995; Rothschild and Dublin 1994). Post-abandonment treatment of the structure is also a part of the negotiation of social relations and access to resources. For example, several ethnographic studies have indicated that abandonment of a structure does not indicate a

49

relinquishing of rights of access to that structure as long as individuals and families remain part of the broader social fabric. As such, treatment of abandoned structures (scavenging of building materials and artifacts, leaving the structure unused, remodeling the structure, or changing the foundations and architectural footprint of the structure with new construction) is part of an ongoing social dialogue and negotiation of rights and social relations (Bailey 1990; Creel and Anyon 2003; Gillespie 2000a; González-Ruibal 2005; Lightfoot 1993; Shafer 1995; Walker 2002; Waterson 2000; Wilson 2010). These structures may be revisited by previous inhabitants to scavenge building materials for new structures (Cameron 1999a; Rothschild and Dublin 1994). Conversely, ritual activity may accompany abandonment to symbolically reinforce the death of the structure and the social relations it represents (Creel and Anyon 2003; Lightfoot 1993; Shafer 1995; Walker 2002). Therefore, a chronology of room abandonment, pueblo-wide shifts in occupation, and post-abandonment treatment must be determined. The timing of a room's abandonment can be determined by both the density and dates of the ceramics in the room fill. Specifically, both Ciolek-Torrello (1985) and Lowell (1991) argue that rooms abandoned early in a site's occupation have a higher density and a greater diversity of ceramics than those abandoned late in its occupation.

Excavation Methods at Point of Pines Pueblo

Haury (1989) estimated that Point of Pines Pueblo consisted of 800 rooms at its height, most of which were encircled by a compound wall (Figure 5.1); 130 of these rooms, many with multiple floors, were excavated by the University of Arizona, resulting in data from 204 floors. These rooms overlay a series of pithouses that, based on ceramic cross dates, are contemporaneous with the earliest masonry rooms at the site (see below and Stone 2005b); 36 of these pithouses were excavated. Four small kivas, one Great Kiva, and one formal plaza also were excavated. Finally, numerous sections of the compound wall surrounding large portions of the pueblo

were tested, and some trenching was undertaken to determine the location of additional room walls. Based on these excavations, a chronology of the site defining five building sequences was constructed using stratigraphy, ceramic deposition, and wall bonding/abutting patterns.

When first identified on survey, Point of Pines Pueblo consisted of a large rubble mound on a northeast-southwest-trending ridge adjacent to a tributary of Point of Pines Creek. Several depressions and elevated areas were evident on the surface, as well as numerous artifacts. Topographic features at the site were investigated through excavation between 1946 and 1960 using judgmental samples. Two types of excavations were conducted: 1) test trenches, used to define walls and investigate areas where architectural features were not evident on the surface, such as plazas and middens; and 2) excavations that explored entire architectural features (evident either on the surface or during excavation of adjacent structures). These two types of excavations were tied together through a 15 × 15 m grid placed over the site. Four areas of the pueblo (two inside the compound wall surrounding the pueblo and two outside of it) were evident on the surface: they were designated W:10:50A, W:10:50B, W:10:50C, and W:10:51 (referred to here as Room Blocks A, B, C, and W:10:51). The surface ceramics were late, suggesting use at the end of the pueblo's occupation. These areas were investigated as discrete units, ranging from tests of individual rooms to excavation of an entire room block (Morris 1957; Wasley 1952; Wendorf 1950). All of these areas contained evidence of use at the end of the pueblo's occupation as well as during earlier phases. Rooms were numbered in order of excavation, but each with its own sequence. When excavation occurred in other areas of the pueblo, rooms were numbered in order of excavation as well. The result is five rooms designated "Room 1" (one in each of the four room blocks as well as one in the main pueblo). Two room blocks that were constructed when the pueblo was established received considerable attention. The central room block used by the Kayenta migrants and a large room block to the north inhabited by Mogollon resi-

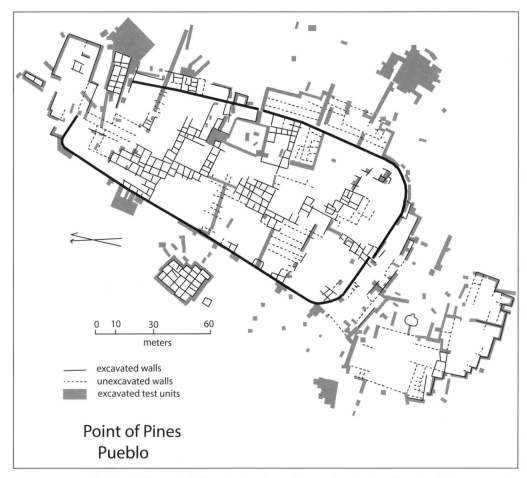

FIGURE 5.1. Map of Point of Pines Pueblo showing locations of excavation by the University of Arizona archaeological field school.

dents were extensively excavated. Though not designated as such by the excavators, the central room block is referred to in this study as Room Block D. The room block in the northern portion of the pueblo, surrounding the Great Kiva and Kiva 2, is referred to as Room Block E.

Test trenches were used in areas lacking architectural features on the surface and generally started as 1 × 2 m trenches that were excavated to sterile in arbitrary levels. These units were extended if features such as walking surfaces, burials or walls were encountered. These extensions took two forms: long trenches that helped define wall alignments, and large-scale stripping. The results of both types of explorations were described in the excavator's running field notes

and, if architecture was encountered, standardized forms.

When an architectural feature was excavated, it was assigned the next consecutive room number. The walls of the unit were first defined with the use of trenches starting from a known point and extending out until all of the walls were defined. Known points included wall alignments visible on the surface, those identified in a test trench, and those defined in the excavation of adjacent architectural structures. These trenches extended from the known wall alignment on the surface until a floor was encountered. Once all of the walls and strata were defined using this method, the interior was excavated using natural stratigraphic levels (fill, roof fall, wall fall, and floor). In most architectural structures, though not all, subfloor excavation occurred and extended to sterile.

For architectural features, standardized forms and running field notes were recorded. Although the amount and type of data recorded in field notes vary considerably from room to room, the standardized architectural forms provide baseline data regarding floor features, wall and roof construction, the presence of doors and windows, and a map of features for each floor identified within an architectural structure, which allows comparisons to be made in the analysis. Three types of architectural features were investigated: aboveground masonry rooms, semi-subterranean pithouses, and kivas. In addition to these features, two other architectural structures were investigated. The first of these "other structures" is a formal plaza on the eastern side of the site, and the second is the compound wall surrounding the pueblo. Both were evaluated with test units as discussed above and were recorded in field notes rather than with standardized forms.

In both types of excavations (architectural features and test units), whole and reconstructable vessels were cataloged by excavation unit and level and saved, as were diagnostic collections of whole chipped and ground stone formal tools and unusual artifacts. These are now housed at the Arizona State Museum at the University of Arizona in Tucson. Lithic debitage and informal lithic tools were not recorded, and sherds were not saved. Rather, in keeping with the standards of the day, they were typed using the standard ceramic typologies, counted in the field laboratory for most excavation units, and not transported back to Tucson. Ceramic types were sometimes merely noted as present or absent. Other times they were systematically listed with counts and related to natural stratigraphic levels of fill, floor fill (10 cm above the floor), floor contact, and subfloor. Occasionally, they were tabulated by 10 cm arbitrary level without reference to stratigraphy. On rare occasions, sherd tabulations were not made. For most rooms, ceramic counts were listed only for some ceramic types, such as polychromes. This allowed the rooms and, in cases of rooms with multiple plastered floors, each occupation of the room to be dated by ceramics found on the floor but precluded calculations of sherd density and diversity, important ratios for understanding abandonment patterns.

Excavators assigned phase designations to the fill, floor, and subfloor levels of both architectural features and test excavation units based on the ceramics present. The field identification of ceramic types and counts are accepted here; however, considerable adjustment has been made to ceramic production spans in the last 50 years, and our understanding of formation and abandonment processes have become considerably more sophisticated. Therefore, all phase assignments of deposits have been reevaluated for this study.

Chronological Considerations

No radiocarbon dates exist for Point of Pines Pueblo, and dendrochronological dates were recovered only from the earliest floors within Room Block D in the center of the pueblo, which apparently burned in a single episode. These dates correspond with ceramic cross dates from these floors. Dendrochronological samples were not obtained from rooms built above the burned floors. For these upper floors and the remainder of the pueblo, relative dating methods must be used.

To determine phase designations through relative dating for individual rooms lacking dendrochronological samples, three pieces of data were examined simultaneously: 1) datable ceramics in the floor and subfloor levels; 2) subfloor deposits (cultural versus sterile deposits); and 3) bonding/abutting patterns. None of these is sufficient alone, but when combined they provide a robust data set with which to analyze chronological placement of individual architectural features. For example, dates from ceramic deposits found on room floors and in subfloor tests can be used to make a chronological phase assignment. Ceramic dates are not sufficient by themselves, however, because floor/floor fill ceramics may be more reflective of post-abandonment behaviors than actual occupation (Schiffer 1975, 1987). Whole vessels on floor sur-

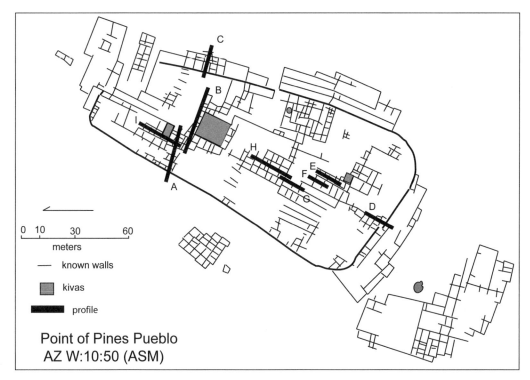

FIGURE 5.2 Location of profiles examined in the stratigraphic analysis of Point of Pines Pueblo.

faces and vessels and sherds embedded in the floor as metate bin baffles are informative, but these are frequently utilitarian wares with long production spans. Subfloor deposits provide data on remains that were present before the floor was laid down, but subfloor tests were not always conducted. Even when subfloor tests did occur, the ceramics were not always recorded or had production spans that were too long to allow a phase designation. Therefore, these data are supplemented with information from soil stratigraphy and bonding/abutting patterns.

In terms of soil stratigraphy, subfloor deposits can be particularly informative regarding the early sequence of construction. Specifically, structures built during the pueblo's earliest occupation had sterile soil in the subfloor tests. As occupation continued and a sheet midden developed, later structures were built on trash that was used to fill in and level the building surface. Sheet midden may be removed during construction of semi-subterranean structures such as kivas and pithouses. Examination of the

full extension of belowground walls and deposits behind wall plaster revealed trash deposits against the upper walls. Specifically, the extension of wall plaster up onto trash indicates that sheet midden existed but was removed during construction. In the process of leveling a location for construction of masonry rooms within the same area, walls of semi-subterranean rooms were sometimes removed. The resulting superposition of newer masonry rooms over earlier semi-subterranean structures indicates relative ages in that location. However, this practice may make it difficult to date construction of the semi-subterranean rooms in the chronology of the larger community.

Based on currently available excavation data, stratigraphic profiles can be constructed for several areas of the site that include the compound wall circling the pueblo and masonry rooms. Figure 5.2 shows the locations for these profiles, and Figures 5.3 and 5.4 present east-west and north-south profiles, respectively. These profiles provide data on several aspects of Point of Pines

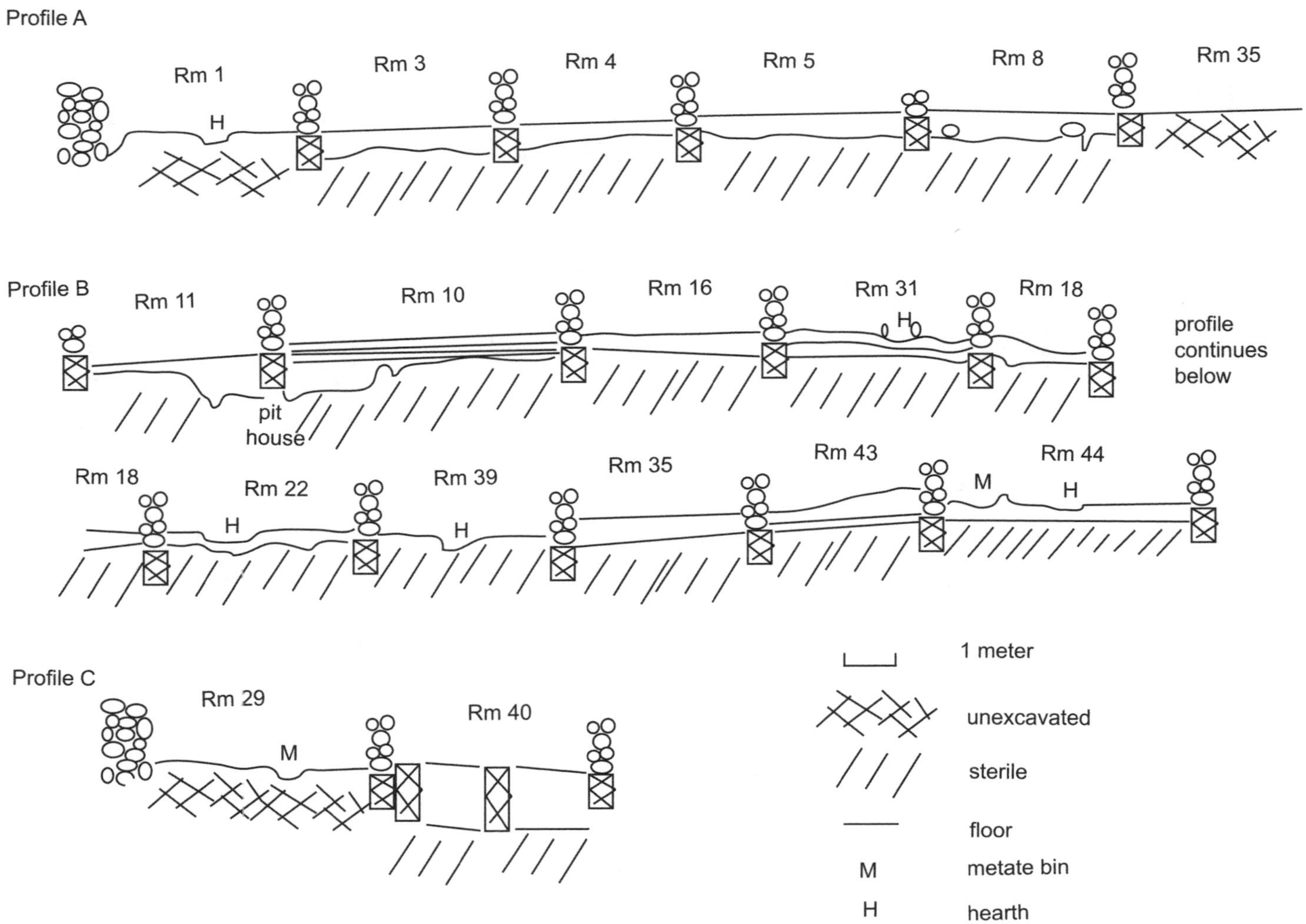

FIGURE 5.3. East-west profiles at Point of Pines Pueblo.

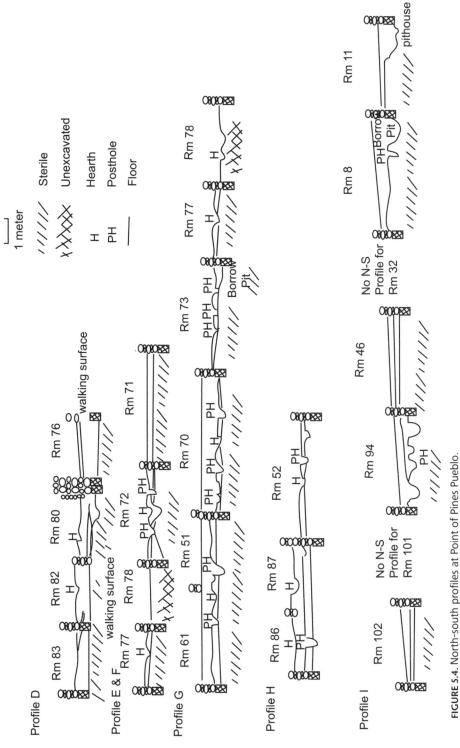

FIGURE 5.4. North-south profiles at Point of Pines Pueblo.

Pueblo. For example, in all cases where subfloor tests were done on the compound wall and adjacent deposits, it is clear that the compound wall was a late addition to the site, built on thick deposits of trash. This is particularly noticeable in Figure 5.4, where the trash deposits underlying the south gate of the compound wall are evident in Profile D.

In addition to ceramic dates and stratigraphy, wall bonding/abutting patterns for masonry rooms also were examined. Walls that are bonded were built at the same time, while walls that abut were added after the first wall was constructed. These can be distinguished by interdigitation of the building stones. (The stones in bonded joints are interdigitated, while abutted walls are not.) Both bonding and abutting can occur either at corners or on long, straight walls. When several rooms share long, continuous bonded walls, it can be assumed that they were built at the same time. The chronological relationship between abutted walls is more difficult to ascertain. The abutted wall could have been added the next day, and therefore be contemporaneous, or it could have been added several decades later.

Construction Methods at Point of Pines Pueblo

Data on construction methods used by the inhabitants of Point of Pines Pueblo are uneven. Some of the earliest structures were partially destroyed by later construction, and construction methods were not recorded for all masonry rooms that were excavated. Despite these limitations, enough data exist for all periods of occupation to allow a discussion of building methods.

The pithouses at Point of Pines Pueblo are substantially smaller and less formal than those recorded for the Pithouse period in the region (Stone 2005b). At the time of excavation, it was suggested that the pueblo's pithouses may have served as temporary shelter for the migrant population while masonry rooms were constructed (Haury 1958; Wendorf 1950). Ethnographic accounts from Third Mesa in Hopi provide descriptions of the use of pithouses as temporary

structures by migrants from the village of Orayvi prior to completion of masonry structures at their new home in the village of Bacavi (Whiteley 1988b). In contrast, the indigenous Mogollon at Point of Pines would not have needed these temporary structures and likely lived at Tularosa phase sites identified on survey like Turkey Creek Pueblo.

All of the pithouses at Point of Pines Pueblo were constructed by excavating into sterile soil. They are predominately square in shape, relatively small (mean = 7.1672 m^2) and shallow (mean depth = .3517 m). In accordance with their small size, they have few main support posts (mean 2.8). Additionally, they contain little evidence of investment in internal features; half lack floor plaster and/or wall plaster, and though most have a hearth, few contain any other type of feature.

Raw material for the construction of masonry structures at the pueblo is recorded for 85 of the 130 excavated rooms. Most of the excavated rooms were constructed using tuff boulders and spalls ($n = 74$, 87%). The remainder were a mixture of tuff and basalt boulders and spalls ($n = 11$, 13%), both of which are readily available at the site. In most cases, at least some of the larger tuff boulders have clear evidence of pecking and shaping ($n = 61$, 64%). The foundation stones of the rooms show greater variability. Material used for foundations was recorded for 69 rooms. Although most consisted of large tuff boulders ($n = 35$, 51%), some were made of basalt ($n = 16$, 23%) or a mixture of basalt boulders and smaller tuff stones ($n = 15$, 22%). A very small number ($n = 3$, 4%) sat on coursed adobe foundations. Foundation stones were generally placed directly on trash or sterile soil.

Upper walls evidence two types of masonry style (Figure 5.5). The first is a coursed masonry of large and small rocks cemented together with liberal amounts of mud mortar. The mud mortar frequently contains small amounts of trash and was evidently mined from the numerous borrow pits found in subfloor excavations and large-scale stripping. Additional material for mud mortar may have been obtained from the excavation of the semi-subterranean pithouses

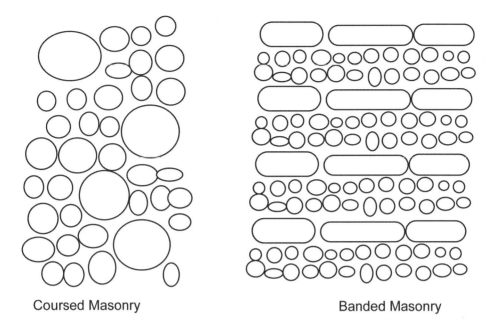

Coursed Masonry   Banded Masonry

FIGURE 5.5. Masonry styles used at Point of Pines Pueblo.

used during early occupation of the site (cf. Wilshusen 1989). The stones in this masonry style, at least some of which were shaped, are dominated by tuff and occasionally by a mixture of tuff and basalt.

The second type of masonry is banded, with rows of large, usually shaped stones interspersed by several rows of very small ones. Similar to the coursed masonry style, liberal amounts of mud mortar were used in construction. Masonry style was either drawn or discussed in the field notes for 125 rooms; banded masonry was the most common ($n = 56$, 45%), followed by coursed masonry ($n = 45$, 36%). The remaining 24 rooms (19%) had both styles of masonry on different walls. There is a relationship between the masonry style and the type of stone used for wall construction ($x^2 = 10.314$; p-value = .006), though the association is weak to moderate (Cramer's V = .350). Specifically, rooms with only banded or with a mixture of masonry types have a lower than expected frequency of walls made of a mixture of basalt and tuff stones and a higher than expected frequency of walls using only tuff boulders.

Excavators determined the number of stories

present for 118 rooms associated with 193 separate floors (or occupations); 106 rooms (89.8%) were classified as one-story structures, and 12 as having two stories (10.1%). Rooms with two-story construction were concentrated in the central room block (Room Block D), believed to be inhabited by the Kayenta migrants and dated to the Pinedale/Maverick Mountain phase. Specifically, 8 of the 12 two-story rooms (66.67%) are in Room Block D, 3 are in Room Block E adjacent to the Great Kiva, and one was constructed adjacent to the compound wall late the pueblo's occupation.

The determination of two-story construction was made based on the nature of the fill encountered during excavation. In three rooms, two distinct sets of roof fall, separated by floor features such as hearths, were evident. In most, however, the determination was made based on the quantity of wall fall in the fill. (Two-story rooms have greater amounts of wall fall than one-story rooms.) These differences also can be seen in the recorded wall height, but not the width of the base of the wall. Specifically, rooms that were identified as having two stories had significantly higher standing walls at the time of excavation (t-score = 5.749; p-value = .000; difference = .68 m). Interestingly, the width of the walls did not differ significantly for rooms identified as one- and two-story (t-score = .577; p-value = .568).

Differences in the number of stories that are present do not appear to have affected roof construction. Of the 204 floors excavated, most had no postholes (n = 131, 63.9%). Floors where postholes were recorded included both one- and two-story rooms. Room size is moderately correlated with the number of postholes present (r = .413), and floors that completely lack postholes are significantly smaller than those that have postholes (t-test = 4.22; p-value = .000; difference = 3.9 m²).

Based on the roof fall reported in field notes, roof construction was consistent throughout the site. Specifically, a series of primary roof beams were socketed into the top of the room walls. Sockets for primary roof beams were found in the highest standing walls at the site (n = 24, 19%). Primary beams were covered with a series of smaller stringers. Finally, mud was used to cover the entire roof. Mud with impressions of small stringers was the most common roof fall material found at the pueblo.

Subfloor tests were conducted in 113 of the 130 excavated masonry rooms (86.9%); most (n = 69, 61.1%) had only one floor. When multiple distinct floors were separated by trash layers, they ranged in number from two to five. In 37 cases (29.4% of the rooms with subfloor tests), the new floors were on a different footprint than previous ones, indicating that older construction was leveled and new structures with independent foundations were built. In other areas, new foundations were added to existing structures to allow the space to be subdivided.

Building Phases
at Point of Pines Pueblo

Based on the stratigraphic profiles, ceramic deposits on and beneath the floors, and wall bonding/abutting patterns, five building phases were identified at Point of Pines Pueblo. The changes from one building phase to the next provide a history of the community and its evolving social relationships. These are detailed below. Individual room and floor designations for each phase are contained in the appendix.

Building Phase I (Early Tularosa Phase)

Excavated rooms from the earliest construction phase at Point of Pines Pueblo are evident in structures built directly on sterile soil (Figure 5.6). Included are all of the pithouses, three small kivas (Kivas 2 and 3, and PH 13), and nine one-story masonry rooms. Each of the rooms was built using what Cameron (1999b) refers to as "agglomerative layouts" (i.e., they do not share long runs of continuous, bonded walls). One room was constructed on the east side of the community in Room Block B. Two rooms, not connected to each other, in the center of the pueblo formed the core of Room Block D. Finally, the remaining rooms were built in the north half of the pueblo, adjacent to Kiva 2 in Room Block E.

Kiva 3 is a small (12.49 m²), D-shaped kiva at the south end of the site. It contains a bench around its perimeter, and a ventilator opens onto the kiva floor through the bench on the east wall. A sipapu (a ceremonial hole representing the emergence of humans into this world) and floor grooves, which when covered by boards served as foot drums, are also present. This kiva shape is unique in the region. It has been suggested that it, along with pithouses constructed as temporary housing and the rooms in Room Block D, were used by the migrant group from the Kayenta region (Haury 1958, 1989; Wendorf 1950; see Chapter 6 for more detail).

Also present is Kiva PH 13 at the northwest end of the site (in the area designated W:10:51). PH 13 is semi-subterranean (1.2 m below surface) and small (10.6 m²). It contained a sipapu, hearth, and ventilator shaft, along with several burials. The walls were lined with coursed masonry covered with plaster. In contrast to these isolated kivas, aboveground masonry domestic structures are present and clustered around Kiva 2, at the north end of the site. Kiva 2 is rectangular and the largest of the three small kivas (28.37 m²). The walls were constructed of coursed masonry of shaped tuff boulders coated

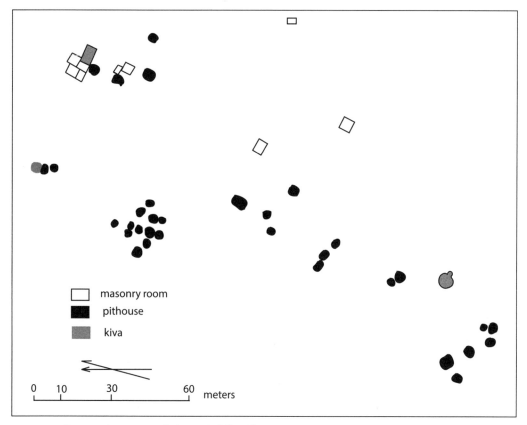

FIGURE 5.6. Excavated structures dating to Building Phase I.

with plaster. It lacks a sipapu but contains post-holes, three floor pits, a hearth and associated ash pit, as well as a ventilator shaft through adjacent architectural walls in the north wall. There is a stone slab on the floor that may have served as a hatch cover and two ladder holes. Combined, this suggests a roof entrance; however, a door is present in the eastern wall.

Recent statistical analysis of the architectural features of the pithouses confirms that they were, in fact, temporary structures used while more permanent housing was constructed (Stone 2005b). Specifically, when compared to pithouses used as domestic structures in the Circle Prairie through Stove Canyon phases, the pithouses at Point of Pines Pueblo are smaller, have fewer primary and secondary post supports, fewer storage pits, and lack ramp entrances. It should be noted, however, that pithouses were used as domestic structures in the Kayenta re-

gion until the beginning of the Tsegi phase in AD 1250 (Dean 1996; Geib 2011). If the pithouses and the D-shaped kiva were used by the migrants, as Haury suggests, their stratigraphic position indicates that the newcomers were present in the region at the pueblo's earliest occupation and created the community of Point of Pines Pueblo in conjunction with indigenous people who had been living in large, aggregated settlements at nearby sites such as Turkey Creek Pueblo. Additionally, the presence of three small kivas and the lack of either a formal plaza or a kiva large enough to accommodate the entire pueblo indicate integration of small groups occurred, but village-wide integration was informal at best. Additionally, the variability in size, shape, construction, and internal features of the kivas indicates differences in the concept of ritual space by the groups using them. Based on the ceramics in structures built on sterile soil

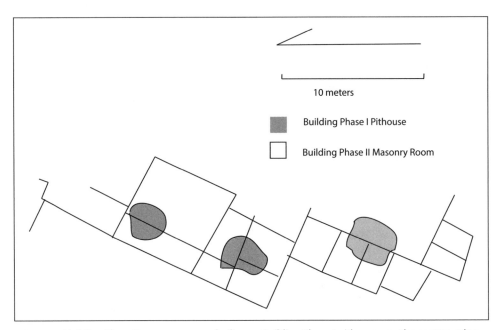

10 meters

☐ Building Phase I Pithouse

☐ Building Phase II Masonry Room

FIGURE 5.7. Building Phase II masonry rooms built over Building Phase I pithouses on the eastern edge of the plaza in Room Block E.

(McDonald Corrugated, Tularosa Black-on-White, and [in the pithouses and Kiva 3] Maverick Mountain Polychrome), the community was founded during the Tularosa phase.

Building Phase II (Late Tularosa Phase)

The second phase of construction at the site was built above thin deposits of trash and occasionally on top of pithouses (Figure 5.7). The pithouses of the earliest occupation at the site were no longer used, and domestic structures were restricted to aboveground masonry. The construction of new rooms over the pithouses symbolically indicates a break with the earliest occupation of the site and a more permanent presence of the migrants in the community as they moved into more substantial and longer-lived masonry structures.

The D-shaped kiva found in the previous phase continued to be used during the second stage of construction, as did Kiva 2, located at the north end of the site in Room Block E. The lowest floors of the 9 rooms founded during Building Phase I continued to be used, and 23 new masonry rooms were constructed. In other words, 33 of the 130 rooms (25%) excavated at the

pueblo were occupied at this time. Two of them (Rooms 60 and 35) contained two floors, both dated to this building phase, indicating there was time enough to afford replastering of domestic floors in some instances.

Three clusters of domestic masonry rooms are evident, indicating continued construction in the areas established during Building Phase I (Figure 5.8). The first cluster is Room Block E and incorporates Kiva 2. In Building Phase II, this room block was expanded both to the south and east by appending new rooms to existing structures. Excavators estimated that one room constructed at this time was two stories based on the amount of wall fall. The eastern extension in Room Block E began to encompass a formal plaza area. Gerald's (1957) analysis of the plaza indicates a compacted surface that served as a communal space bounded by rooms on at least two sides. This space lacks postholes, indicating it was not roofed and therefore visible from the surrounding rooftops. The two-story masonry room constructed in Room Block E during this phase overlooks the plaza.

The second cluster of rooms, Room Block D, lies between this group and the D-shaped kiva

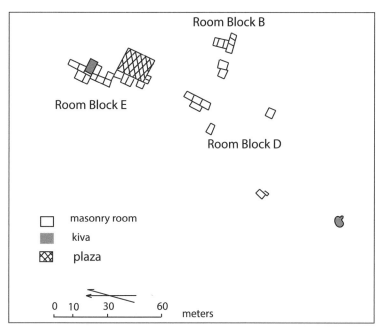

FIGURE 5.8. Excavated rooms at Point of Pines Pueblo dated to Building Phase II.

to the south and consists of several large rooms, one of which is two stories. Four of these rooms (including the two-story structure) were built in a tight room block, and several additional isolated rooms are evident nearby. Finally, a cluster of rooms, Room Block B, is found to the east of this room block built over sheet trash. These rooms were appended to each other and do not share a single, continuous wall.

The ceramics found on the room floors suggest that this building sequence dates to the end of the Tularosa phase. Specifically, Reserve, Tularosa, and McDonald Corrugated are found throughout the pueblo, as are Tularosa and Pinedale Black-on-White, and St. Johns and Springerville Polychromes. In Kiva 3 (the D-shaped kiva) and Room Block D, Kayenta Black-on-White and Maverick Mountain Polychrome also are found.

From the founding of the site until the end of Building Phase II, considerable growth occurred in three areas of the site in a very short period of time. Temporary pithouse architecture was replaced by more permanent masonry structures. The clustering of structures in three separate areas, two with their own small kiva, indicate

the beginnings of three defined room blocks. Excavation of individual rooms elsewhere at the site indicates other room blocks were likely established at this time as well. The concentration of rooms in Room Block D, the D-shaped kiva (Kiva 3) and the presence of Kayenta Black-on-white and Maverick Mountain Polychrome suggest the migrant community established itself in more permanent housing and concentrated activities associated with signaling their ethnic otherness in a single area of the pueblo. Despite this apparent small group divide, a very large public plaza was defined by the construction of rooms in Room Block E and a compacted surface. This large space was capable of holding more individuals than just those housed in Room Block E and was open on two sides, allowing easy access to the broader community. As such, it may represent an attempt at community integration at a larger scale.

Building Phase III
(Pinedale/Maverick Mountain Phase)
Testing of individual rooms at the north and south ends of the pueblo indicated occupation in numerous room blocks during Building

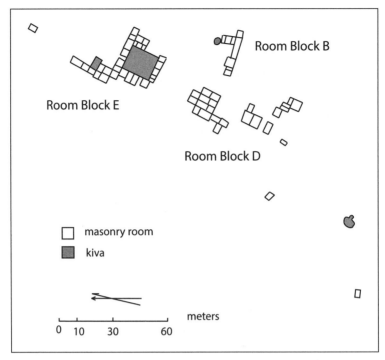

FIGURE 5.9. Excavated rooms at Point of Pines Pueblo dated to Building Phase III.

Phase III. However, excavation was concentrated in the center of the pueblo, and consequently this part of the community is best understood. Specifically, 65 of the 130 rooms (50%) excavated at the pueblo have evidence of occupation during Building Phase III (Figure 5.9). Twenty rooms built during Building Phase II continued to be used with no evidence of remodeling, and 38 new rooms were added. (Note: three rooms in Room Block E built at this time were destroyed in subsequent expansion of the Great Kiva in Building Phase IV and are too incomplete to include in the discussion here.) The remaining seven rooms occupied during Building Phase III have evidence of remodeling ranging from new plastered floors within the same footprint to changes in the footprint with new foundation stones.

Considerable construction occurred in Room Block E during Building Phase III. New masonry rooms were added and existing rooms were remodeled with a new plaster floor, sometimes with leveling of the old structure and construction of rooms on new foundations. The most dramatic change can be seen in the rooms surrounding Kiva 2 where they were leveled and rebuilt on top of those of the previous periods with a new footprint (Figure 5.10). The rooms that surrounded the plaza in the previous building phase were still present, and new ones were added to fully enclose the area. Additionally, the floor of the plaza became considerably more formalized; massive postholes were added, indicating that the space was roofed. The addition of a roof indicates that the function of the plaza changed to that of a large (220 m²) Great Kiva (Gerald 1957) whose walls were formed by the exterior walls of the adjacent rooms rather than by a single, continuous, bounded one. The entrance to the Great Kiva was on the east, consisting of a break in the adjacent rooms.

Rooms also were added to Room Block B, including one that was remodeled with a new plaster floor. Also added was a very small (69.8 m²), semi-subterranean kiva (Kiva 5), which was round and contained a single posthole and sipapu.

The north and south halves of Room Block

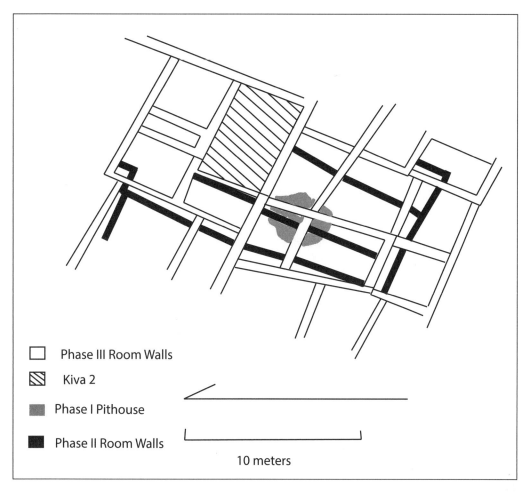

FIGURE 5.10. Superimposed rooms surrounding Kiva 2 in Room Block E at Point of Pines Pueblo.

Phase III Room Walls

Kiva 2

Phase I Pithouse

Phase II Room Walls

10 meters

D grew with the addition of 17 appended rooms. Additional unexcavated rooms were present between the two halves of the room block, indicating the presence of a single large room block. Based on the amount of wall fall, seven of these rooms were interpreted as two-story structures, and they were present in both the north and south clusters of the room block. No remodeling is evident in any of the rooms built in Room Block D during Building Phase III, and Kiva 2 continued to be used. At the end of this building phase, 19 of the 23 rooms (82.6%) in Room Block D had abundant artifacts and stores of corn covered with burned roof fall (see discussion of abandonment below). It is from these rooms, burned at the end of Building Phase III, that

all of the dendrochronological samples from the site were recovered. The roof of Kiva 3 also burned. Only three other burned floors were found for the entire pueblo, regardless of building phase. The recovery of whole artifacts on the floors of rooms elsewhere in the site was also unusual (Haury 1989).

Ceramics found in Room Blocks B and E are dominated by Tularosa Corrugated as well as numerous sherds of McDonald Corrugated. Imported painted wares include Tularosa and Pinedale Black-on-White and Springerville Polychrome, with small amounts of Pinedale Polychrome. The same ceramics are evident in the isolated rooms at the south end of the pueblo. The room clusters that form Room Block D and

Kiva 3 included large amounts of Kayenta Black-on-White and Maverick Mountain Polychrome in addition to the ceramics noted above. Based on these ceramics, this building sequence dates to the Pinedale/Maverick Mountain phase.

This building sequence represents a dynamic period in the community's biography. In the excavated areas, community expansion involved the use of three small kivas, one for each room block. The kivas are different from each other in size, shape, construction, and internal features, indicating small group affiliation with different concepts of the nature of ritual space. Considerable expansion of habitation rooms is evident in the southern portion of the site. Building and remodeling were prevalent in the northern portion of the site as well, which resulted in construction over earlier rooms with new foundations in a different orientation in some cases. In contrast to these differences, the roofing of the plaza in the north portion of the site to form a large Great Kiva indicates an attempt to integrate the individual room clusters.

Finally, this building sequence apparently ends with the destruction of Room Block D and Kiva 3. The presence of abundant artifacts on room floors suggests that there was little warning of the fire and apparently little attempt to salvage artifacts or building material afterwards.

Building Phase IV (Canyon Creek Phase)

The fourth building sequence provides evidence of dramatic changes in the Point of Pines community. First, a compound wall was built around the major occupation of the site, although an isolated room excavation at the south end indicates that the entire site was not contained by the wall (Figure 5.11). The compound wall averages 1.23 m in height and 0.73 m in width at its base, indicating a considerable investment of labor. The construction of the wall was examined through a number of test units and during excavation of abutting rooms. In some test units, the wall appears to be constructed completely of shaped basalt boulders, but in others it is a mixture of shaped basalt and tuff boulders. In all cases it consists of coursed (rather than banded) masonry. It has four formal openings (Figure 5.12). The wall restricted access into and out of the pueblo and channeled the movement of people in very specific ways. The opening of the east wall led into the formal plaza, also constructed during the Building Phase IV. The openings in the west and south walls were blocked soon after construction by the addition of a series of rooms. The north gate remained open from the time of construction until abandonment of the pueblo. Shortly after construction of the wall, several rooms were built directly against it, interior cross walls of the rooms abutting the Great Wall itself. This is particularly noticeable at the south end and eastern edge of the pueblo.

Habitation of the pueblo remains similar to the previous building phase with 58 of the 130 excavated rooms (44.6%) occupied. Kiva 2 and Room Block E continue to be occupied, though the locations of inhabited rooms shifted slightly. Specifically, 14 rooms continued to be used, but 11 rooms used during the previous phase were abandoned at the beginning of Building Phase IV. Additional rooms ($n = 11$) were appended to the north end of this room block and around the Great Kiva. Four of the rooms constructed during the previous phase were remodeled with new plastered floors, and three rooms on the eastern edge of the Great Kiva were leveled during this phase to increase the size of the Great Kiva (from 220 m^2 264 m^2). Walls on the south, west, and north edges of the Great Kiva also were remodeled to facilitate the increased size. Specifically, room walls on the southern and western edges of the Great Kiva were demolished, and a single continuous, bonded wall was constructed, which created smaller rooms. In addition, the Great Kiva itself was remodeled: 15 postholes were placed in a rectangular pattern in the floor, a single storage pit was located in the north, and a hearth was placed in the center. Additionally, there are four large depressions radiate from the hearth in four directions and appear similar to foot drums noted elsewhere in the region (Stone 2002a). Contrary to other sites in the region, however, parts of the depressions in the Great Kiva were covered with large, flat stones,

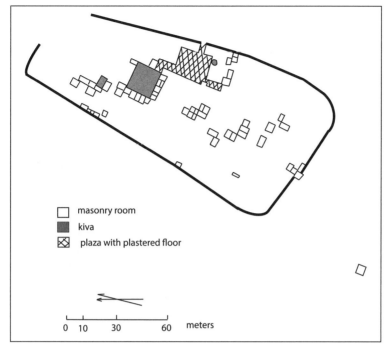

FIGURE 5.11. Excavated rooms at Point of Pines Pueblo dated to Building Phase IV.

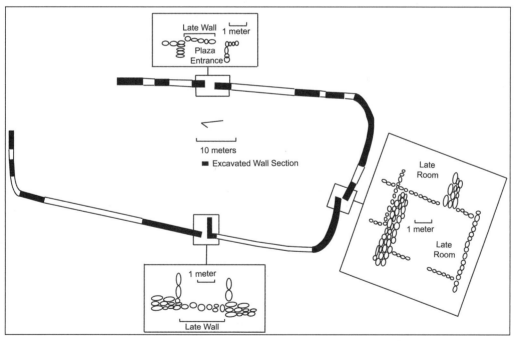

FIGURE 5.12. Compound wall at Point of Pines Pueblo. Black sections indicate excavated areas, and close-ups are of later modifications to the openings.

the purpose of which is unknown. Finally, floor plaster in the Great Kiva was extended through the entrance on the east side into a formal plaza that was added to the southeast, uniting the two ritual spaces (Gerald 1957). The continuous plaster floor suggests the plaza may have played some role in ritual performances. The eastern entrance to the plaza is through a break in the wall surrounding the pueblo. There is another entrance to the plaza area to the south, adjacent to Room Block B. Some of the rooms established during Building Phase III in Room Block B continued to be used. The northern edge of Room Block B was located on the southern edge of the plaza, and the edge of Kiva 5 is adjacent to this public space.

Many of the burned rooms in Room Block D were abandoned, while others were remodeled. The room block is considerably smaller in size. Four of the rooms received plaster coatings over the burned roof fall and burned walls, and were subdivided to form smaller houses. Additionally, the doors in these rooms were sealed. The burned remains were capped with fresh plaster in five additional rooms and reoccupied without alteration in terms of size. The doors to other rooms were sealed in three cases. Additionally, four new rooms were built, one of which contained no doors to additional rooms. The result overall was a decrease in room suite size in this room block. The D-shaped kiva in the southern portion of the site was filled and no longer used.

Ceramics in all of the rooms dated to this building sequence are similar. Prieto Corrugated was found for the first time, as were sherds from San Carlos Red-on-Brown. Pinedale Black-on-White continued to be present. Polychromes recovered are dominated by Pinedale and Cedar Creek Polychrome, with relatively limited amounts of Fourmile and Pinto Polychrome. There is no Gila Polychrome, indicating that Building Phase IV dates to the Canyon Creek phase.

Building Phase V (Point of Pines Phase)

Structures associated with the fifth and final building sequence contain Gila Polychrome, indicating a Point of Pines phase. This was a

dynamic time for the community, with some structures being abandoned but others remodeled. New construction is evident in a number of places. A large percentage of the excavated rooms ($n = 107$, 82.3%) were occupied during this phase, many containing multiple plastered floors.

Neither the Great Kiva of the previous period nor Kivas 2 and 5 were in use during the final building phase (Figure 5.13); however, two new kivas (Kivas 4 and 6) are evident. Both are small (Kiva 4 = 10.78 m^2; Kiva 6 = 12.95 m^2), rectangular, and remodeled from previously constructed domestic rooms. Benches, slab-lined hearths, and ventilator shafts are present in both, and Kiva 4 contains a sipapu. Neither kiva has a door, so a roof entrance is assumed for both. This interpretation is supported in Kiva 6 by the presence of ladder holes and a broken sandstone slab that may have served as a hatch cover.

The compound wall surrounding the pueblo was still present, though numerous rooms were found outside its confines. New rooms are evident inside the wall as well, some of which were remodeled within the same footprint of those from the previous periods. Others were constructed on new footprints, shifting the foundations from earlier rooms. Additionally, more building of domestic structures occurred. Specifically, Room Block A was built during this phase. It was occupied long enough to warrant multiple replasterings of floors in many of the rooms. The 18 masonry rooms in W:10:51 also were constructed at this time. A small number of remodeled rooms in Room Block D established in the previous phase continued to be occupied. Room Block E witnessed continued occupation and construction of additional rooms on the western edge of the room block, approaching the Great Wall. Construction also occurred in Room Block B, where new rooms were built on top of the masonry rooms and Kiva 5 used in previous phases. This construction resulted in a lack of access to Kiva 5 and the southern edge of the plaza from this room block (Figure 5.14). Tests in individual rooms elsewhere in the site suggest considerable occupation both inside and outside of the compound wall. The end of the building

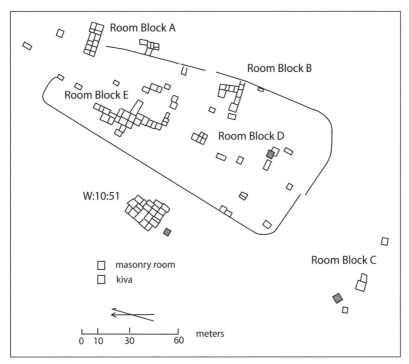

FIGURE 5.13. Excavated rooms at Point of Pines Pueblo dated to Building Phase V.

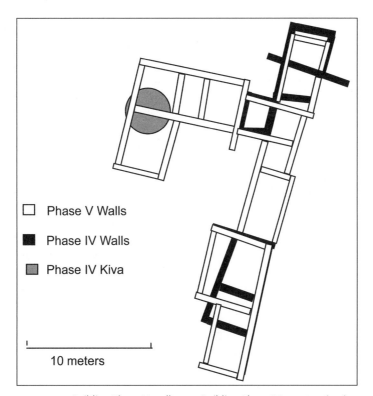

FIGURE 5.14. Building Phase V walls over Building Phase IV construction in Room Block B.

phase represents abandonment not only of Point of Pines Pueblo, but the entire region.

Room Abandonment Patterns

The dynamic nature of community organization is clearly demonstrated in the discussion of community growth above. Equally important is room abandonment. Abandonment of entire room blocks co-occurring with construction in other areas of the pueblo is an indication of shifting community organization that involved groups larger than individual households. This can be contrasted with the abandonment of individual rooms within room blocks, which likely reflects changing household size through time and can be seen in each of the five building sequences throughout the pueblo.

Room abandonment is generally measured through discussions of de facto versus secondary refuse (Cameron 1999a; Lightfoot 1993; Lowell 1991; Montgomery 1993; Schiffer 1975, 1987; Stevenson 1982; Varien and Mills 1997). One of the most frequently used data sources to examine this issue in the American Southwest relates to the distribution of whole vessels on room floors and the density of ceramic sherds in room fill. Specifically, the longer a room is abandoned, the greater the accumulation of trash, including sherds, is expected to be. The density of ceramic sherds in room fill can be used as a proxy for trash accumulation. Finally, the diversity of ceramic types in the fill can also indicate length of abandonment when differences in room volume are accounted for. The earlier a room is abandoned in the life of a community, the greater the number of ceramic types that can be deposited there as trash. However, the diversity of types present at any given time varies considerably through time. To account for this diversity, ratios comparing material found on the floor to material in the fill are calculated. In other words, ratios of the number of pots on the floor to sherd density in room fill, and number of pots on the floor to sherd type diversity in the room fill are calculated. The lower these two ratios, the longer the room has been abandoned.

These deposits can be impacted by a number of factors, however. For example, it has been well documented ethnographically that the amount and types of material culture left in a room at abandonment are impacted by a series of factors including the distance of the move, motive for the move, length of time to prepare for the move, and anticipation of return to the room by individuals and families when they abandon a structure (Rothschild and Dublin 1994; Rothschild et al. 1996; Stevenson 1982; Tomka and Stevenson 1993). If inhabitants abandon rooms and move to another location within the same community, they are still geographically close and supposedly still have good relations with other community members—in particular, their former neighbors. Therefore, scavenging of material culture and building material is expected. The longer the remainder of the community continues to be occupied, the more complete the scavenging is expected to be. Conversely, the degree of scavenging can be curtailed by a number of cultural factors. For example, several studies have demonstrated that both ceremonial and domestic structures may be ritually burned and/or buried upon abandonment (Creel and Anyon 2003; Lightfoot 1993; Montgomery 1993; Walker 2002). This type of cultural behavior would severely limit the amount of material that could be scavenged from the room floor and in the case of ritual burial (Montgomery 1993) may considerably increase the amount (density) of trash in the fill of the rooms after abandonment from a single period. Additionally, if alliances with neighbors and other community members were broken at the time of abandonment, former inhabitants of abandoned rooms may have been prevented from scavenging material. In this case, large amounts of material may have been left on the floors, but the density and diversity of ceramics would not represent rapid filling in a single period. Thus the variety of ceramic types in the trash would reflect a greater diversity than in cases of ceremonial abandonment and infilling, as noted above.

To determine the pattern of the site's final room abandonment, the number of whole vessels on the floor, the density of ceramic sherds in the fill (count/room volume) and typological diversity ratio (number of types/room volume) of those ceramics were measured. To investigate the impact of cultural processes, including ritual abandonment and burning, the ordering of room abandonment suggested by the sherd density and diversity and number of whole vessels was compared to the last phase of construction. If this data can be used to help determine the process of abandonment within any one phase, there should be differences in these variables between rooms that were last occupied in different phases. One compounding factor should be noted, however. Specifically, sherd density figures could be calculated for only 34 rooms and the diversity ratio for 30 rooms due to the incomplete recording of the full ceramic assemblage in the field notes.

The number of pots found on the highest floor could be determined for 122 floors based on maps of floor deposits and exhibited a difference between the floors that were burned and those that were not. Specifically, 24 rooms were burned, 9 of which were reoccupied (all with evidence of remodeling) in subsequent building phases. When only the last floor occupied in a room is examined, there is a significant difference in the number of pots found on the floor for rooms that were burned versus those that were not (two-tailed t-test = 3.487; p-value = .001). The number of pots on the burned floor ranged from zero to 47 with an average of 7.63 pots per floor (Figure 5.15). This can be compared to the highest floors found in rooms with no evidence of burning, where the counts ranged from zero to 25 and average 1.336. A significant difference (F-ratio = 4.340; p-value = .015) is present when the mean number of pots on the highest floor present within a room structure is compared for the rooms assigned to the Pinedale/Maverick Mountain, Canyon Creek, and Point of Pines phases for their last phase of occupation using a one-way analysis of variance. (The Tularosa phase rooms were not included because the sample size was too small.) The least standard differences (LSD) post hoc analysis indicates that the Pinedale/Maverick Mountain phase rooms had significantly more vessels on the floor than either the Canyon Creek or Point of Pines phase rooms (p-value = .007 and .009, re-

spectively)—likely due to the large number of vessels found in burned rooms that were not reoccupied in later phases. Interestingly, there is no significant difference in the sherd density or diversity ratio of ceramic types in the room fill for these three phases (p-value = .832 and .143, respectively), indicating that although the reasons for abandonment may have affected the nature of the floor assemblages, it did not affect the nature of refuse dumping after abandonment as would be expected if the burning was due to ceremonial abandonment. A one-way analysis of variance of the ratio of the number of pots on the floor divided by the sherd density also indicates the Pinedale/Maverick Mountain phase is significantly different from both the Canyon Creek and Point of Pines phases (p-value = .011 and .033, respectively). The Canyon Creek and Point of Pines phases, however, are not different from each other (p-value = .985). Again, rooms that were occupied last during the Pinedale/Maverick Mountain phases had the highest ratios. This is most likely due to the large number of pots on the floors of burned rooms that were not reoccupied. Similar results are found when the ratio of the number of pots divided by the diversity ratio is used.

In summary, the social processes involved in the abandonment of the central room block occupied by the migrant enclave were different from those of the nonmigrant rooms. Specifically, most were burned, and all were abandoned at the same time, indicating a social dynamic beyond changes in family size and makeup. Further, the burning of this room block at the end of the Pinedale/Maverick Mountain phase appears to structure the nature of the post-abandonment treatment of these rooms in a way that is not seen in any other area of the site. These processes were so powerful in terms of the organization of the community that when the burned rooms are removed from the analysis, there is no difference between rooms dated to different phases in terms of the ratio of the number of pots on the floor/sherd density in the fill (F-ratio = .675; p-value = .570) and the ratio of the number of pots on the floor/diversity of ceramic types (F-ratio = .143; p-value = .934).

FIGURE 5.15. Field photographs of Room 51, Floor 3, with broken pots and ground stone (*top*) and Room 68, Floor 1, with whole pots. (Photographed by Emil Haury and reproduced with permission from Arizona State Museum Photo Archives, University of Arizona.)

Architectural Changes
at Point of Pines Pueblo Through Time

The construction and abandonment of domestic and ritual structures at Point of Pines Pueblo is indicative of various community dynamics. These processes are evident in all five of the defined building phases, with considerable evidence of community growth during Phases II, III, and V. In each building phase, new construction of domestic structures was agglomerative. Cameron (1999b) argues this type of construction is indicative of individual family activity in response to family needs rather than coordinated action by larger social groups, though the building activities are likely sanctioned (or at least tolerated) by their neighbors.

Construction and remodeling activities occurred in all areas of the pueblo throughout its existence. However, based on the excavated data these activities were not equally intense in all areas. Furthermore, though these conclusions may be impacted somewhat by sampling error, what is evident in the five areas that received the most intensive excavation (Room Blocks A, B, D, E, and W:10:51) provide evidence that they were not occupied equally in all building phases. Specifically, Room Block E was established during the founding of the pueblo adjacent to important public structures (Kiva 2 and the Great Kiva/Plaza complex). It is the largest room block (in terms of room counts) in every building phase. Additionally, four of the rooms constructed during Building Phase I (Rooms 9, 10, 46, 94) have evidence of occupation in every subsequent building phase. These four rooms were joined by seven additional rooms during Building Phase II (Rooms 15, 21, 23, 33, 34, 58, 101/102) that had evidence of occupation in every subsequent building phase (see Appendix). Combined, these 11 rooms likely represent core houses of the social group occupying this portion of the pueblo. Within Room Block D, believed to house the migrant population, six rooms were constructed during Building Phases I and II and occupied until the burning of the room block. As such, Rooms 52, 64/65, 68, 69, 89, and 95 should be considered core rooms for the migrant population. Core rooms are not found elsewhere in the pueblo.

Each building phase also included remodeling. Often this activity involves construction of a new plastered floor within the same footprint. In at least four instances, however, remodeling extended to creation of rooms on a new footprint. The earliest example of this occurred during Building Phase II, when pithouses constructed in the previous phase in several areas of the pueblo were filled in, and masonry rooms were constructed over them. The second period of major remodeling occurred during Building Phase III, when two areas of Room Block E were remodeled. The first of these occurred in domestic rooms adjacent to Kiva 2, and the second was the conversion of the plaza into the Great Kiva. The rooms around the Great Kiva were further modified in Building Phase IV when the Great Kiva was enlarged, resulting in the destruction of three rooms on the east and the movement of the walls in other areas. Shifts in foundations are also evident in Room Block D in Building Phase IV, when several rooms were subdivided. Doors were sealed in numerous rooms as well. The result was both smaller rooms and smaller room suites. Finally, during Building Phase V, Room Block B witnessed considerable remodeling, with new domestic room foundations laid over both Kiva 5 and rooms from previous building phases.

Finally, each building phase has evidence of abandoned rooms. In most instances, these were isolated rooms spread throughout the pueblo, indicating changes in individual family dynamics or shifts in alliances. In three cases, however, abandonment was concentrated in a specific area, indicating a community-wide dynamic. The first episode occurred at the end of Building Phase I when the temporary pithouses were abandoned in favor of more permanent masonry rooms. The second occurred at the end of Building Phase III when most of Room Block D, as well as Kiva 3, were burned and abandoned. The third episode occurred at the end of Building Phase IV when the Great Kiva and two smaller kivas were abandoned, indicating a shift in ritual concepts at the pueblo. This occurred despite an apparent expansion in domestic structures and new construction indicating a population increase in Building Phase V. The pueblo itself, as well as the region as a whole, was abandoned at the end of Building Phase V.

The architectural chronology presented in this chapter provides the background data needed to understand the complex community dynamics at Point of Pines Pueblo. The nature of the relationships between individual households and small group formation (including ethnic interaction between the Kayenta migrants and indigenous Mogollon population) can now be examined by comparing domestic and ritual structures at the pueblo with those found elsewhere in the Point of Pines and Kayenta regions.

CHAPTER 6

Migrant-Host Interactions

The First Fifty Years at Point of Pines Pueblo

As noted in Chapter 5, the stratigraphic position of the pithouses and masonry rooms in Room Blocks D and E indicates the presence of a considerable number of Kayenta migrants at the founding of Point of Pines Pueblo along with their Mogollon hosts. If the house and, by extension, the ethnic group were an important organizing principle (as suggested in Chapter 2), this axis of identity should be evident at the site in the engagement of space through architecture from the earliest occupation of the pueblo (Figure 6.1). In particular, differences should be evident in a comparison of the subconscious (building techniques) and conscious (internal organization of domestic space and public architectural displays) construction and manipulation of architecture at the pueblo from its founding until the burning of the migrant room block (i.e., the first 50 years of occupation, Building Phases I–III). Domestic architecture inhabited by the two groups should show considerable differences, especially in the core houses—the earliest houses built at the site by the two groups. In addition, because the preservation of ceremony was so important to the model, there should be evidence of differences in preservation of ritual paraphernalia and traditional organization of ritual space between the Kayenta migrants and Mogollon hosts. Ritual differences, in fact, may have been emphasized by the migrants with the encouragement of at least a segment of the host community as they invited the newcomers in and allowed them to maintain their ritual and

ethnic "otherness" in exchange for their support in the political dynamics of the pueblo; however, there are limits, or thresholds, of differentiation that aggregated communities in middle-range societies can tolerate as they balance the tensions of community integration and subgroup factionalism. Once those limits are surpassed, the community is threatened with fissioning, and differences may no longer be tolerated to the same degree. To eliminate an axis of differentiation such as ethnicity, the symbols of that identity in terms of architecture and ritual paraphernalia may be written out of the community's social memory by constructing new buildings on a new footprint over the migrant structures and restricting the scavenging of abandoned areas by former inhabitants.

Migrant households and ritual space were identified by the presence of at least five or more sherds of Kayenta and Maverick Mountain ceramics or whole vessels on the floor, or connection to rooms through doors or shared walls that have these ceramics. Additionally, these rooms burned ca. 1300 and contain large amounts of floral material (particularly corn) that differs from plant remains elsewhere at the site.

Domestic Space

Engagement with space through the construction of architecture is particularly noticeable in domestic structures. They loom so large because they are the center of enculturation and the earliest experience and engagement with socially

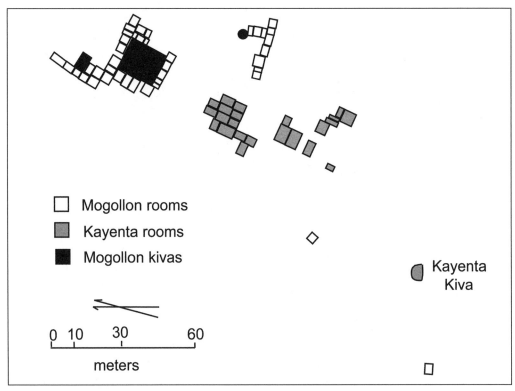

FIGURE 6.1. Excavated rooms occupied during the first 50 years of occupation showing Kayenta and Mogollon occupations.

structured space. Creese (2012:366) encapsulates this point eloquently when he states, "Houses are not only made in the image of persons; people also construct themselves using houses and house-images, in and through the routine material and social engagement of domestic living" (see also Carsten and Hugh-Jones 1995; Rapoport 1990). Domestic spaces are the locus in which personal and group identities and histories are created through the daily activities that occur within their walls (Creese 2012; Gamble 2007; Johnson 2012; Thomas 1996). When domestic structures are considered in relation to others in a community, especially with reference to their public (as opposed to their interior, private) appearance, they stand as personal statements about identity (including ethnicity), status, and public face (Blanton 1994; Wilk 1990). Therefore, the domestic structures of the Kayenta migrants (Room Block D) can be compared to other rooms in the pueblo in terms of their construction, internal organization of space, and exterior/public appearance and location within the community.

House Construction

As noted in Chapter 5, building techniques were recorded in excavation notes for some, though not all, of the rooms in terms of the types of stone used in foundations and wall construction (tuff or basalt), the shaping of stones in terms of pecking, and the use of banded or course masonry. Because the room walls have evidence of plaster (both interior and exterior) covering the masonry, the use of these different construction methods probably reflect subconscious learning frameworks rather than intentional signaling of identity and allegiance to a house/ethnic group.

The foundations were recorded for 69 masonry rooms constructed at the pueblo. Four different types of foundations were used: adobe ($n = 3$, 4.4%), basalt boulders ($n = 16$, 23.2%), tuff boulders ($n = 35$, 50.7%) and rooms with

TABLE 6.1. Room functions defined at Point of Pines Pueblo

Room Type	n	Mean Size (m²)	Distinguishing Features
Mogollon Rooms			
Habitation Type I	17	12.981	hearth and metate bin
Habitation Type II	4	14.950	hearth and storage bin
Habitation Type III	82	11.711	hearth only
Special Purpose	2	15.355	storage bin or metate bin only
Storage	71	9.072	none
Kayenta Rooms			
Habitation Type I	2	22.055	hearth and storage bin
Habitation Type II	5	23.790	hearth and metate bin
Habitation Type III	14	23.790	hearth only
Storage	7	10.711	none

Source: After Stone 2009:75.
Note: Only rooms that were completely excavated are included.

different foundations for different walls due to the appended nature of their construction ($n = 15$, 21.7%). Unfortunately, the foundations for only four of the migrant rooms were recovered. In all four cases they consisted of tuff boulders. Because the majority of all recorded foundations were of tuff, its use in these rooms likely represents an adaptation to available building material rather than a different learning framework.

The types of stones used in wall construction (tuff or a mixture of tuff and basalt) were recorded for 85 rooms, including 9 rooms in the migrant room block. Additionally, the presence of shaping, in the form of pecking of the wall stones, was recorded for 96 rooms, including 9 of the migrant rooms. Chi-square analysis indicates no relationship between these two variables and whether the room was constructed by Kayenta migrants or their Mogollon hosts (wall stones $x^2 = 0.03$, p-value = .863; shaping $x^2 = .869$, p-value = .351), again suggesting no difference between the learning frameworks of the migrants and their hosts. Finally, masonry style (coursed or banded) was recorded for 101 rooms, 10 of which were in the migrant room block. As before, chi-square analyses demonstrate no relationship between who constructed the room and masonry style ($x^2 = 2.709$, p-value = .10). In other words, construction methods do not appear to have varied significantly between rooms built by the two groups.

Internal Organization of Domestic Space
Previous analysis of room function indicates considerable flexibility in how domestic space was organized in the Mogollon Highlands (Ciolek-Torrello 1985; Lowell 1991; Reid and Whittlesey 1982; Riggs 2001; Stone 2009). Similarly, at Point of Pines Pueblo there is also variability in the types of rooms and how they are arranged into house suites. One axis of variability at Point of Pines is the ethnicity of the house; another is the date at which the room was constructed (see Chapter 7). In terms of ethnicity, previous studies of room size and features (Stone 2009) indicate five different types of functionally distinct rooms used by the Mogollon hosts and four types used by the Kayenta migrants (Table 6.1).

When only the rooms occupied during the Pinedale/Maverick Mountain phase are compared, the Kayenta rooms are significantly larger than the Mogollon rooms (t-score = 4.12, p-value = .000, difference = 8.059 m²). Additionally, the Kayenta rooms have more doors than the Mogollon rooms (t-score = 1.891, p-value = .066, mean difference = .333 doors), suggesting they were arranged into larger suites. Most rooms contain at least one door, although 33 rooms have no evidence of doors at any time during their use, and an additional 12 rooms had all of the doors sealed at some point, indicating at least some one-room houses. Rooms in one-room house suites are not, however, larger than rooms connected to other domestic space through doors (t-score = .212, p-value = .932).

The vast majority of rooms had at least one door (n = 122, 67.8%). In every case that the space adjacent to a door was excavated, it led into another room rather than extramural space (Stone 2009). The number of suites that were completely excavated is relatively small (n = 15), but those that were indicate a variety of different organizations. Two- and three-room suites (n = 13 and 2, respectively) are both present and are in linear arrangements created by appending rooms to each other rather than the use of a continuous wall. These suite types are found in both Kayenta and Mogollon room blocks.

Three types of arrangements were found among the two-room suites. The first type (n = 2) is characterized by a lack of floor features in both rooms. The second type (n = 2) contains a hearth in both rooms. One of these suites also contains a milling bin in one room. All of the remaining suites (n = 9) have a hearth in one room but not the other. Three of these suites also contained a milling bin in the room with the hearth.

Among the three-room suites, no single pattern is evident. One suite has hearths in adjacent rooms but lacks them in the third. Also, milling bins were found in each of the rooms with a hearth. Conversely, in the other suite, a hearth is present only in one room. Due to the small number of completely excavated room suite complexes, no statement can be made regarding differences between Kayenta and Mogollon organization of internal space beyond the fact that migrant rooms have more doors and thus were likely connected to more rooms.

Public Indicators of
Ethnicity in Domestic Architecture

Public indicators of ethnic differences between the Kayenta and Mogollon inhabitants during the first 50 years of occupation at Point of Pines Pueblo can be seen in the distribution of houses at the site, the use of two-story construction and differences in ritual architecture. The first issue is the segregation of space. When the site was first founded, both masonry architecture and pithouses were constructed. As noted in Chapter 5,

the pithouses appear to be temporary structures used by the Kayenta migrants for a short period of time. This designation is made based on the temporary nature of the pithouse structures and the presence of Kayenta and Maverick Mountain ceramics. When the location of these structures is examined, it is clear that the Kayenta migrants were concentrated on the west and south sides of the site, and the indigenous Mogollon were located on the north and east sides (Figure 6.2).

As occupation continued and the pithouse structures were abandoned in favor of masonry rooms, this pattern continued. Figure 6.3 shows the structures occupied through the first 50 years of the pueblo, with those constructed during Building Phases I and II marked as core houses for both groups. The Kayenta houses are concentrated on the western side of the pueblo, while the Mogollon houses are found to the north (surrounding the Great Kiva), in a room block to the east of the Kayenta houses, and additional rooms to the south.

In addition to spatial segregation, the Kayenta room block differs from the Mogollon in terms of the number of rooms that were two stories in height. A total of 12 two-story rooms were constructed at Point of Pines Pueblo, 10 of them during the first 50 years of occupation (Figure 6.4). Although some of the two-story rooms were found in the northern Mogollon room block (n = 3, 7.5% of the Mogollon rooms occupied during the first 50 years), the vast majority were in areas occupied by the Kayenta migrants, clustered in the center of the pueblo (n = 7, 31.8% of the excavated Kayenta rooms occupied in the first 50 years). The remaining two rooms were dated to later occupations. Additionally, none of the Mogollon core rooms identified in Chapter 5 is two stories, but Room 52, a core room for the Kayenta room block, was two stories at its initial construction.

Public Indicators
of Ethnicity in Ritual Architecture

Both small kivas associated with individual room blocks and a large Great Kiva were constructed during the first 50 years of occupation at Point of Pines Pueblo. Three of the first buildings constructed at the site were small kivas (Kiva 2,

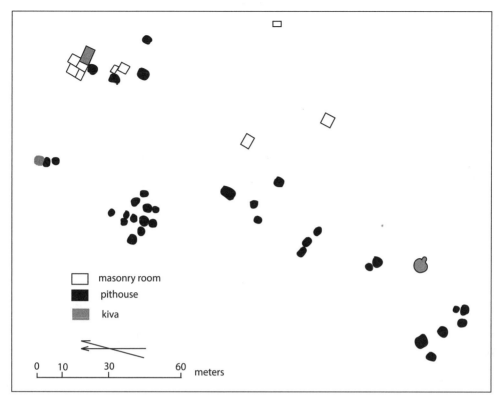

FIGURE 6.2. Locations of the earliest structures (those built on or into sterile soil) at Point of Pines Pueblo.

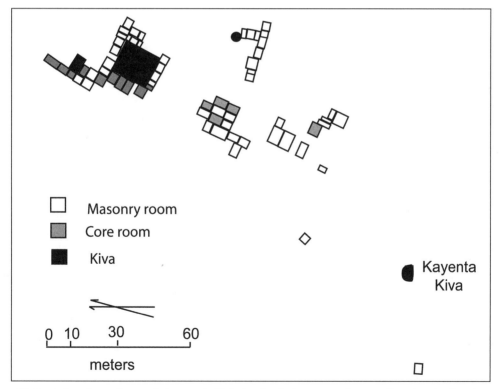

FIGURE 6.3. Locations of excavated rooms built during the first 50 years of occupation, showing location of the core room.

FIGURE 6.4. Locations of excavated one- and two-story rooms built during the first 50 years of occupation.

Kiva 3, PH 13 at W:10:51). One of them (PH 13) was used during Building Phase I but was no longer in use by the start of Building Phase II. A very large plastered plaza was added during Building Phase II. The plaza is bordered on two sides by rooms and lacked postholes so is believed to have been unroofed (Gerald 1957). During Building Phase III, the plaza was surrounded by rooms and covered by a roof, changing its function to a large (220 m²) Great Kiva. Kivas 2 and 3 continued to be used at this time, and a third small kiva (Kiva 5) was added on the western side of the pueblo. Kiva 5 was associated with Room Block B.

The meaning, in terms of ritual and social organization, of small versus large kivas has been a topic of considerable debate in Southwestern archaeology (Adler 1989, 1993; Adler and Wilshusen 1990; Lekson 1988, 1989; Stone 2013; Ware 2002; Wilshusen 1989). Based on a cross-cultural analysis of ritual structures in 28 middle-range societies described in the Human Area Relation Files (HARF), Adler (1993) argues that we can make a distinction between "generalized-use facilities" and "high-level integrative facilities." As the name implies, generalized-use facilities house both secular and ritual activities, are generally of restricted size, and are used by relatively small groups; in large communities they are used by a segment of the community only. Conversely, high-level integrative facilities tend to be more ritually specialized in their function and are used by larger groups, such as the entire village or multiple small settlements linked together by ritual (Gilman and Stone 2013). Adler and Wilshusen (Adler 1993; Adler and Wilshusen 1990; Wilshusen 1989) have argued we can use this cross-cultural analogy to understand the differences in scale of the groups that use small, corporate group kivas and large community ones in the American Southwest.

Ware (2002; see also Bernardini 2008 and

TABLE 6.2. Small kivas used at Point of Pines Pueblo during the first 50 years of occupation

Kiva	Shape	Size (m²)	Affiliation
PH 13 (W:10:51)	rectangular	10.60	possible Kayenta
Kiva 3	D-shaped	12.49	Kayenta
Kiva 2	rectangular	28.37	Mogollon
Kiva 5	round	8.81	Mogollon

Stone 2013) has taken this argument a step further and argued that political organizations that we see among ethnographic groups in the northern Southwest are associated with these different types of ritual structures. Based on the presence of small kivas and Great Kivas in the archaeological record, these political organizations have deep histories. Small, corporate kivas facilitate the meeting of kin groups (specifically, matriclans of the Western Pueblos) to participate in clan rituals and the education of uninitiated members about clan history and ritual away from the prying eyes of other kin groups. Conversely, Great Kivas provide space for meetings of groups larger than individual clans and are used by moieties or sodalities for ritual performances of importance to the entire community.

Interestingly, however, Great Kivas are not found in the Kayenta region, suggesting its inhabitants lacked the ritual sodalities or moieties associated with them (Stone 2013). Additionally, a mixture of small, corporate kivas and large Great Kivas at the same site is not characteristic of communities in the Mogollon region (Gilman and Stone 2013; Stone 2002a). Specifically, although kiva size varies in Mogollon communities, it is tied to site size (as measured by room counts) in the Point of Pines region ($r = .617$, Stone 2002a:403). Additionally, although there are recorded instances of Mogollon sites with multiple Great Kivas (Gilman and Stone 2013; Stone 2002a), the combination of small kivas and Great Kivas at the same site is unique to Point of Pines Pueblo. Given the importance of ritual and its maintenance in house societies, both the Kayenta and Mogollon inhabitants of Point of Pines Pueblo may have utilized small kivas as Ware (2002) suggests, not only to perform rituals

important to the house but also to educate the uninitiated in its history and ritual, away from the prying eyes of the members of other room blocks, corporate groups, or ethnic groups. In contrast, the Great Kiva would serve to house ceremonies that integrate the entire community. This integration would balance the factional tendency of house-specific organizations. If the house society model is correct, the small kivas should demonstrate considerable variability as each kin group builds its corporate kiva to serve its own needs for history and ritual. Further, there should be some similarity between the Kayenta kivas and those found in the Kayenta homeland. The Great Kiva, although used by the community as a whole at Point of Pines Pueblo, was not a tradition in the Kayenta region. Therefore, the model of Mogollon Great Kivas would have been predominate, and the structure at Point of Pines Pueblo should share characteristics with those found at other communities in the Mogollon Highlands, particularly Turkey Creek in the Point of Pines region; Grasshopper Pueblo on the Grasshopper Plateau to the west; and WS Ranch, Foote Canyon Pueblo, and Higgins Flat Pueblo in the Pinelawn/Reserve region to the east.

Small Kivas at Point of Pines Pueblo

Four small kivas (Table 6.2) were used during the first 50 years of occupation at Point of Pines Pueblo, though PH 13 at W:10:51 was restricted to Building Phase I, and Kiva 5 was not constructed until Building Phase III. The small kivas appear to be associated with specific room blocks or the pithouses, supporting the model of their use by small segments, or house groups, within the pueblo. The construction of these small kivas

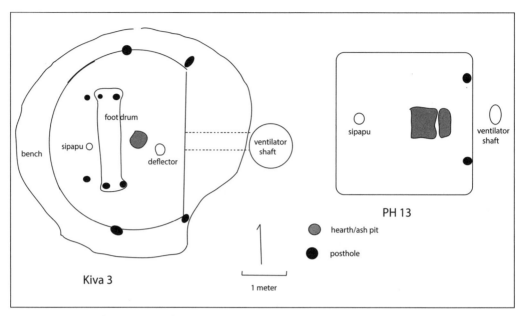

FIGURE 6.5. Migrant kivas at Point of Pines Pueblo.

at the earliest stage of occupation indicates the importance of ritual associated with small segments of the community, in keeping with a model emphasizing the importance of the house group/ethnicity as a source of identity.

A recent analysis of kivas in the Kayenta area (Stone 2013) indicates considerable variability in these structures, as would be expected if they were used by matriclans to perform clan-specific ceremonies and impart unique history and esoteric knowledge to uninitiated members of the clans in secret. Only two characteristics are consistently present. The first is the semi-subterranean nature of the kiva and the second is a hearth, deflector, and ventilator shaft complex. Both PH 13 and Kiva 3 are semi-subterranean and contain a hearth and ventilator shaft; PH 13 lacks a deflector stone, but Kiva 3 contains one (Figure 6.5). Both also contain a sipapu.

PH 13 is rectangular and contains no floor features other than the hearth and sipapu. Its assignment to the Kayenta pithouses is based on its proximity, its semi-subterranean construction, and the presence of a hearth and ventilator shaft complex. No artifacts were found on the floor, and no Kayenta or Maverick Mountain ceramics were found in association with PH 13. However,

if the Kayenta residents abandoned the kiva early in the pueblo's occupation in favor of Kiva 3, these items may have been removed as part of the abandonment process. At the moment, however, the suggestion that PH 13 was used by the Kayenta migrants is tentative at best.

More data are available to assign Kiva 3 to the Kayenta room block. In addition to its semi-subterranean construction and the presence of the hearth, deflector, and ventilator shaft complex are its shape and additional features and artifacts found on the floor. Kiva 3 is D-shape (Figure 6.6), a shape not found elsewhere in the Point of Pines region; they are present, though unusual, in the Kayenta region. Additionally, support posts were embedded in the walls of Kiva 3, a common practice in the Kayenta region (Stone 2013). A foot drum and a bench circling the kiva are also present; these features are common to both Kayenta and Mogollon kivas. The kiva was used long enough so that the floor was replastered at least once. The highest floor was not cleared prior to abandonment, and a variety of locally made ceramics along with Kayenta Polychrome and Maverick Mountain Polychrome sherds were found under the burned roof. Possible ceremonial paraphernalia

FIGURE 6.6. Field Photograph of Kiva 3. (Photographed by Ken Sharp and reproduced with permission from the Arizona State Museum Photo Archives, University of Arizona.)

on the floor include two deer vertebrae found at the base of postholes on either side of the foot drum, a sheep horn on the floor, and a metate. The deer vertebrae may represent dedicatory offerings given their location at the bottom of the postholes.

Kivas 2 and 5 (Figure 6.7) are associated with the Mogollon room blocks on the east and north sides of the pueblo. Kiva 2 is an aboveground masonry structure surrounded by domestic rooms (Room Block E) and contains a hearth and ventilator. Conversely, Kiva 5 is semi-subterranean, though it lacks the hearth, deflector, and ventilator shaft associated with Kayenta kivas. Additionally, neither kiva had Kayenta or Maverick Mountain Polychrome ceramics on the floors, though they were present in the trash fill of each. Finally, Kiva 5 is directly adjacent to the Mogollon room block on the eastern side of the pueblo (Room Block B), and Kiva 2

is surrounded by rooms that form part of the northern Mogollon Room Block E.

Kiva 2 sits on sterile soil and was one of the earliest structures built at the site. It is similar in construction and internal features to other kivas in the Point of Pines region (Stone 2002a), though it is rather small. It contains a central hearth, an ash pit, a deflector stone, and a ventilator opening at floor level in a north-south alignment. Additionally, five pits are present, as are two ladder holes and a large number of postholes, many of which were not evident until the kiva floor was removed. There is also a door in the north wall. That room was not excavated and its function is unknown. The kiva was used long enough that the floor was replastered at least once. Based on the amount of roof fall, the excavators suggested that there may have been a second story above the kiva, but this cannot be confirmed. A second possibility suggested by the

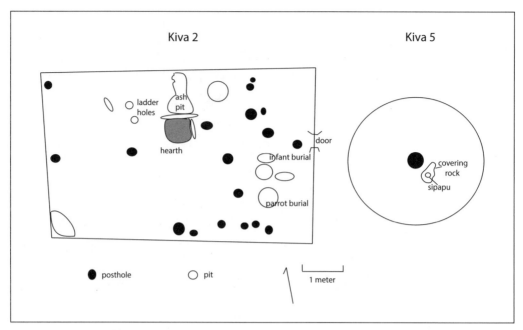

FIGURE 6.7. Early Mogollon kivas at Point of Pines Pueblo.

excavators was later reoccupation of the area. A hearth is evident 0.4 m above the kiva floor, but the floor with which this hearth was associated was not defined. Therefore, the remains were too incomplete to distinguish between these two possibilities. Artifacts found on the floor include two caches of cores, formal chipped stone tools, two manos, and abrading stones. Of possible ceremonial importance is a parrot burial and an infant burial (approximately nine months of age), each in a shallow pit in the kiva floor. A parrot burial was also found in a shallow pit in the earliest floor (Floor 2) of Room 31, a Mogollon room built on the north side of the Great Kiva during Building Phase III. No other parrot burials are known from the site.

Kiva 5 is a round, semi-subterranean kiva adjacent to the Mogollon room block on the east side of the site (Room Block B). Its only floor features are a single posthole and a sipapu covered by a stone slab. Possible ceremonial paraphernalia found on the floor of the kiva include a piece of azurite, a chalcedony core and biface, an antler wrench, and a rubbing stone.

The small kivas used during the first 50 years of occupation at Point of Pines Pueblo demon-strate a considerable amount of variability in terms of shape, size, internal features, and artifacts. This is consistent with the idea of their use by individual segments of the community and the importance of the house group and ethnicity as loci of identity.

Early Great Kiva at Point of Pines Pueblo

During Building Phase II, a plastered plaza was constructed on the north side of the site, with domestic rooms that were part of Room Block E on the west and south sides. During Building Phase III, domestic rooms were also constructed on the north and east sides, largely encircling the area to form a large (220 m²) public space. Additionally, the presence of 13 postholes indicates the Great Kiva was roofed at this time. There are no other floor features evident in this lowest floor of the Great Kiva (though other features were added later).

A comparison of the Point of Pines Great Kiva to other Tularosa phase Great Kivas in the Mogollon Highlands shows remarkable similarity (Table 6.3, Figure 6.8). Specifically, comparisons are made to Great Kivas at Turkey Creek Pueblo (Johnson 1965) in the Point of

TABLE 6.3. Great Kivas found at aggregated communities in the Mogollon Highlands

Pueblo	Size (m²)	Entrance	Number of Postholes	Other Features
Point of Pines (Earliest Floor)	220	east, extramural space	13	none
Turkey Creek Pueblo	192	east, extramural space	14	hearth, foot drum
Grasshopper Pueblo	182	east, room	12	hearth, foot drum, small pits
WS Ranch	134.6	east, extramural space	0	hearth, foot drums
Higgins Flat Pueblo	128.4	southeast, extramural space	11	hearth, foot drum, small pit
Foote Canyon Pueblo*	135	northeast, extramural space	8	none

Sources: Gerald 1957; Johnson 1965; Martin et al. 1957; Riggs 2001; Rinaldo 1959; and Tomka 1988.
Note: Rinaldo (1959) initially classified the Great Kiva at Foote Canyon Pueblo as a plaza but notes it contains postholes and was roofed. Therefore, Great Kiva is a more appropriate designation.

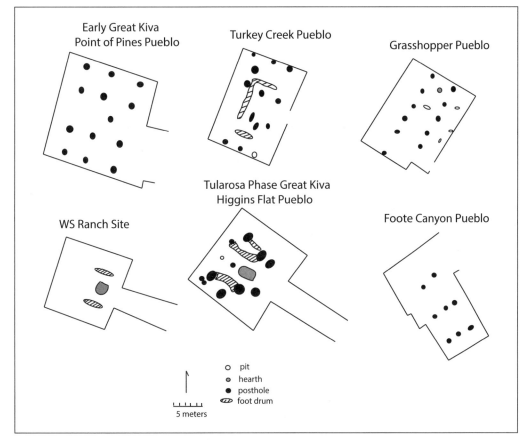

FIGURE 6.8. Excavated Great Kivas from aggregated sites in the Mogollon Highlands.

Pines region, Grasshopper Pueblo (Riggs 2001) on the Grasshopper Plateau to the west, and three to the east in the Pinelawn/Reserve region (WS Ranch [Tomka 1988], Higgins Flat Pueblo [Martin et al. 1957], and Foote Canyon Pueblo [Rinaldo 1959]). In five of the six Great Kivas the entrance is through an opening in the wall facing east/southeast. At Grasshopper Pueblo, the Great Kiva entrance leads into a room with no floor features, but in the other five kivas they open onto extramural space. All but the WS Ranch and Higgins Flat Pueblo Great Kivas are incorporated into a room block. In addition to the orientation of their entrances and location within room blocks, five of the six Great Kivas have a series of large postholes arranged in parallel lines. At Grasshopper, Turkey Creek, WS Ranch, and Higgins Flat Pueblos additional floor features include hearths and foot drums (and small pits in the case of Grasshopper Pueblo and Higgins Flat Pueblo). The large size of the Great Kivas at all six sites suggests the structures served as a high-level integrative facility in which ceremonial activities could be conducted that would integrate the entire village and balance the factional tensions created by subgroup-specific ceremonies in the small, corporate group kivas.

Political Dynamics in the Host Community during the First Fifty Years of Occupation

The above comparison of domestic and ritual architecture provides evidence of the migrant group's efforts to maintain their ethnic and ritual "otherness" separate from their host. The Kayenta migrants were not alone, however, in terms of active negotiations within and between small group alliances at Point of Pines Pueblo. In addition to the construction of the small kivas associated with different room blocks occupied by the Mogollon inhabitants and the increasing formalization of community-wide space (plaza to Great Kiva), political dynamics within the host community are evident in the domestic architecture. As noted in Chapter 3, remodeling of structures—particularly when it involves razing old structures and building new ones with their foundations in a different footprint—is part of an ongoing social dialogue and negotiation of rights and social relationships between community members. Prior to the end of Building Phase III, when the migrant room block was burned, there were two instances of abandonment and dismantling of houses followed by the building of new domestic structures over the old ones using a new footprint. The first is the abandonment and filling in of pithouses used as temporary structures during Building Phase I and the construction of masonry rooms over them

(Figure 6.9). This action, coupled with construction of masonry rooms in Room Block D during Building Phases II and III, indicates changes in the status of the migrants from temporary to permanent members of the pueblo.

The construction of masonry rooms over the pithouses was not the only incidence of remodeling on a new footprint during the first 50 years of occupation. During Building Phase III, remodeling of masonry domestic rooms that involved the razing of structures built during the previous phase and the construction of new rooms on foundations with a different footprint (Figure 6.10) also occurred. These actions represent a shift in alliances within at least one room block/corporate group within the Mogollon community, foreshadowing the dramatic events that occurred at the end of Building Phase III and the destruction of the migrant enclave.

Kayenta Abandonment Patterns after the First Fifty Years of Occupation

As noted in Chapter 5, the abandonment processes exhibited in the Kayenta and Mogollon rooms at Point of Pines Pueblo at the end of Building Phase III were dramatically different. Although there were realignments of the footprints of some Mogollon rooms (especially in Room Block E) during the first 50 years of occupation, none of the Mogollon rooms were burned as part of this process, and relatively little was left on the floors. In contrast, the Kayenta rooms were burned with large amounts of macrobotanical remains and material culture left on the floors (Figures 6.11). Additionally, the roof of Kiva 3 was burned, and the presence of ceramics, a metate, and sheep horn indicate cultural material was not removed prior to this event. The model of host-migrant/migrant-host relationships presented in Chapter 3 indicates the importance of ritual not only in the maintenance of ethnic differences, but also as a potential source of conflict. More specifically, tolerance, or even encouragement, of ethnic and ritual otherness by at least part of the host community when the migrants first arrived appears to have shifted to hostility as the community grew. Hostility between ethnic groups over differences

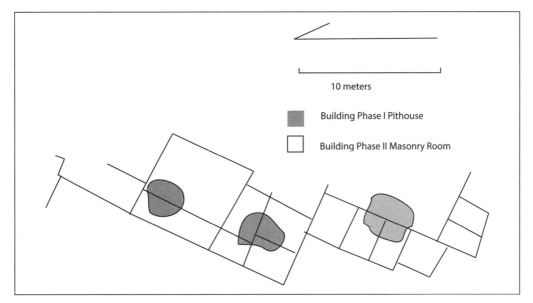

FIGURE 6.9. Construction of masonry rooms over early pithouses during Building Phase II.

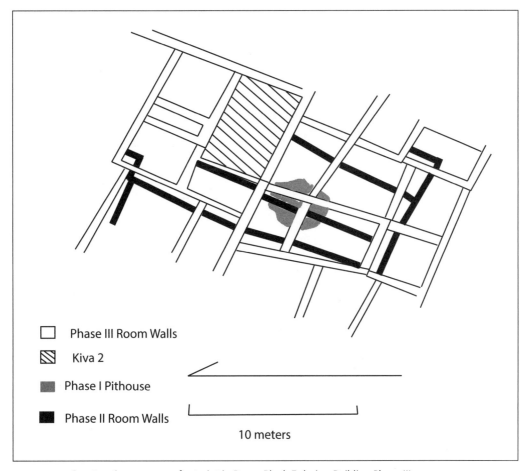

Phase III Room Walls

Kiva 2

Phase I Pithouse

Phase II Room Walls

10 meters

FIGURE 6.10. Construction on a new footprint in Room Block E during Building Phase III.

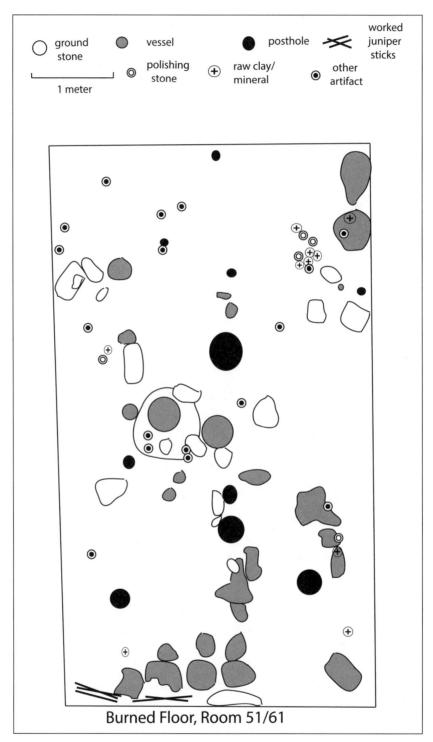

FIGURE 6.11. Burned floor of Room 51/61 in Room Block D with cultural material remaining on the floor.

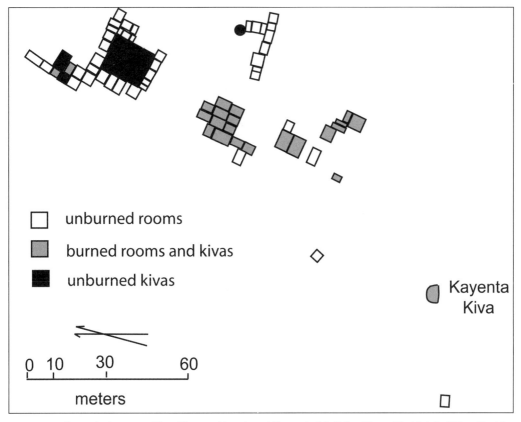

FIGURE 6.12. Excavated rooms with evidence of burning at the end of Building Phase III at Point of Pines Pueblo.

in ritual calendars is well-known ethnographically in multiethnic pueblos (Dozier 1954, 1966; Ellis 1979; Stanislawski 1979). I argue that as the community grew, they reached a threshold in which the ritual calendar became full and conflicts began to occur. As a result, the ritual otherness of the migrant groups became less tolerated. Support for this contention can be found in the abandonment of the migrants' D-shaped kiva and rooms. Though it is not the only kiva to have material of possible ritual significance on the floor, Kiva 3 is the only one that was burned. This occurred at the end of Building Phase III, at the same time the migrant room block burned. The only two rooms burned outside of Room Block D during the first 50 years of occupation were in Room Block E, where remodeling on a new footprint occurred earlier in the building phase (Figure 6.12). Scavenging of these rooms did occur, as did replastering and reoccupation

of the room in the same footprint of subsequent periods. The burning of Room Block D and Kiva 3, combined with the failure to scavenge material culture from the floors, is further evidence that the host community attempted to delegitimize the ritual and ethnic differences of the migrants and remove them from the community's social memory.

Despite conscious attempts by the Mogollon inhabitants of Point of Pines Pueblo to rewrite history and social memory after the first 50 years of occupation, the presence of the migrants did affect the community in the long run. Specifically, numerous aspects of the pueblo demonstrate the migrants' continued impact on community dynamics, even after their identity as a separate segment within the pueblo was no longer expressed. These impacts are discussed in Chapter 7.

The Indigenous Community
at Point of Pines Pueblo

The Next One Hundred Years

The presence of migrants in any region has an impact not only on the economic, ritual, social, and political organization of the incoming group but on the host population as well. As noted in Chapter 3, the nature of the relationship between hosts and migrants and the impact on the host community of newcomers entering the region varies considerably depending on the temporal, social, and spatial scales of the migration. Minimally, the impact is demographic as additional people are added to the regional population. In cases where the migrant group is large and the host population is densely settled in aggregated communities, as was the case with the Point of Pines region, there are additional factors to consider. Specifically, the introduction of a large group of people and an additional axis of differentiation (i.e., ethnicity) can introduce a new source of stress and tension to the already tenuous balance of factional tendencies versus community integration that is always present in aggregated communities. That is, aggregated communities are fluid, dynamic structures in which power relationships are constantly negotiated, challenged, and renegotiated as myriad issues are addressed and decisions made in everyday life. Factions within the host community may encourage and support the migrants' attempts to maintain their ethnic "otherness" in terms of ritual and social structures in exchange for the newcomers' support of the spon-

soring group in disputes within the established settlement.

Within Point of Pines Pueblo this dynamic can be seen in the presence of multiple room blocks, each with its own small, corporate group kiva. There also is evidence of integration of groups within the community as a whole in the construction of the large Great Kiva. The presence of both small, corporate kivas and a Great Kiva is a combination of ritual spaces that is unique in the Mogollon Highlands (Gilman and Stone 2013; Stone 2002a). The migrant community extended the concepts of affiliation and kinship associated with the "house" to form an ethnic enclave. As demonstrated in Chapter 6, the Kayenta enclave is evident architecturally by differences in ritual structures, internal organization of domestic space, and the external appearance of their room block, particularly with reference to its concentration of two-story rooms.

There must be limits, or thresholds, to ritual and social differentiation, however, if aggregated communities are to balance the tensions of subgroup factionalism versus community integration in the long run. When these thresholds are reached or surpassed, communities can experience increased stress and conflict at a variety of scales. Ethnographically, disputes over the ritual calendar within aggregated communities (McGuire and Saitta 1996; Stone 2005a) may escalate when multiple ethnic groups are present, creating a major source of tension (Dozier 1954, 1966; Ellis 1979; McGuire 1986; Stanislawski 1979). Further, although rules of exogamy and the use of increasing numbers of different, sometimes competing, social identities in which membership crosscuts kin ties (such as sodalities) can serve as a mechanism to mitigate the factional tendencies of aggregated communities, other axes of identity and affiliation can increase these tensions. Specifically, social identities that inhibit the forming of crosscutting ties by limiting membership and encouraging small group endogamy (like ethnicity) have the opposite effect, increasing the tendency toward factionalism. These exclusionary groups, combined with differing ritual calendars, can lead to factional fighting that escalates to the level of village fissioning and abandonment of the community by one or more groups (Levy 1992; Stone 2005a; Titiev 1944; Whiteley 1988a, 1988b).

This appears to have happened at Point of Pines Pueblo. Specifically, around AD 1300 tensions rose to the level of conflict along ethnic lines. As noted in Chapter 6, a result of this tension was the burning of the Kayenta room block (Room Block D) and kiva (Kiva 3). After this episode, if any members of the Kayenta group were left at Point of Pines Pueblo, they no longer expressed their ethnic and ritual "otherness." Further, the remaining Mogollon inhabitants undertook several actions both to write the Kayenta migrants out of the architectural history of the pueblo and to reinforce community integration by altering social memory through changes in domestic and ritual spaces through which individuals moved and lived on a daily basis. On some level these efforts were successful enough that the community continued to be occupied, and even grew in size, for at least another 100 years. However, tensions between small groups remained, and mechanisms through which they expressed these differences that began during the first 50 years of occupation (such as the use of small, corporate kivas) continued to be used and, through time, appear to have increased in importance at the cost of community-wide institutions. These social dynamics are evident in the remodeling of domestic space using new footprints and in the construction and elaboration of communal space.

Elimination of Ethnicity as an Axis of Identity

During the first 50 years of occupation, the Kayenta enclave was identified by the use of flexed burials, differences in ceramic manufacture and decoration, internal organization of domestic space, use of two-story construction, and a D-shaped kiva. Most burials lacked sufficient grave goods to assign them to a specific phase at Point of Pines Pueblo (Rodrigues 2008). Therefore, chronologically fine-grained analysis of changes in burial patterns is not possible. There is evidence, however, that all of the other conscious signifiers of ethnic differentiation were eliminated after 1300 and a more unified Mogollon identity dominated the community. In terms of ceramics, the migrants were associated with imported Kayenta Black-on-Red and Polychrome ceramics and the manufacture of Maverick Mountain Black-on-Red and Polychrome ceramics (using Kayenta designs on local clays). An examination of the artifact catalogs associated with room floors reveals a highly restricted distribution of Kayenta and Maverick Mountain ceramics in space and time. Specifically, only 19 of the 204 excavated floors (9%) had either whole vessels or substantial numbers (more than five) of Kayenta and/or Maverick Mountain sherds in floor fill (floor contact and the first 10 cm of fill). Fifteen of these rooms (78.9%) were located in the Kayenta room block (Room Block D) and independently dated to the Pinedale/Maverick Mountain phase with dendrochronological samples, stratigraphic positioning, and ceramic cross dating of associated materials. Two floors were in rooms elsewhere at the site but dated to the Point of Pines phase and likely represent redeposited trash associated with room abandonment. Rooms 39 and 44, in Room Block E on the north side of the Great Kiva, have Maverick Mountain ceramics on floors dated to the Pinedale/Maverick Mountain phase. Specifically, Room 39 had two small, Maverick Mountain Black-on-Red vessels on the floor, and Room

44 had Maverick Mountain Polychrome sherds in the floor fill and one Maverick Mountain sherd embedded in the floor as a metate baffle. Elsewhere in the pueblo, both during the first 50 years of occupation and subsequent to this time, painted ceramics are dominated by Cibola Black-on-White and White Mountain Black-on-Red/Polychrome ceramics imported from the Zuñi region to the north. It is unclear what the presence of Maverick Mountain ceramics in these two rooms indicates, but possibilities include marriage across ethnic lines or ceramic gifts between allies.

In addition to painted ceramics, all other aspects of material culture that signaled Kayenta ethnic boundaries were eliminated after AD 1300. For example, the roof of Kiva 3 was burned and collapsed onto the floor at the end of Building Phase III. Burning is not a characteristic of kiva abandonment in the Kayenta Region (Stone 2013). Although there is no evidence of construction over Kiva 3, it was abandoned and filled in at this time. Additionally, considerable remodeling and new construction are evident in what was formerly the Kayenta room block. As noted in Chapter 3, remodeling in new footprints and construction of new structures over old buildings is an engagement of architecture that is inherently tied to ongoing political action within the community. These actions deny the rights of the previous inhabitants and give them to their replacements. In addition, these activities prevent the former inhabitants from scavenging material culture and building materials, and remove visual evidence of the previous occupants. These actions effectively write the migrants out of the architectural history of the community and remove them from its social memory. The construction of new structures also affects pathways of movement through the community, and thus how the space and the history it creates are experienced and perceived.

Remodeling of domestic space in Room Block D during Building Phase IV occurred in two ways. The first was demolition and new construction. Specifically, 11 rooms that were occupied during Building Phase III were abandoned during Building Phase IV (though one of these

was remodeled and reoccupied during building Phase V). Additionally, new rooms were built on the edge of the room block during the Canyon Creek phase (Building Phase IV). All of the new rooms resemble Mogollon rooms at the pueblo in terms of size (mean 13.13 m²), and all have just one story. The second change in the use of Room Block D was reoccupation after the remodeling of the internal space. Five rooms were subdivided (Figure 7.1), resulting in rooms smaller than those in other room blocks at the pueblo. A Oneway ANOVA of floor area for floors dated to the Canyon Creek phase indicates rooms in Room Block D are significantly smaller (f-ratio = 2.446, p = .087) than rooms in other room blocks in the pueblo by between 2 and 5 m².

The other form of remodeling of rooms in Room Block D had a similar effect. Specifically, internal space was remodeled by sealing doors during the Canyon Creek and Point of Pines phases (Figure 7.1). The sealing of doors was relatively common at pueblos in the Mogollon Highlands (Stone 2009) and may relate to changes in family size through its life cycle (Cameron 1996; Reynolds 1981). At Point of Pines Pueblo, however, it appears to be tied more closely to the restructuring of internal space, as Kayenta rooms were remodeled to comply with Mogollon concepts of organizing domestic areas. This conclusion is based on the distribution of sealed doors at the pueblo. Specifically, 119 floors can be securely dated to Canyon Creek and/or Point of Pines phases with no other phases of occupation indicated. The association of sealed doors with these specific floors is based on the overlapping of plaster between walls and floors noted by excavators in the field. A chi-square analysis of the presence of sealed doors versus the room block in which the room was located during the Canyon Creek and Point of Pines phases indicates a significant association (x^2 = 10.2, p = .001, V = .293). Specifically, there is a higher than expected number of rooms with sealed doors in Room Block D (13 of 19 floors occupied during these phases, 68%) and lower than expected number of rooms with sealed doors in all other room blocks (30 of 100 rooms, 30%) during these phases. Both the remodeling

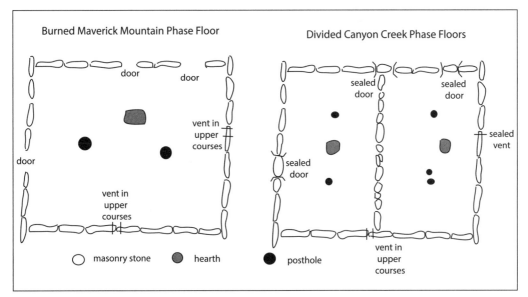

FIGURE 7.1. Comparison of the burned Pinedale/Maverick Mountain phase floor to the remodeled Canyon Creek floor of Room 72 in Room Block D (note dividing wall and sealed doors).

and new construction at Point of Pines Pueblo after AD 1300 resulted in houses that are similar to Mogollon houses throughout the Mogollon Highlands (Stone 2009).

Strengthening of Community Ties During the Canyon Creek Phase

In addition to eliminating ethnic signals associated with domestic space in Room Block D during the first 50 years of occupation of Point of Pines Pueblo, the community members engaged the pueblo's space and architecture in a number of ways that strengthened and integrated community ties. For example, there was continued occupation of the 11 core rooms constructed in Room Block E at the very beginning of the pueblo's occupation, as well as the two room blocks inhabited by Mogollon groups during the first 50 years (Room Blocks B and E). Additionally, the two small kivas associated with these room blocks (Kiva 2 and Kiva 5) continued to be used. The Great Kiva was further elaborated, and a large plaza with a plastered floor connected with the Great Kiva floor was constructed. As noted in Chapter 6, Great Kivas have a long history of use in the Mogollon region (Gilman and Stone 2013), and Riggs (2013) argues they

represent an important overt signal of Mogollon identity. The Great Kiva at Point of Pines Pueblo is similar to Mogollon Great Kivas found to both the east and west. Its continued use and elaboration at this time is an indication of intensification of Mogollon ritual after AD 1300.

One of the most striking aspects of public architecture, however—and one that considerably impacted the way individuals could move through the pueblo and perceive space inside versus space outside of the pueblo community—is the compound wall that was constructed around the site (Figure 7.2). As noted in Chapter 5, the wall averages 1.23 m in height and is .73 meters wide at its base, representing a massive undertaking and considerable labor. There were only four entrances into the pueblo through the wall in its initial construction (Figure 7.3). Two of them (on the south and west portions) were blocked with construction almost immediately, or at least by the end of the Canyon Creek phase (Figure 7.2). The east wall entrance is very narrow and would have channeled individuals directly into the formal plaza connected to the Great Kiva. The largest opening is in the northeast edge of the wall. The pueblo grew during the subsequent Point of Pines phase, forming

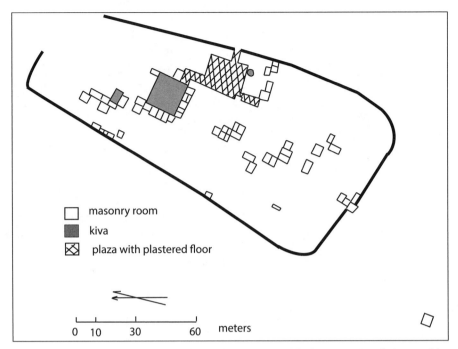

FIGURE 7.2. Excavated rooms occupied during the Canyon Creek phase at Point of Pines Pueblo.

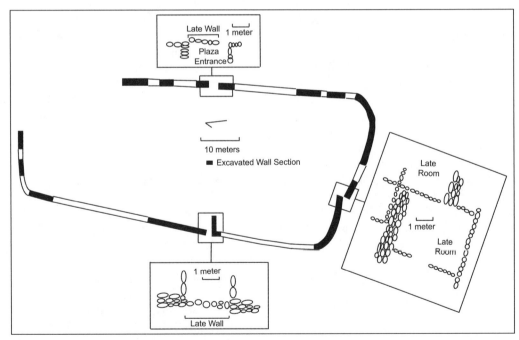

FIGURE 7.3. Details of the compound wall excavations at Point of Pines Pueblo (dark shading indicates excavated segments).

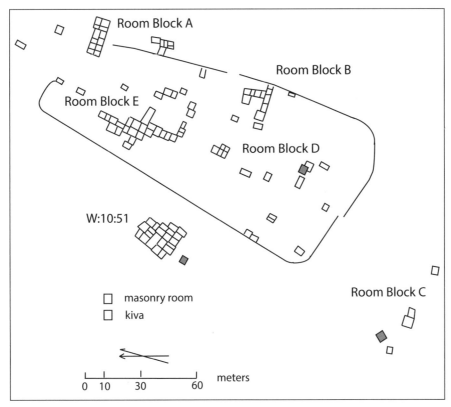

FIGURE 7.4. Excavated rooms occupied during the Point of Pines phase at Point of Pines Pueblo.

additional room blocks and reaching its greatest number of occupied rooms (Figure 7.4), suggesting the success of these methods of village integration for the next 100 years.

The construction of the compound wall is interesting for several reasons. First, Point of Pines Pueblo is the only Mogollon community (including both the Mogollon Highlands and the southern lowlands of the Mimbres, Gila, and San Simon Valleys) that had a compound wall. Its massive scale and chronological position following the burning of the Kayenta room block at the end of Building Phase III suggests that the Mogollon inhabitants who remained may have feared retaliation by the migrant group. The final abandonment of the Kayenta region also occurred around AD 1300, and there is evidence of Kayenta migrants moving farther south into the southern Basin and Range region at this time (Clark 2001; Dean 1996; Haas 1989; Lyons et al. 2008; Reid 1989). Migrants from the Mo-

gollon Rim and the Little Colorado and Upper Gila Rivers were also moving into the Mogollon Highlands to the west of Point of Pines (Reid and Whittlesey 1982, 1999; Whittlesey and Reid 2012). Concern over retaliation at Point of Pines Pueblo may have been heightened due to the possibility of the Kayenta enclave forming alliances with new groups moving through neighboring regions.

The compound wall not only served as a defensive structure by limiting access to the pueblo from the outside; it also had an impact on the residents and their ability to move around and through the community (Stone 2000). Due to its height (averaging 1.23 m), many residents of the pueblo would not have been able to see over the wall when standing next to it. This would have been particularly noticeable in the plaza, a formal public space tied to the Great Kiva by a continuous plaster floor. Additionally, every time individuals left the pueblo to tend agricultural

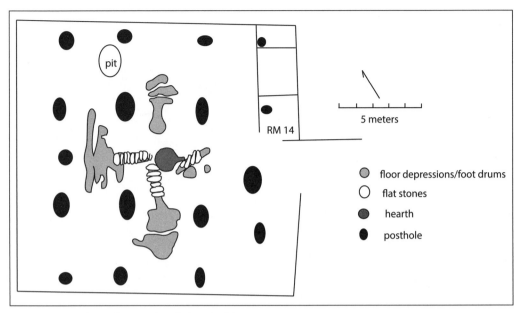

FIGURE 7.5. Late Great Kiva at Point of Pines Pueblo.

fields, gather wild resources, hunt, or collect raw materials used to manufacture material culture, they would have had to pass through a limited number of openings. This restriction of movement into and out of the pueblo would have had an impact on the daily activities, bodily experiences, and perception of community and history. Thus even though the remodeling of Room Block D removed the Kayenta migrants from the architectural history and social memory of the community, the compound wall, in a sense, gave them a more enduring presence and provided a daily reminder of their place in history.

The other locus of considerable labor was the remodeling of the Great Kiva, which was enlarged to 264 m² (adding 44 m²). The increase in size was accomplished by demolishing walls of rooms on the south, west, and north edges of the Great Kiva and creating a new continuous wall in this area. Additionally, three rooms on the eastern side of the Great Kiva were razed, and the space was pulled into the Great Kiva (Figures 7.5 and 7.6). The Great Kiva is open on the east side to the plaza, and a continuous plaster floor extends from the Great Kiva out into the plaza (Gerald 1957). Also, according to the excavation notes and maps of the Great Kiva, there

is an entrance into Room 14 just to the north of the plaza entrance. Room 14 is relatively small (13.32 m²) and contains a hearth but no other features. Unfortunately, excavation notes for Room 14 are somewhat limited, but they suggest a formal door was not present. As a result, the relationship of Room 14 to the Great Kiva is unclear, as is the role that subsequent remodeling may have played in this interpretation. If a door did exist between the Great Kiva and Room 14 at some point, the room may have served as an area in which to store ritual paraphernalia or to stage ritual performances. The Great Kiva at Grasshopper Pueblo has an opening into a room on the eastern side of the pueblo that may have served a similar function (Riggs 2001).

In addition to increasing its size and connecting it to the open plaza to the east, the community added a number of additional features to the Great Kiva. Specifically, a hearth was placed in the center, and a single storage pit was added in the northwest corner. Additionally, a series of large depressions starting at the hearth and radiating out toward the kiva walls were added. According to the field maps, these depressions ranged in depth from 40 to 55 cm, similar to foot drums found in other kivas in the Point of

FIGURE 7.6. Field photo of late Great Kiva floor with students standing on the postholes. (Photographed by E. B. Sayles and reproduced with permission from the Arizona State Museum Photo Archives, University of Arizona.)

Pines region (Stone 2002a). At the hearth end of three of these depressions, a series of flat rocks had been placed over the depressions, but their function is unknown.

The largest area of the plaza is located southeast of the Great Kiva and abuts the compound wall on its east side. Its presence was first identified when the east entrance through the wall was investigated and a plastered surface was encountered. The surface in this area is a corridor approximately 6.5 m long that leads from the wall, between room blocks, and into the plaza

area. The plaza's outlines were further defined by the northern edge of Room Block B on the south and room blocks to its north and west that were not excavated but whose walls were evident on the surface. A corridor on the northwest side of the plaza led into the Great Kiva, and one on the southwest corner extended from the plaza, between room blocks, to the south. The entire plaza was not cleared during excavation, but numerous test pits were excavated over a three-year period. Test excavations revealed several extramural surfaces under the plastered

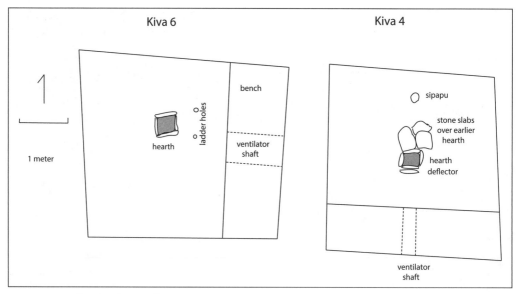

FIGURE 7.7. Small Point of Pines phase Mogollon kivas.

floor, along with several hearths and pits. Trash deposits on top of the plaster floor indicate the plaza was abandoned as an extramural space at the beginning of the Point of Pines phase.

Remnants of Differentiation in Canyon Creek and Point of Pines Phases

Despite these apparent attempts to decrease social and ritual heterogeneity and increase community integration at Point of Pines Pueblo, the differentiation that began during the first 50 years of occupation continued. This can be seen in the continued organization of domestic space into room blocks and the use of the small kivas associated with them (Kivas 2 and 5) during the Canyon Creek phase. This differentiation is even more evident during the Point of Pines phase. During this final phase of occupation, the Great Kiva and plaza fell out of use. The compound wall remained, but increasing numbers of rooms were constructed outside of it, including W:10:51 to the west, Room Block C to the south, and Room Block A in the middle of the northern entrance to the pueblo. Finally, Kivas 2 and 5 were abandoned, but two new kivas (Kiva 4 and Kiva 6) were constructed (Figure 7.7).

These small kivas are interesting for several reasons. Both were relatively small (Kiva 4 =

10.78 m²; Kiva 6 = 12.95 m²) and roughly rectangular in shape. Both contained a bench, a hearth, and a ventilator shaft beneath the bench. Kiva 6 also contained ladder holes, and Kiva 4 had a sipapu and deflector. Both were built over earlier habitation rooms that were partially razed and leveled to allow construction of the kivas. In the case of Kiva 4, part of the earlier room wall was used to build the east wall of the kiva and part of the bench. Kiva 6 was built over the southeastern corner of Room 95, one of those occupied by the Kayenta migrants during the pueblo's first 50 years of occupation. Excavation in areas surrounding the new kivas does not, however, indicate their incorporation into or association with a specific room block during the Point of Pines phase, when both were constructed and used (Figure 7.4). Additionally, construction in three room blocks (Room Blocks A, B, and W:10:51) occurred at this time, but each of these lacked an associated kiva. In the case of Room Block B, earlier domestic rooms and Kiva 5 were razed, and new construction occurred over these older rooms, indicating a shift in the alliance formations and rights of the inhabitants in this area (Figure 7.8). Further, Room Block E continued to grow at this time, containing more rooms than in any previous phase.

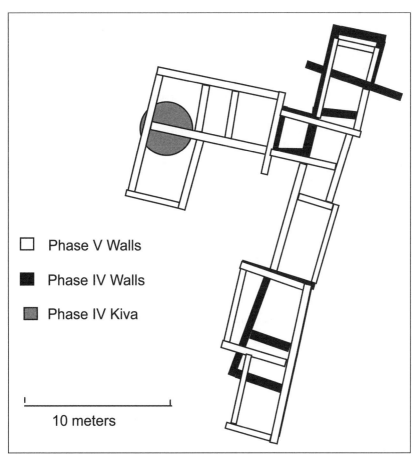

FIGURE 7.8. Point of Pines phase construction (Building Phase V) over earlier domestic and ritual structures in Room Block B.

The lack of a Great Kiva and plaza, along with the disassociation of the small kivas from densely occupied room blocks, indicates a shift in ritual organization of the pueblo. Interestingly, this occurred at the same time as the pueblo appeared to be at its greatest extent. Specifically, 107 of the 130 rooms excavated at the main pueblo and all of the W:10:51 masonry rooms had evidence of occupied floors at this time. Many of these rooms had multiple plaster floors in the same footprint, suggesting continued, stable occupation for a long enough period to require maintenance of the floors. The realignment of rooms in Room Block B does, however, suggest some shifting of small group alliances and renegotiation of rights to the architectural structures in this portion of the pueblo.

Although the reorganization of ritual at the pueblo appears to have allowed its inhabitants to negotiate the tensions between factionalism and village integration, and the community to grow during this 50-year period, it was ultimately unsuccessful. Point of Pines Pueblo, and the region as a whole, was abandoned at the end of the Point of Pines phase and not reoccupied until protohistoric Apache groups entered the area in the 1500s. The pueblo's final abandonment did not include the dramatic fires witnessed by the Kayenta enclave 100 years earlier, but the abandonment pattern indicates a number of different behaviors were followed. Specifically, 42 of the 108 floors in the main pueblo (38.9%) contained whole pots. Additionally, 116 whole pots were recovered on the floors from W:10:51 (Wendorf

1950). In contrast, many of the floors were swept clean and contained no artifacts in floor contact. There is no association, however, between where the rooms were located and whether whole vessels were left on the floor ($x^2 = 4.135$; $p = .388$). It is possible that the pueblo was abandoned in stages, and those that left earlier had time to return prior to final abandonment to recover material left behind. However, current data do not allow this possibility to be tested.

The long occupation of Point of Pines Pueblo makes it an excellent case study in which to examine the political dynamics of a large, aggregated community as exhibited in its architectural history. The presence of a Kayenta ethnic enclave at the site for the first 50 years of its occupation and its continued habitation for another 100 years after the destruction of the ethnic enclave adds to the complexity of community dynamics. The extensive excavation of the site and relative lack of disturbance prior to

work there have made it an ideal community in which to investigate the importance of the house as a source of identity for migrant groups, the extension of house identity to the formation of an ethnic enclave, and the interactions between ethnic groups. The creation of an architectural biography of the pueblo has allowed us to gain a nuanced understanding of the nature of interaction and community dynamics at this one site; however, Point of Pines Pueblo is but one example of these dynamics in middle-range societies. As demonstrated in Chapter 1, migration and migrant-host interactions in middle-range societies were, in fact, a worldwide phenomenon in prehistory. Similar interactions and political dynamics occurred elsewhere in the world. Placing the architectural biography of Point of Pines Pueblo within this broader view aids our understanding of both the commonality and diversity of interactions that occur during migration processes in middle-range societies.

Migration and Ethnicity
in Middle-Range Societies

The View from Point of Pines Pueblo and Beyond

Although the last several chapters have dealt extensively with a single case study (Point of Pines Pueblo), it is, in fact, but one example of a phenomenon that has occurred many times in prehistory in many locations throughout the world in middle-range societies. Migration, and the resulting host-migrant interactions, was a common occurrence as peoples related to and engaged with complex natural and social landscapes. Although common, it is a complex process. For us to understand it, we must move beyond linear modeling in which we expect similar outcomes for every migration. As the case studies in Chapter 1 clearly demonstrate, peoples in middle-range societies migrated over varying distances in groups of different sizes and organizational structures. When they arrived at their destinations, they encountered landscapes that had already been settled. The resulting host-migrant interactions ranged from complete assimilation of the newcomers to the formation of multiethnic communities which, in some cases, were dominated by the host group and in others by the migrants in terms of economics, ritual, and politics.

To understand why and how people migrate both in general and particular situations, we must change our conception of migration as a solitary event taken only as a last resort that severs ties with a place and a landscape, to an understanding that migration can occur at many scales, temporally, geographically and socially.

Further, rather than being rare or unusual, migration is viewed by many groups as a common undertaking in their history. It has been integral to the formation of concepts of their relationship with the landscape, and with other people, and is an essential aspect of who they are as a people, engaged in and part of the landscape (Basso 1996; Bernardini 2005; Ferguson et al. 2009; Fowles 2010; Naranjo 1995).

Not all migrations are identical, however, even for a single group. The process itself is highly variable in terms of distance traveled, length of time of both the movement and the stay at the new destination, and the social interactions that occur. Additionally, the nature of changes in the social structure of both the migrant and host populations can vary considerably depending on the initial conditions of demographics, population density, social and ritual structures, and mechanisms for gaining access to both material (land, water, wild resources, raw material) and nonmaterial (marriage partners, status, ceremonial participation) resources. The conditions encountered by the Northern Iroquois differed considerably from those encountered by the pastoralists of the Canaan Highlands or the Norse in the Outer Hebrides. Even within a single area, like the Mogollon Highlands, considerable variability occurred in host-migrant interaction due to differences in demographics, population density, and flexibility of the social structure of both the host and migrant groups

(Stone 2003; Stone and Lipe 2011). In the case of Point of Pines Pueblo, a relatively large group of Kayenta migrants entered an area that was densely populated by Mogollon peoples living in large, aggregated communities. These communities had political and ritual structures in place to balance the tensions between factional tendencies of kin affiliations with crosscutting integrating ties that held large villages together. Although the majority of the migrants' trade relations appeared to exist with groups from other areas (see Chapter 4), they did have contacts in the Point of Pines region prior to their arrival. Specifically, there is evidence at sites like Turkey Creek Pueblo of very small-scale migrations (individual or, at most, a family) between the Kayenta and Point of Pines regions prior to the major migration (Rodrigues 2008). These earlier migrants likely provided information to the large group that followed, as well as eased their way once they arrived in the Point of Pines region.

To understand the nature of host-migrant interaction in situations like Point of Pines Pueblo, where a large migrant group moves over long distances and enters an area with a high population density living in aggregated communities, we need to remember that the latter are highly fluid, heterogeneous mosaics full of individuals, families, and small groups with different personal goals and positions within the community power structure. Individuals, families, and small groups—be they members of the migrant or host group—must navigate these complex mosaics in terms of alliance formation and access to material and nonmaterial goods. In middle-range societies, community political, economic, ritual, and social structures are often dominated by kin relations and sodalities that crosscut kin groups to help balance the tensions between factionalism and integration. These kin relations and sodality memberships are the mechanisms through which access to material and nonmaterial resources are channeled and through which alliances are formed, negotiated, contested, and/or reified.

For migrants, their original kin and sodality ties are broken during the migration process. To reestablish these organizational structures in their new homes, concepts of kinship, affinity, and alliance are manipulated and extended in new ways. The house is a likely institution to which these ideas may be attached (Bernardini 2008; Gillespie 2000a, 2000b, 2000c; González-Ruibal 2005; Lévi-Strauss 1979, 1984; Waterson 1995), thus becoming the center of identity and affiliation. The house can be small and restricted to a single domestic structure or, when a sufficiently large group is present, extended to a large group to form an ethnic enclave. House societies and ethnic groups share characteristics of history, assumed rather than demonstrated relationships, and the extension of kinship concepts to larger groups. The formation of these larger groups of affiliation (the house and ethnic enclave) would be attractive to migrant groups because they would anchor them in a new community, in a place and a time. As a nexus of identity it provides them alliances with others and routes of access to material and nonmaterial resources. At the same time, however, it differentiates them from others in the community. Because of this distinction, the formation of ethnic enclaves also represents a challenge to the tenuous balance between factionalism and integration that always exists within large, aggregated communities in middle-range societies. As such, we must ask ourselves why the hosts would allow migrants to take these actions and effectively manipulate existing ritual, social, and political organizations and mechanisms for determining rights and access to resources that were in place prior to the migrants' arrival.

To answer this question we must remember that communities are fluid and dynamic affairs. Even in the absence of multiple ethnic groups, they are heterogeneous collectives that form complex mosaics in which groups of individuals, families, and small groups (factions) with differing personal goals, places in the power structure, and perceptions of the existing ritual, social, and political organization exist side by side (Alt 2006; Isbell 2000; O'Gorman 2010; Pauketat and Alt 2003; Stone 1999, 2008). Multiple interest groups are present and the status quo is constantly negotiated, challenged, contested, reified, and sometimes overturned. Hosts or, more likely, segments of the host communities may welcome a new group with a different source of identity (house) and encourage ethnic otherness in an attempt to gain political allies to challenge the status quo (McGuire and Saitta 1996). This appears to have happened at Point of Pines Pueblo. Specifically, prior to the formation of Point of Pines Pueblo, very small numbers of Kayenta migrants were present in the region at sites like W:10:56, a small masonry pueblo, and Turkey Creek Pueblo, a large (300 room) aggregated community. When a new and relatively large group of Kayenta migrants entered the Point of Pines region during the Tularosa phase, Mogollon inhabitants of villages like Turkey Creek Pueblo joined with them to form a new community in which a new axis of identity (ethnicity rooted in the house) was not only expressed but encouraged. The temporal overlap of Turkey Creek and Point of Pines Pueblos and evidence of construction of domestic and ritual structures associated with both the migrant and host populations on sterile soils indicate that segments of the Mogollon population challenged the status quo by constructing a new community. Not all members of the host population in the Point of Pines Region embraced this new situation, and at least one other aggregated community (Willow Creek Pueblo) was occupied at the same time as Point of Pines Pueblo. There is no evidence of a migrant population that actively signaled its ethnic identity at Willow Creek Pueblo, though it must be noted that archaeological investigation of the site has been extremely limited.

The integration of large groups of people in the absence of centralized decision making is, however, a tenuous affair, and alliances, like the communities in which they are grounded, are fluid and fragile in middle-range societies. "Otherness" that was embraced and encouraged at one time may become the locus of tension and even conflict at another. Additionally, there are thresholds to differentiation that can be accommodated. When these thresholds are approached and exceeded, the presence of an endogamous exclusionary organization, like ethnicity, which hinders multiple crosscutting ties and channels of alliance formation, may heighten fac-

tional tendencies, resulting in village fissioning or conflict. Again, this appeared to happen at Point of Pines Pueblo at the end of the Pinedale/Maverick Mountain phase, when the Kayenta room block and kiva were burned. If members of the migrant enclave remained at the pueblo after this time, they did so without expressing their ethnic otherness through architecture, burials, and material culture. In short, ethnicity—and the social and ritual differences it encompassed relative to the host population—ceased to be an axis of identity that was actively expressed in the region.

Because the house is so important in rooting migrants in their new home, providing a social structure in which they can live their everyday lives and ensure ceremonial continuity with their place of origin, domestic and ritual architecture is a particularly powerful medium in which these identities, alliances, and social structures are engaged (Byrd 1994; Carsten and Hugh-Jones 1995; Ferguson 1996; Gamble 2007; Johnson 2012; Silliman 2001, 2009; Tilley 1994; Wilson 2010). Further, people deliberately engage space and architecture to create history and social memory to justify their actions. We can see these political dynamics play out by constructing an architectural biography of communities in which these types of interactions occur. Specifically, space in general and architecture in particular is *not* a neutral background against which people live their everyday lives. Rather, space is imbued with social meaning tied to history and to current relationships of people to the landscape and to each other. Because architecture is both a daily, visible reminder of place and the past, and because it structures movement through space in the course of daily activities, it is a particularly powerful force in the creation, negotiation, and reification of history and the rights of groups. In other words, architecture is consciously created and manipulated as well as subconsciously experienced and interpreted (Creese 2012; Gamble 2007; Johnson 2012; Thomas 1996). Like alliances, however, architecture is not static. Remodeling of existing architectural structures and treatment of abandoned ones (whether unused, scavenged, remodeled in the same footprint, or razed and rebuilt on a new footprint) is part of this ongoing social dialogue. The continued existence of structures is a reminder of the past, and therefore a powerful tool in the creation and reification of social memory. Alternatively, the destruction of architectural structures and their replacement with new ones associated with new meanings is a very real tool in the rewriting of history and social memory. Removal of domestic and ritual structures of a segment of the society not only denies them the right to salvage material from their former homes, it removes evidence of their existence in the community. History, and the active construction of social memory that supports it, is a complex thing, however, and not all residents may perceive it in the same way. This is especially true when a new structure, such as the compound wall surrounding Point of Pines Pueblo, may serve as a daily reminder of past conflict, not only by its visual presence, but also by the way it impacts bodily movement and experience of the space it defines. Therefore, the creation of a community's architectural biography can tell us a great deal about the political dynamics of its inhabitants.

The architectural biography of Point of Pines Pueblo presented in this volume illustrates the usefulness of this approach for understanding the process of migration and host-migrant interactions. This biography allows an in-depth examination of the engagement of space and manipulation of bodily experience and movement to negotiate, contest, and renegotiate identity through the creation, destruction, and manipulation of history and social memory in one community. Any community, however, exists within a larger regional context, and a history of interaction that pulls in a larger area is a necessary part of the biography. As noted above and in Chapter 4, the inhabitants of the Point of Pines region did not live in isolation. Rather, they had extensive trade relations with other areas as evidenced by the presence of imported painted ceramics. During the early Pithouse period phases (Circle Prairie and Stove Canyon), the majority of imported ceramics originated to the south in the Mimbres area. Starting in the Nantack phase, however, trade shifted to the north. Specifically,

Cibola White wares begin to be imported from the Zuñi region, and Zuñi continued to be the source for most of the imported ceramics found in the Point of Pines region until its abandonment around AD 1400.

There is evidence of contact with the Kayenta region as well. Although no Kayenta ceramics were found in regional ceramic assemblages prior to the founding of Point of Pines Pueblo (see, for example, Lowell 1991; Stone 2002b), there is evidence of very small numbers of Kayenta migrants in the burial assemblages of two sites dated to the Tularosa phase (Rodrigues 2008). The assignment of these burials to Kayenta migrants was made based on the use of a flexed body position, which can be contrasted with the use of extended inhumations and cremations in the Point of Pines region. Using these criteria, Rodrigues (2008) identified two Kayenta burials at the small masonry site of W:10:56 and 20 Kayenta burials at Turkey Creek Pueblo. The burials include males and females of all ages, including children. Although this small number of migrants may have been welcome at these sites during the Tularosa phase, their ethnic otherness was not expressed outside the use of the flexed burial pattern.

This relationship changes with the establishment of Point of Pines Pueblo by Mogollon and Kayenta migrant groups. Both ethnic groups are evident from the founding of the pueblo with the establishment of domestic and ritual structures on sterile soils. The domestic structures in the Mogollon room block (Room Block E) consisted of masonry rooms and can be contrasted with the Kayenta structures, which included both masonry rooms (Room Block D) and pithouses that were used for a short time during Building Phase I (Tularosa phase). For both groups, ritual structures consisted of small kivas (Kivas 2 and 3). The small kivas and masonry rooms established at this time became the core houses, or axes, around which the two ethnic groups orbited for the first 50 years of the pueblo's occupation. Differences in the internal organization of space and external appearances—as well as the establishment of two separate room blocks at the pueblo during Building Phase I and the restriction of Kayenta and Maverick Mountain ceramics to the Kayenta room block, pithouses, and kiva—indicate the importance of ethnicity as an axis of identity from the beginning of the establishment of the Point of Pines community. As the community grew, however, and new room blocks and ritual structures were added, there is evidence of shifting alliances and conscious political actions. Four major episodes in which the architectural history of the pueblo was re-written and social memory was manipulated are evident.

The first of these is evident in Building Phase II during the late Tularosa phase. At this time new rooms were constructed by both the migrants and indigenous members of the community in their existing room blocks as well as in a newly established Mogollon room block (Room Block B) and associated small kiva (Kiva 5). Much of the new construction of domestic rooms in all three room blocks, as well as the formal plaza, were built over the temporary pit-houses used by Kayenta migrants during Building Phase I. This action symbolically indicated a break with the earliest occupation of the site and a more permanent presence of the migrants in the community as they moved into more sub-stantial and longer-lived masonry structures.

The beginning of Building Phase III (Pinedale/ Maverick Mountain phase) is characterized by additional construction of both domestic and communal space in several areas of the site. Re-modeling of existing domestic architecture also occurred at the beginning of Building Phase III. Specifically, the rooms in Room Block E were built on top of those of the previous two building phases with a new footprint, indicating a realign-ment of alliances and claims to rights. As the architectural history of the previous phase was removed from view in this part of the site, it re-mained intact elsewhere. These shifts in alliances and negotiations of rights might have been due to increasing tensions inherent in a community growing in size and social complexity. Village integration was accommodated with the remod-eling of the informal plaza of the previous phase into a formal, roofed structure (Great Kiva) large enough (at 220 m²) to house the entire village.

Building Phase III ended, however, with dra-matic changes in the pueblo's social, ritual, and political organization, as can be seen through changes in the engagement of space. Specifi-cally, the end of Building Phase III is signaled by the simultaneous burning of the entire migrant room block (Room Block D) and its associated small, D-shaped kiva (Kiva 3). The burned rooms contained numerous whole vessels and ground stone on the floor under the roof fall, as well as corn in storage facilities, indicating the residents had little or no warning and no opportunity to scavenge materials from the rooms afterward. Burned rooms and the lack of scavenging of whole artifacts and food stores is absent at the site outside of this incidence. During the next phase, the shift in the organization of the pueblo became even more evident, as ethnicity was eliminated as an axis of identity in the community.

Building Phase IV (Clear Creek phase) is characterized by considerable remodeling of both public and domestic space. In particular, the Great Kiva was enlarged and connected to an unroofed plaza by a continuous plaster floor. The enlargement of the Great Kiva occurred at the expense of the domestic spaces that surrounded it. Specifically, three rooms on the eastern side were leveled, and rooms on the other four sides of the Great Kiva decreased in size as their exte-rior walls were demolished and a new continu-ous wall was constructed, expanding the overall dimensions of the Great Kiva. Additionally, a compound wall was built around the pueblo, se-verely limiting access and influencing movement both into and out of the pueblo. Finally, new rooms were built on top of the burned structures in Room Block D. These new rooms included the remodeling of existing rooms by subdividing the spaces and/or sealing doors so that the internal space was similar to those found elsewhere at the pueblo, though slightly smaller. New rooms were also built in the area.

Finally, during Building Phase V (Point of Pines phase), the Great Kiva, plaza, and small kivas of earlier times were abandoned. In their place, two new small kivas were constructed in space that was remodeled from domestic rooms. Additionally, Room Block B was demolished, and new domestic structures were built over the rooms and kiva of the previous phase using new foundations in a different footprint. Despite the apparent changes in political and ritual organization which these architectural changes represent, and the loss of facilities for village wide integration, the community continued to grow. Point of Pines Pueblo was at its largest extent at this time and included both space inside the compound wall and a large number of newly constructed structures outside of it. The end of the Point of Pines phase, however, represents the last phase of indigenous occupation in the region, and both the pueblo and the region as a whole were abandoned at the end of this period, ca. AD 1400.

This architectural biography of Point of Pines Pueblo demonstrates a complex, dynamic community in which alliances were highly fluid. Social relationships and ritual and political structures were constructed, contested, and reconfigured through time. During the first 50 years of its occupation, a major axis of these dynamics was ethnicity. Despite the disappearance of the Kayenta enclave at the end of the Pinedale/

Maverick Mountain phase and attempts by the remaining Mogollon inhabitants to remove evidence of the enclave from the history and social memory of the pueblo, its continuing influence on the pueblo's social relationships are evident. This is particularly marked in the compound wall that constrained movement into and out of the pueblo, in the continued use of both small kivas and the Great Kiva, and in the frequent remodeling of domestic and ritual space. The events that occurred at Point of Pines Pueblo are indicative of a larger issue, however. Similar social actions occurred prehistorically, though with different results due to differing initial conditions, in many places around the world. Migration, the reconceptualization of identity that results from host-migrant interactions, and the manipulation of kinship, affinity, and affiliation were common events in middle-range societies. To understand these complex occurrences we must investigate how individuals, families, and small groups engaged with place and manipulated concepts of history and social memory through the active transformation of architecture.

APPENDIX

Assignment of Individual Architectural Structures to Building Phases

Structure Type	Location	Structure and Floor Numbers (X.X)
Building Phase I (Early Tularosa Phase)		
Communal Structures	Room Block E	Kiva 2
	W:10:51	P13
	Isolated / Room Block D	Kiva 3
Pithouses	W:10:50	1, 2, 3, 4, 5, 6, 7, 8, 9, 10, 11/12, 13, 14, 15, 16, 17, 18, 19, 20
	W:10:51	1, 2, 3, 4, 5, 6, 7, 8, 9, 10, 11, 12, 14, 15
Masonry Rooms	Room Block B	3.5
	Room Block D	89.1, 95.2
	Room Block E	9.1, 10.2, 46.4, 49.2, 94.3, 104.3
Building Phase II (Late Tularosa Phase)		
Communal Structures	Room Block E	Kiva 2, Plaza under Great Kiva I
	Isolated	Kiva 3
Masonry Rooms	Room Block B	2.3, 3.5, 4.2, 5.2, 6.2, 8.4, 9.2, 12.3
	Room Block D	52.1, 64/65.2, 68.1, 69.2, 89.1, 95.2
	Room Block E	8.2, 9.1, 10.2, 11.2, 15.1, 21.1, 23.1, 32.5, 32.6, 32.7, 33.3, 34.1, 46.4, 49.2, 58.2, 94.3, 101/102.2, 104.3
	Isolated room excavations	57.4, 60.1, 60.2
Building Phase III (Pinedale/Maverick Mountain Phase)		
Communal Structures	Room Block B	Kiva 5
	Room Block E	Kiva 2, Great Kiva I
	Isolated	Kiva 3
Masonry Rooms	Room Block B	1.4, 2.3, 3.5, 4.1, 5.2, 6.2, 8.4, 9.2, 11.2, 12.3
	Room Block C	107.2
	Room Block D	50.1, 51/61.2, 52.2, 62.2, 64/65.2, 66/67.2, 68.1, 69.2, 70.2, 71.1, 72.2, 73.1, 84.1, 86.2, 87.1, 89.1, 90 east.1, 90 west.1, 92.1, 92.2, 95.2, 96.2, 99.1, 110.1

Structure Type	Location	Structure and Floor Numbers (X.X)
	Room Block E	Three unnumbered rooms under Great Kiva II remodel, 8.2, 9.1, 10.2, 15.1, 16.1, 17.1, 19/30.1, 21.1, 22.1, 23.1, 24.1, 25.2, 26.1, 27.2, 31.2, 32.3, 32.4, 33.2, 34.1, 35.1, 39.1, 43.1, 44.1, 46.3, 58.1, 94.2, 101/102.2
	Isolated room excavations	57.4, 75.2, 75.3
Building Phase IV (Canyon Creek Phase)		
Communal Structures	Room Block B	Kiva 5
	Room Block E	Kiva 2, Great Kiva II/Plaza Complex
	W:10:50	Great Wall
Masonry Room	Room Block B	1.2, 1.3, 1.4, 3.4, 4.1, 5.1, 6.1
	Room Block C	111.1
	Room Block D	64.1, 65.1, 66.1, 67.1, 69.1, 70.1, 72 east.1, 72 west.1, 77.1, 78.1, 85.1, 86A.1, 86B.1, 87.1, 89.1, 95.1, 96.1, 98.1, 99.1
	Room Block E	2.1, 3.1, 9.1, 10.1, 12.1, 14.1, 15.1, 16.1, 17.1, 21.1, 23.1, 26.1, 30.1, 33.1, 34.1, 35.1, 46.2, 53.1, 55.1, 55.2, 56.1, 58.1, 94.1, 101/102.2, 104.2, 105.1
	Adjacent to Great Wall	74.1, 76.1, 80.1, 82.1, 83.1, 84.1, 91.2
Building Phase V (Point of Pines Phase)		
Communal Structures	Room Block C	Kiva 4
	Room Block D	Kiva 6
	W:10:51	Structure A
	W:10:50	Great Wall
Masonry Room	Room Block A	1.1, 1.2, 1.3, 2.1, 3.1, 4.1, 5.1, 6.1, 7.1, 8.1, 9.1, 10.1, 11.1, 11.2, 12.1, 12.2
	Room Block B	1.1, 2.1, 2.2, 3.1, 3.2, 3.3, 4.1, 5.1, 6.1, 7.1, 8.1, 8.2, 9.1, 10.1, 11.1, 12.1, 12.2
	Room Block C	1.1, 103.1, 107.1, 111.1
	Room Block D	64.1, 65.1, 66.1, 67.1, 70.1, 78.1, 85.1, 87.1, 95.1, 98.1
	Room Block E	1.1, 4.1, 5.1, 8.1, 9.1, 10.1, 11.1, 13.1, 15.1, 16.1, 17.1, 18.1, 20.1, 21.1, 23.1, 24.1, 25.1, 26.1, 27.1, 31.1, 32.1, 32.2, 33.1, 34.1, 35.1, 46.1, 48.1, 49.1, 53.1, 58.1, 94.1, 101.1, 102.1, 104.1
	Adjacent to Great Wall	28.1, 29.1, 36.1, 37.1, 38.1, 40.1, 54.1, 57.1, 57.2, 57.3, 59.1, 63.1, 75.1, 79.1, 88.1, 91.1, 97.1, 97.2, 97.3,
	Isolated room excavations	93.1, 93.2, 106.1, 108.1, 109.1, 109.2
	W:10:51	1.1, 2.1, 3.1, 4.1, 5.1, 6.1, 7.1, 8.1, 9.1, 10.1, 11.1, 15.1, 16.1, 17.1, 18.1, 19 east.1, 19 west.1, 20.1

Notes:

– Room designation is to the left of the decimal, floor designation to the right (e.g., Room 35.4 is Room 35, Floor 4).

– Rooms designated east or west are rooms from a later building phase that have been subdivided. Room designations with two numbers (101/102) are rooms from an earlier building phase, prior to subdivision. Pithouses with two numbers are superimposed structures.

– Rooms 45 and 60, both located adjacent to the Great Wall, contained insufficient data to date.

– No excavation occurred for Rooms 6, 7, 41, 42, 47, and 81.

References Cited

Adams, Jenny L.
1994   The Development of Prehistoric Grinding Technology in the Point of Pines Area, East-Central Arizona. Unpublished PhD dissertation, Department of Anthropology, University of Arizona, Tucson.

Adams, William Y., Alexander J. Lindsay Jr., and Christy G. Turner II
1961   *Survey and Excavations in Lower Glen Canyon, 1952–1958*. Bulletin No. 36. Museum of Northern Arizona, Flagstaff.

Adams, William Y., Dennis P. Van Gerven, and Richard S. Levy
1978   The Retreat from Migrationism. *Annual Review of Anthropology* 7:483–532.

Adler, Michael A.
1989   Ritual Facilities and Social Interaction in Non-ranked Societies. In *The Architecture of Social Integration in Prehistoric Pueblos*, edited by William D. Lipe and Michelle Hegmon, pp. 35–52. Occasional Paper No. 1, Crow Canyon Archaeological Center, Cortez, CO.
1993   Why Is a Kiva? New Interpretations of Prehistoric Social Integrative Architecture in the Northern Rio Grande of New Mexico. *Journal of Anthropological Research* 49: 319–346.

Adler, Michael A., Todd Van Pool, and Robert D. Leonard
1996   Ancestral Pueblo Population Aggregation and Abandonment in the North American Southwest. *Journal of World Prehistory* 10: 375–438.

Adler, Michael A., and Richard H. Wilshusen
1990   Large-Scale Integrative Facilities in Tribal Societies: Cross-Cultural and Southwestern US Examples. *World Archaeology* 22:133–146.

Alt, Susan M.
2006   The Power of Diversity: The Roles of Migration and Hybridity in Culture Change. In *Leadership and Polity in Mississippian Society*, edited by Brian M. Butler and Paul D. Welch, pp. 289–308. Occasional Paper No. 33. Center for Archaeological Investigations, Southern Illinois University, Carbondale.

Ambler, J. Richard
1985   *Navajo National Monument: An Archaeological Assessment*. Archaeological Series No. 1. Northern Arizona University, Flagstaff.
1994   The Shonto Junction Doghouse: A Weaver's Field House in the Klethla Valley. *Kiva* 59: 455–473.

Ambler, J. Richard, Alexander J. Lindsay Jr., and Mary Anne Stein
1964   *Survey and Excavations on Cummings Mesa, Arizona and Utah 1960–1961*. Bulletin No. 39. Museum of Northern Arizona, Flagstaff.

Ambler, J. Richard, and Alan P. Olson
1977   Salvage Archaeology in the Cow Springs Area. Technical Series No. 15. Museum of Northern Arizona, Flagstaff.

Anderson, Keith M.
1971   Excavations at Betatakin and Keet Seel. *Kiva* 37:1–29.
1980   *Highway Salvage on Arizona State Hwy 98: Kayenta Anasazi Sites between Kaibito and Klethla Valley*. Archaeological Series No. 140. Arizona State Museum, University of Arizona Press, Tucson.

Andrews, Peter P., Robert W. Layhe, Deborah Nichols, and Shirley Powell
1982   *Excavations on Black Mesa 1980: A Descriptive Report*. Research Paper 24. Center for Archaeological Investigations, Southern Illinois University, Carbondale.

Anthony, David W.
1990   Migration in Archaeology: The Baby and the Bathwater. *American Anthropologist* 92:895–914.

Archer, Margaret
2000   *Being Human: The Problem of Agency.* Cambridge University Press, Cambridge.
Asch, C. M.
1961   Post-Pueblo Occupation at the Willow Creek Ruin, Point of Pines. *The Kiva* 26(2): 31–42.
Bailey, Douglass W.
1990   The Living House: Signifying Continuity. In *The Social Archaeology of Houses,* ed. by R. Samson, pp. 19–48. Edinburgh University Press, Edinburgh.
Bannister, Bryant, and William J. Robinson
1971   *Tree-Ring Dates from Arizona U-W, Gila Salt River Areas.* Laboratory of Tree-Ring Research, University of Arizona Press, Tucson.
Barth, Fredrik
2007   Overview: Sixty Years in Anthropology. *Annual Review of Anthropology* 36:10–16.
Basso, Keith H.
1996   *Wisdom Sits in Places: Landscape and Language Among the Western Apache.* University of New Mexico Press, Albuquerque.
Beals, Ralph L., George W. Brainerd, and Watson Smith
1945   *Archaeological Studies in Northeast Arizona.* Publications in American Archaeology and Ethnology Vol. 44(1). University of California, Berkeley.
Beck, Robin A. Jr., Douglas J. Bolender, James A. Brown, and Timothy K. Earle
2007   Eventful Archaeology: The Place of Space in Structural Transformation. *Current Anthropology* 48:833–860.
Beekman, Christopher W., and Alexander F. Christensen
2003   Controlling for Doubt and Uncertainty Through Multiple Lines of Evidence: A New Look at Mesoamerican Nahua Migrations. *Journal of Archaeological Method and Theory* 10:111–164.
2011   Power, Agency and Identity: Migration and Aftermath in the Mezquital Area of North-Central Mexico. In *Rethinking Anthropological Perspectives on Migration,* edited by Graciela S. Cabana and Jeffery J. Clark, pp. 147–171. University Press of Florida, Gainesville.
Bennett, Kenneth A.
1967   The Indians of Point of Pines: A Comparative Study of Their Physical Characteristics. Unpublished PhD dissertation, Department of Anthropology, University of Arizona, Tucson.
1973   *The Indians of Point of Pines, Arizona: A Comparative Study of Their Physical Characteristics.* Anthropological Paper 23. University of Arizona Press, Tucson.
Bernardini, Wesley
2005   Reconsidering Spatial and Temporal Aspects of Prehistoric Cultural Identity: A Case Study from the American Southwest. *American Antiquity* 70:31–54.
2008   Identity as History: Hopi Clans and the Curation of Oral Tradition. *Journal of Anthropological Research* 64:483–509.
2011a North, South and Center: An Outline of Hopi Ethnogenesis. In *Religious Transformation in the Late Pre-Hispanic Pueblo World,* edited by Donna Glowacki and Scot Van Keuren, pp. 196–220. University of Arizona Press, Tucson.
2011b Migration in Fluid Social Landscapes. In *Rethinking Anthropological Perspectives on Migration,* edited by Graciela S. Cabana and Jeffery J. Clark, pp. 31–44. University Press of Florida, Gainesville.
Berry, Brian J. L., Kiel Douglas, and Elliot Euel (editors)
2002   *Adaptive Agents, Intelligence, and Emergent Human Organization: Capturing Complexity Through Agent-Based Modeling.* Supplement No. 3, Proceedings No. 99. National Academy of Sciences of the United States of America, Washington, DC.
Binford, Lewis R.
1962   Archaeology as Anthropology. *American Antiquity* 28:217–225.
1965   Archaeological Systematics and the Study of Cultural Process. *American Antiquity* 31:203–210.
1968   Some Comments on Historical Versus Processual Archaeology. *Southwestern Journal of Anthropology* 24:267–275.
1972   *An Archaeological Perspective.* Seminar Press, New York.
Blanton, Richard E.
1994   *Houses and Households: A Comparative Study.* Plenum Press, New York.
Blier, Suzanne P.
1987   *The Anatomy of Architecture.* Cambridge University Press, Cambridge.
Bliss, Wesley L.
1960   Impact of Pipeline Archaeology on Indian Prehistory. *Plateau* 33(1):10–13.

Bohrer, Vorsila L.
1973 Ethnobotany of Point of Pines Ruin, Arizona W:10:50. *Economic Botany* 27:423–437.

Bond, Mark, Toni Sudar-Murphy, and Fred P. Frampton
1977 *Highway Salvage Archaeology in the Vicinity of Chilchinbito, AZ: Excavation and Interpretation of Seven Kayenta Anasazi Sites in Navajo and Apache Counties, AZ*. CRM Division, Department of Anthropology and Sociology, New Mexico State University, Las Cruces.

Breternitz, David A.
1956 The Archaeology of Nantack Village, Point of Pines, Arizona. Unpublished MA thesis, Department of Anthropology, University of Arizona, Tucson.
1959 *Excavations at Nantack Village, Point of Pines, Arizona*. Anthropological Paper No. 1. University of Arizona Press, Tucson.

Breternitz, David A., James C. Gifford, and Alan P. Olson
1957 Point of Pines Phase Sequence and Utility Pottery Type Revisions. *American Antiquity* 22:412–416.

Bunzell, Ruth L.
1932 *Zuñi Ceremonialism*. Smithsonian Institution, Washington, DC. Reprint, University of New Mexico Press, Albuquerque, 1992.

Burmeister, Stefan
2000 Archaeology and Migration: Approaches to an Archaeological Proof of Migration. *Current Anthropology* 41:539–567.

Butler, Kim D.
2001 Defining Diaspora, Refining a Discourse. *Diaspora: A Journal of Transnational Studies* 10(2):189–219.

Byrd, Brian
1994 Public and Private, Domestic and Corporate: The Emergence of the Southwest Asian Village. *American Antiquity* 59:639–666.

Cabana, Graciela S.
2011 The Problematic Relationship Between Migration and Culture Change. In *Rethinking Anthropological Perspectives on Migration*, edited by Graciela S. Cabana and Jeffery J. Clark, pp. 16–28. University Press of Florida, Gainesville.

Cameron, Catherine M.
1995 Migration and the Movement of Southwestern Peoples. *Journal of Anthropological Archaeology* 14:104–124.
1996 Observations on the Pueblo House and Household. In *People Who Lived in Big Houses: Archaeological Perspectives on Large Domestic Structures*, edited by Gary Coupland and E. B. Banning, pp. 71–88. Monographs in World Archaeology No. 27. Prehistory Press, Madison, WI.
1999a *Hopi Dwellings: Architecture at Orayvi*. University of Arizona Press, Tucson.
1999b Room Size, Organization of Construction, and Archaeological Interpretation in the Puebloan Southwest. *Journal of Anthropological Archaeology* 18:201–239.

Cameron, Catherine M., and Andrew I. Duff
2008 History and Process in Village Formation: Context and Contrasts from the Northern Southwest. *American Antiquity* 73:29–58.

Carlson, Roy L.
1979 *White Mountain Red Ware: A Pottery Tradition of East-Central Arizona and Western New Mexico*. Anthropological Paper No. 19. University of Arizona Press, Tucson.

Carsten, Janet, and Stephen Hugh-Jones
1995 Introduction: About the House: Lévi-Strauss and Beyond. In *About the House: Lévi-Strauss and Beyond*, edited by Janet Carsten and Stephen Hugh-Jones, pp. 1–46. Cambridge University Press, Cambridge, UK.

Chapman, John
1997 The Impact of Modern Invasions and Migrations on Archaeological Explanation. In *Migrations and Invasions in Archaeological Explanation*, edited by John Chapman and Helena Hamerow, pp. 11–20. BAR International Series 664.

Chapman, John, and Helena Hamerow
1997 On the Move Again: Migrations and Invasions in Archaeological Explanation. In *Migrations and Invasions in Archaeological Explanation*, edited by John Chapman and Helena Hamerow, pp. 1–10. BAR International Series 664.

Chenoweth, John M.
2009 Social Identity, Material Culture and the Archaeology of Religion. *Journal of Social Archaeology* 9:319–340.

Childe, V. Gordon
1950 *Prehistoric Migrations in Europe*. Harvard University Press, Cambridge.

Christenson, Andrew L.
2003 Archaeological Survey in Tsegi Canyon, 1988–1995. In *Climbing the Rocks: Papers in Honor of Helen and Jay Crotty*, edited by Regge N. Wiseman, Thomas C. O'Lauflin,

and Cordelia T. Snow, pp. 69–82. Paper
No. 29. Archaeological Society of New Mexico, Albuquerque.

Christenson, Andrew L., and William J. Perry
1985 *Excavations on Black Mesa, 1983: A Descriptive Report.* Research Paper 46. Center for
Archaeological Investigation, Southern
Illinois University, Carbondale.

Ciolek-Torrello, Richard
1985 A Typology of Room Function at Grasshopper Pueblo, Arizona. *Journal of Field
Archaeology* 12:41–63.

Clark, J. Grahme D.
1952 *Prehistoric Europe: The Economic Basis.*
Methuen, London.

Clark, Jeffery J.
2001 *Tracking Prehistoric Migrations: Pueblo
Settlers among the Tonto Basin Hohokam.*
Anthropological Paper No. 65, University of
Arizona Press, Tucson.

Clark, Jeffery J., and Paul F. Reed
2011 Chacoan Immigration and Influence in the
Middle San Juan. *Kiva* 77:251–274.

Clifford, James
1994 Diasporas. *Cultural Anthropology* 9(3):302–
338.

Cobb, Charles R.
2005 Archaeology and the "Savage Slot": Dis-
placement and Emplacement in the Premod-
ern World. *American Anthropologist* 107:
563–574.

Cobb, Charles R., and Brian M. Butler
2006 Mississippian Migration and Emplacement
in the Lower Ohio Valley. In *Leadership
and Polity in Mississippian Society,* edited
by Brian M. Butler and Paul D. Welch,
pp. 328–347. Occasional Paper No. 33. Center
for Archaeological Investigations, Southern
Illinois University, Carbondale.

Cohen, Robin
1997 *Global Diasporas: An Introduction.* University of Washington, Seattle.

Colwell-Chanthaphonh, Chip, and T. J. Ferguson
2006 Memory Pieces and Footprints: Multivocality and the Meanings of Ancient Times and
Ancestral Places among the Zuñi and Hopi.
American Anthropologist 108:148–162.

Cook, Edwin A.
1961 A New Mogollon Structure. *Kiva* 26(3):24–32.

Cordell, Linda S.
1995 Tracing Migration Pathways from the Re-
ceiving End. *Journal of Anthropological
Archaeology* 14:203–211.

Cordell, Linda S., and Judith A. Habicht-Mauche
2012 *Potters and Communities of Practice: Glaze
Paint and Polychrome Pottery in the American Southwest, AD 1250–1700.* University of
Arizona Press, Tucson.

Cordell, Linda S., and Fred Plog
1979 Escaping the Confines of Normative
Thought: A Reevaluation of Puebloan Prehistory. *American Antiquity* 44:405–429.

Crawford, Gary W., and David G. Smith
1996 Migration in Prehistory: Princess Point and
the Northern Iroquoian Case. *American
Antiquity* 61:782–790.

Creel, Darrell, and Roger Anyon
2003 New Interpretations of Mimbres Public Architecture and Space: Implications for Culture Change. *American Antiquity* 68:67–92.

Creese, John L.
2012 The Domestication of Personhood: A View
from the Northern Iroquoian Long House.
Cambridge Archaeological Journal 22:365–
386.

Crown, Patricia
1991 Evaluating the Construction Sequence and
Population of Pot Creek Pueblo, Northern
New Mexico. *American Antiquity* 56:291–314.
1994 *Ceramics and Ideology: Salado Polychrome
Pottery.* University of New Mexico Press,
Albuquerque.

Cummings, Byron
1945 Some Unusual Kivas Near Navajo Mountain. *The Kiva* 10:30–35.

Dean, Jeffrey S.
1969 *Chronological Analysis of Tsegi Phase Sites in
Northeastern Arizona.* Papers of the Labora-
tory of Tree-Ring Research No. 3. University
of Arizona Press, Tucson.
1970 Aspects of Tsegi Phase Social Organization:
A Trial Reconstruction. In *Reconstructing
Prehistoric Pueblo Societies,* edited by William A. Longacre, pp. 140–174. University of
New Mexico Press, Albuquerque.
1990 Intensive Archaeological Survey of Long
House Valley, Northeastern Arizona. In *The
Archaeology of Regions: A Case for Full-
Coverage Survey,* edited by Suzanne K. Fish
and Stephen A. Kowalewski, pp. 173–88.
Smithsonian Institution Press, Washington, DC.
1996 Kayenta Anasazi Settlement Transforma-
tions in Northeastern Arizona, AD 1150
to 1350. In *The Prehistoric Pueblo World,
AD 1150–1350,* edited by Michael A. Adler,

pp. 29–47. University of Arizona Press, Tucson.

2000   Subsistence Stress and Food Storage at Kiet Siel, Northeastern Arizona. In *Environmental Change and Human Adaptation in the Ancient American Southwest*, edited by David E. Doyel and Jeffrey S. Dean. University of Utah Press, Salt Lake City.

2002   Late Pueblo II–Pueblo III in Kayenta-Branch Prehistory. In *Prehistoric Culture Change on the Colorado Plateau: Ten Thousand Years on Black Mesa*, edited by Shirley Powell and Francis Smiley, pp. 121–157. University of Arizona Press, Tucson.

2006   Subsistence Stress and Food Storage at Kiet Siel, Northeastern Arizona. In *Environmental Change and Human Adaptation in the Ancient American Southwest,* edited by David E. Doyel and Jeffrey S. Dean, pp. 160–179. University of Utah Press, Salt Lake City.

Dean, Jeffrey S., Robert C. Euler, George J. Gumerman, Fred Plog, Richard H. Hevly, and Thorn V. Karlstrom

1985   Human Behavior, Demography, and Paleoenvironment on the Colorado Plateaus. *American Antiquity* 50:537–554.

Dean, Jeffrey S., Alexander J. Lindsay Jr., and William J. Robinson

1978   Prehistoric Settlement in Long House Valley, Northeastern Arizona. In *Investigations of the Southwestern Research Group: An Experiment in Archaeological Cooperation: The Proceedings of the 1976 Conference*, edited by Robert C. Euler and George J. Gumerman, pp. 25–44. Museum of Northern Arizona, Flagstaff.

Di Peso, Charles C.

1950   Painted Stone Slabs of Point of Pines, Arizona. *American Antiquity* 16:57–65.

1958   *The Reeve Ruin of Southeastern Arizona*. Amerind Foundation, Dragoon, AZ.

Dongoske, Kurt E., Michael Yeatts, Roger Anyon, and T. J. Ferguson

1997   Archaeological Cultures and Cultural Affiliation: Hopi and Zuñi Perspectives in the American Southwest. *American Antiquity* 62:600–608.

Dozier, Edward P.

1954   *The Hopi-Tewa of Arizona*. Publications in American Archaeology and Ethnology 44(3):259–376. University of California Press, Berkeley.

1966   *Hano, a Tewa Indian Community in Arizona*. Holt, Rinehart and Winston, New York.

Duff, Andrew I.

1998   The Process of Migration in Late Prehistoric Southwest. In *Migration and Reorganization: The Pueblo IV Period in the American Southwest*, edited by K. A. Spielmann, pp. 31–52. Anthropological Research Papers No. 51. Arizona State University Press, Tempe.

Duff, Andrew I., and Richard H. Wilshusen

2000   Prehistoric Population Dynamics in the Northern San Juan Region, AD 950–1300. *Kiva* 66:167–190.

Duncan, James S.

1981   Introduction. In *Housing and Identity: Cross-Cultural Perspectives*, edited by James S. Duncan, pp. 1–5. Croom Helm, London.

Effland, Richard Wayne, Jr.

1979   A Study of Prehistoric Spatial Behavior: Long House Valley, Northeastern Arizona. Unpublished PhD dissertation, Department of Anthropology, Arizona State University, Tempe.

Ellis, Florence Hawley

1979   Laguna Pueblo. In *Handbook of North American Indians*, Vol. 9: *Southwest*, edited by Alfonso Ortiz, pp. 438–449. Smithsonian Institution Press, Washington, DC.

Esman, Milton

2009   *Diasporas in the Contemporary World*. Polity Press, Cambridge.

Ezzo, Joseph A.

1993   *Human Adaptation at Grasshopper Pueblo, Arizona*. Archaeological Series 4, International Monographs in Prehistory. Ann Arbor, MI.

Ezzo, Joseph A., and T. Douglas Price

2002   Migration, Regional Reorganization and Spatial Group Composition at Grasshopper Pueblo, Arizona. *Journal of Archaeological Science* 29:449–520.

Feld, Steven, and Keith H. Basso

1996   Introduction. In *Senses of Place*, edited by S. Feld and K. H. Basso, pp. 1–12. School of American Research, Santa Fe.

Ferg, Alan

1980   Forestdale Black-on-Red: A Type Description and Discussion. *Kiva* 46:69–98.

Ferguson, T. J.

1996   *Historic Zuñi Architecture and Society: An Archaeological Application of Space Syntax*. Anthropological Paper No. 60. University of Arizona Press, Tucson.

Ferguson, T. J., G. Lennis Berlin, and Leigh J. Kuwanwisiwma
2009 Trails of Tradition: Movement, Meaning and Place. In *Landscapes of Movement*, edited by James E. Snead, Clark Ericson, and Andrew Darling, pp. 20–41. University of Pennsylvania Museum of Archaeology and Anthropology, Philadelphia.

Ferguson, T. J., and E. Richard Hart
1985 *The Zuñi Atlas*. University of Oklahoma Press, Norman.

Ford, James A.
1938 A Chronological Method Applicable to the Southeast. *American Antiquity* 3:260–264.

Fowles, Severin
2010 The Southwest School of Landscape Archaeology. *Annual Review of Anthropology* 39: 453–468.

Gamble, Clive
2007 *Origins and Revolutions: Human Identity in Earliest Prehistory*. Cambridge University Press, Cambridge.

Geib, Phil R.
2011 *Foragers and Farmers of the Northern Kayenta Region: Excavations Along the Navajo Mountain Road*. University of Utah Press, Salt Lake City.

Geib, Phil R., J. Richard Ambler, and Martha M. Callahan
1985 *Archaeological Investigations Near Rainbow City, Navajo Mountain, Utah*. Archaeological Report No. 576. Northern Arizona University, Flagstaff.

Gerald, M. Virginia
1957 Two Great Kivas at Point of Pines. Unpublished MA thesis, Department of Anthropology, University of Arizona, Tucson.

Gerald, Rex E.
1975 Drought Correlated Changes in Two Prehistoric Pueblo Communities in Southeastern Arizona. Unpublished PhD dissertation, Department of Anthropology, University of Chicago.

Giddens, Anthony
1991 Structuration Theory: Past, Present, and Future. In *Giddens' Theory of Structuration: A Critical Appreciation*, edited by C. G. Bryant and D. Jary, pp. 201–221. Routledge, New York.

Gifford, Carol A., and Elizabeth A. Morris
1985 Digging for Credit: Early Archaeological Field Schools in the American Southwest. *American Antiquity* 50:395–411.

Gifford, James C.
1957 Archaeological Explorations in Caves of the Point of Pines Region. Unpublished MA thesis, Department of Anthropology, University of Arizona, Tucson.
1960 *Archaeological Explorations in Caves of the Point of Pines Region*. Anthropological Paper No. 36. University of Arizona Press, Tucson.

Gillespie, Susan D.
2000a Beyond Kinship: An Introduction. In *Beyond Kinship: Social and Material Reproduction in House Societies*, edited by Rosemary A. Joyce and Susan D. Gillespie, pp. 1–21. University of Pennsylvania Press, Philadelphia.
2000b Lévi-Strauss and *Maison* and *Société a Maisons*. In *Beyond Kinship: Social and Material Reproduction in House Societies*, edited by Rosemary A. Joyce and Susan D. Gillespie, pp. 22–51. University of Pennsylvania Press, Philadelphia.
2000c Rethinking Ancient Maya Social Organization: Replacing "Lineage" with "House." *American Anthropologist* 102:467–484.

Gilman, Patricia A., and Tammy Stone
2013 The Role of Ritual Variability in Social Negotiations: Great Kiva Homogeneity and Heterogeneity in the Mogollon Region of the North American Southwest. *American Antiquity* 78:607–623.

Gladwin, Harold S.
1957 *A History of the Ancient Southwest*. Bond Wheelwright, Portland, ME.

González-Ruibal, Alfredo
2005 House Societies vs. Kinship-based Societies: An Archaeological Case from Iron Age Europe. *Journal of Anthropological Archaeology* 25:144–173.

Green, Jesse
1979 *Zuñi: Selected Writings of Frank Hamilton Cushing*. University of Nebraska Press, Lincoln.

Gregory, David A., and David R. Wilcox
2007 *Zuni Origins*. University of Arizona Press, Tucson.

Guernsey, Samuel James
1931 *Explorations in Northeastern Arizona: Report on the Archaeological Fieldwork of 1920–1923*. Papers of the Peabody Museum of American Archaeology and Ethnology Vol. 12, No. 1. Harvard University, Cambridge, MA.

Gumerman, George J.

1970   *Black Mesa: Survey and Excavation in North-eastern Arizona 1968.* Occasional Paper. Center for Archaeological Investigations, Southern Illinois University, Carbondale.

1988   *The Anasazi in a Changing Environment.* Cambridge University Press, Cambridge.

Gumerman, George J., and Jeffrey S. Dean

1989   Prehistoric Cooperation and Competition in the Western Anasazi Area. In *Dynamics of Southwestern Prehistory*, edited by Linda S. Cordell and George J. Gumerman, pp. 99–148. Smithsonian Institution Press, Washington, DC.

Gumerman, George J., and Murray Gell-Mann (editors)

1994   *Understanding Complexity in the Prehistoric Southwest.* Addison-Wesley, Reading, MA.

Gumerman, George J., Deborah Westfall, and Carol S. Weed

1972   *Archaeological Investigations on Black Mesa: 1969–1970 Seasons.* Occasional Paper. Center for Archaeological Investigations, Southern Illinois University, Carbondale.

Haas, Jonathan

1986   The Evolution of the Kayenta Anasazi. In *Tse Yaa Kin: Houses Beneath the Rock*, edited by David Grant Noble, pp. 14–23. School of American Research, Santa Fe.

1989   The Evolution of the Kayenta Regional System. In *The Sociopolitical Structure of Prehistoric Southwestern Societies*, edited by Steadman Upham, Kent G. Lightfoot, and Roberta A. Jewett, pp. 491–508. Westview Press, Boulder.

Haas, Jonathan, and Winifred Creamer

1993   *Stress and Warfare among the Kayenta Anasazi of the Thirteenth Century AD.* Fieldiana: Anthropology n.s. 21, Field Museum of Natural History, Chicago.

Hard, Robert J., and William L. Merrill

1992   Mobile Agriculturalists and the Emergence of Sedentism: Perspectives from Northern Mexico. *American Anthropologist* 94:601–620.

Härke, Heinrich

1998   Archaeologist and Migrations: A Problem of Attitude? *Current Anthropology* 39:12–46.

Harrill, Bruce Gilbert

1982   Prehistoric Agricultural Adaptation and Settlement in Long House Valley, Northeastern Arizona. Unpublished PhD dissertation, Department of Anthropology, University of Arizona, Tucson.

Haury, Emil W.

1936   *The Mogollon Culture of Southwestern New Mexico.* Medallion Papers 20. Gila Pueblo, Globe, AZ.

1940   *Excavations in the Forestdale Valley, East-Central Arizona.* University of Arizona Bulletin 12, Social Science Bulletin 11. University of Arizona Press, Tucson.

1945   Archeological Survey on the San Carlos Indian Reservation. *Kiva* 11(1):5–9.

1957   An Alluvial Site on the San Carlos Indian Reservation, Arizona. *American Antiquity* 23:2–27.

1958   Evidence at Point of Pines for a Prehistoric Migration from Northern Arizona. In *Migrations in New World Culture History*, edited by Raymond H. Thompson, pp. 1–8. University of Arizona Bulletin 29, Social Science Bulletin 27. University of Arizona Press, Tucson.

1976   Salado: The View from Point of Pines. *Kiva* 42:81–84.

1989   *Point of Pines, Arizona: A History of the University of Arizona Archaeological Field School.* Anthropological Paper No. 50. University of Arizona Press, Tucson.

Heindl, Leo A.

1955   "Clean Fill" at Point of Pines, Arizona. *Kiva* 20(4):1–8.

Hendon, Julia A.

2000   Having and Holding: Storage, Memory, Knowledge and Social Relations. *American Anthropologist* 102:42–53.

Herr, Sarah

2001   *Beyond Chaco: Great Kiva Communities on the Mogollon Rim Frontier.* Anthropological Paper No. 66. University of Arizona Press, Tucson.

Herr, Sarah, and Jeffery J. Clark

1997   Patterns in the Pathways: Early Historic Migrations in the Rio Grande Pueblos. *Kiva* 62:365–390.

Hillier, Bill, and Julienne Hanson

1984   *The Social Logic of Space.* Cambridge University Press, Cambridge.

Hobler, Philip

1964   The Late Survival of Pithouse Architecture in the Kayenta Anasazi Area. Unpublished MA thesis, Department of Anthropology, University of Arizona, Tucson.

1974   The Late Survival of Pithouse Architecture in the Kayenta Anasazi Area. *Southwestern Lore* 40(2):1–44.

Hornborg, Alf
2005 Ethnogenesis, Regional Interaction and Ecology in Prehistoric Amazonia. *Current Anthropology* 46:589–620.

Howell, Todd L., and Keith W. Kintigh
1996 Archaeological Identification of Kin Groups Using Mortuary and Biological Data: An Example from the American Southwest. *American Antiquity* 61:537–554.

Isbell, William H.
2000 What We Should Be Studying: The "Imagined Community" and the "Natural Community." In *The Archaeology of Communities: A New World Perspective*, edited by Marcello A. Canuto and Jason Yaeger, pp. 243–266. Routledge, London.

Jennings, Jesse
1998 *Glen Canyon: An Archaeological Summary.* University of Utah Press, Salt Lake City.

Johnson, Alfred E.
1961 A Ball Court at Point of Pines, Arizona. *American Antiquity* 26:563–567.
1965 The Development of Western Pueblo Culture. Unpublished PhD dissertation, Department of Anthropology, University of Arizona, Tucson.

Johnson, Matthew H.
2012 Phenomenological Approaches in Landscape Archaeology. *Annual Review of Anthropology* 41:269–284.

Jones, Andrew
2007 *Memory and Material Culture.* Cambridge University Press, Cambridge.

Joyce, Rosemary A.
2000 Heirlooms and Houses: Materiality and Social Memory. In *Beyond Kinship: Social and Material Reproduction in House Societies*, edited by Susan Gillespie, pp. 189–212. University of Pennsylvania Press, Philadelphia.

Khan, Aisha
2007 Good to Think? Creolization, Optimism and Agency. *Current Anthropology* 48:653–673.

Kent, Susan
1990 Activity Areas and Architecture: An Interdisciplinary View of the Relationship Between the Use of Space and Domestic Built Environments. In *Domestic Architecture and the Use of Space: An Interdisciplinary Cross-Cultural Study*, edited by Susan Kent, pp. 1–8. Cambridge University Press, Cambridge.

Kidder, Alfred Vincent, and Samuel James Guernsey
1919 *Archaeological Explorations in Northeastern Arizona.* Bureau of American Ethnology Bulletin 65. US Government Printing Office, Washington, DC.

Klesert, Anthony L.
1978 *Excavation on Black Mesa 1977: A Preliminary Report.* Research Paper 1. Center for Archaeological Investigations, Southern Illinois University, Carbondale.
1982 Standing Fall House: An Early Pueblo Storage and Redistribution Center in Northeastern Arizona. *Kiva* 48:39–61.

Klesert, Anthony L., and Shirley Powell
1979 *Excavations on Black Mesa 1978: A Descriptive Report.* Research Paper 8. Center for Archaeological Investigations, Southern Illinois University, Carbondale.

Kohler, Timothy A., and George J. Gumerman (editors)
2000 *Dynamics in Human and Primate Societies: Agent-Based Modeling of Social and Spatial Processes.* Oxford University Press, Oxford.

Kohler, Timothy A., and Sander E. van der Leeuw (editors)
2007 *The Model-Based Archaeology of Socionatural Systems.* School for Advanced Research, Santa Fe.

Kohler, Timothy A., and Carla R. Van West
1997 The Calculus of Self-Interest in the Development of Cooperation: Sociopolitical Development and Risk among the Northern Anasazi. *In Evolving Complexity and Environmental Risk in the Prehistoric Southwest*, edited by J. Tainter and B. B. Tainter, pp 169–196. Addison-Wesley, Reading, MA.

Kok, Jan
2010 The Family Factor in Migration Decisions. In *Migration History in World History: Multidisciplinary Approaches*, edited by Jan Lucassen and Patrick Manning, pp. 215–250. Brill, Leiden, Netherlands.

Kolb, Michael, and James E. Sneed
1997 It's a Small World After All: Comparative Analysis of Community Organization in Archaeology. *American Antiquity* 62: 609–628.

Kuijt, Ian
2000 People and Space in Early Agricultural Villages: Exploring Daily Lives, Community Size, and Architecture in the Late Pre-Pottery Neolithic. *Journal of Anthropological Archaeology* 19:75–102.

Kus, Susan, and Victor Raharijaona
1990 Domestic Space and the Tenacity of Tradi-

tion Among Some Betsileo of Madagascar. In *Domestic Architecture and Use of Space: An Interdisciplinary Cross-Cultural Study*, edited by Susan Kent, pp. 21–33. Cambridge University Press, Cambridge.

2000 House to Palace, Village to State: Scaling up Architecture and Ideology. *American Anthropologist* 102:98–113.

Lawrence, Denise L., and Setha M. Low

1990 The Built Environment and Spatial Form. *Annual Review of Anthropology* 19:453–505.

Lekson, Stephen H.

1988 The Idea of the Kiva in Anasazi Archaeology. *Kiva* 53:213–234.

1989 Kivas? In *The Architecture of Social Integration in Prehistoric Pueblos*, edited by William D. Lipe and Michelle Hegmon, pp. 161–168. Occasional Paper No. 1. Crow Canyon Archaeological Center, Cortez, CO.

Lekson, Stephen H., and Catherine M. Cameron

1995 The Abandonment of Chaco Canyon, the Mesa Verde Migrations and the Reorganization of the Pueblo World. *Journal of Anthropological Archaeology* 14:184–202.

Lévi-Straus, Claude

1979 *The Way of the Mask*. Translated by Sylvia Modelski. University of Washington Press, Seattle.

1984 *Anthropology and Myth, Lectures 1951–1982*. Translated by Roy Willis. Basil Blackwell, New York.

Levy, Jerrold E.

1992 *Orayvi Revisited: Social Stratification in an "Egalitarian" Society*. School of American Research Press, Santa Fe, NM.

Levy, Thomas E., Russell B. Adams, and Rula Shafia

1999 The Jabal Hamrat Fidan Project: Excavations at the Wadi Fidan 40 Cemetery, Jordan (1997). *Levant* 31:293–308.

Levy, Thomas E., and Agustin F. C. Holl

2002 Migrations, Ethnogenesis, and Settlement Dynamics: Israelites in Iron Age Canaan and Shuwa-Arabs in the Chad Basin. *Journal of Anthropological Archaeology* 21:83–118.

Lightfoot, Ricky R.

1993 Abandonment and Processes in Prehistoric Pueblos. In *Abandonment of Settlements and Regions*, edited by C. M. Cameron and S. A. Tomka, pp. 165–177. Cambridge University Press, Cambridge.

Lilley, Ian

2007 Diaspora and Identity in Archaeology: Moving Beyond the Black Atlantic. In *A Companion to Social Archaeology*, edited by Lynn Meskell and Robert W. Preucel, pp. 287–312. Blackwell, Malden, MA.

Lindsay, Alexander J., Jr.

1969 The Tsegi Phase of the Kayenta Cultural Tradition in Northeastern Arizona. Unpublished PhD dissertation, Department of Anthropology, University of Arizona, Tucson.

1987 Explaining an Anasazi Migration to East-central Arizona. *American Archaeology* 6(3): 190–198.

Lindsay, Alexander J., Jr., Richard Ambler, Mary Anne Stein, and Philip M. Hobler

1968 *Survey and Excavations North and East of Navajo Mountain, Utah, 1959–1962*. Bulletin No. 45. Museum of Northern Arizona, Flagstaff.

Linford, Laurance D.

1982 *Kayenta Anasazi Archaeology: Central Black Mesa, Northeastern Arizona: The Piñon Project*. Navajo Nation Papers in Anthropology No. 10. Navajo National CRM, Window Rock, AZ.

Lister, Robert H.

1959 *The Coombs Site*. Anthropological Papers No. 41. University of Utah Press, Salt Lake City.

Lister, Robert H., J. Richard Ambler, and Florence C. Lister

1960 *The Coombs Site: Part 2*. Anthropological Papers No. 41. University of Utah Press, Salt Lake City.

Lister, Robert H., and Florence C. Lister

1961 *The Coombs Site: Part 3: Summary and Conclusions*. Anthropological Papers No. 41. University of Utah Press, Salt Lake City.

Locock, Martin

1994 Meaningful Architecture. In *Meaningful Architecture: Social Interpretations of Buildings*, edited by M. Locock, pp. 1–13. Ashgate, Brookfield, VT.

Long, Paul V.

1966 *Archaeological Excavations in Lower Glen Canyon, Utah, 1959–1960*. Bulletin No. 42. Museum of Northern Arizona, Flagstaff.

Lowell, Julie C.

1986 The Structure and Function of the Prehistoric Household in the Pueblo Southwest: A Case Study from Turkey Creek Pueblo. Unpublished PhD dissertation, Department of Anthropology, University of Arizona, Tucson.

1988   The Social Use of Space at Turkey Creek
        Pueblo: An Architectural Analysis. *Kiva*
        53:85–100.
1991   *Prehistoric Households at Turkey Creek
        Pueblo, Arizona.* Anthropological Paper
        No. 54. University of Arizona Press,
        Tucson.
1999   The Fires of Grasshopper: Enlightening
        Transformations in Subsistence Practices
        Through Fire-Feature Analysis. *Journal of
        Anthropological Archaeology* 18:441–470.
2007   Women and Men in Warfare and Migration:
        Implications of Gender Imbalance in the
        Grasshopper Region of Arizona. *American
        Antiquity* 72:95–123.

Lyons, Patrick D.
2003   *Ancestral Hopi Migrations.* Anthropological
        Paper No. 68. University of Arizona Press,
        Tucson.
2013   "By their fruits ye shall know them": The
        Pottery of Kinishba Revisited. In *Kinishba
        Lost and Found: Mid-Century Excavations
        and Contemporary Perspectives*, edited by
        John R. Welch, pp. 145–208. Archaeological
        Series 206. Arizona State Museum, Univer-
        sity of Arizona, Tucson.

Lyons, Patrick D., and Jeffery J. Clark
2012   A Community of Practice in Diaspora: The
        Rise and Demise of Roosevelt Red Ware.
        In *Potters and Communities of Practice:
        Glaze Paint and Polychrome Pottery in the
        American Southwest, AD 1250–1700*, edited
        by Linda S. Cordell and Judith A. Habicht-
        Mauche, pp. 19–33. University of Arizona
        Press, Tucson.

Lyons, Patrick D., J. Brett Hill, and Jeffery J. Clark
2008   Demography, Agricultural Potential, and
        Identity Among Ancient Immigrants. In *The
        Social Construction of Communities: Agency,
        Structure, and Identity in the Prehispanic
        Southwest*, edited by Mark D. Varien and
        James M. Potter, pp. 191–213. Altamira, Lan-
        ham, MD.

Lyons, Patrick D., and Alexander J. Lindsay Jr.
2006   Perforated Plates and the Salado Phenome-
        non. *Kiva* 72:7–56.

Marshall, Joan, and Natalie Foster
2002   "Between Belonging": Habitus and the Mi-
        gration Experience. *The Canadian Geogra-
        pher* 46:63–83.

Martin, Paul S., John B. Rinaldo, and Eloise R.
Barter
1957   *Late Mogollon Communities: Four Sites of
        the Tularosa Phase, Western New Mexico.*
        Fieldiana: Anthropology 49(1). Chicago
        Natural History Museum.

Mavroudi, Elizabeth
2007   Diaspora as Process: (De)Constructing
        Boundaries. *Geography Compass* 1(3):
        467–479.

McGuire, Randal H., and Dean J. Saitta
1996   Although They Have Petty Captains, They
        Obey Them Badly: The Dialectics of Prehis-
        panic Western Pueblo Social Organization.
        American Antiquity 61:197–216.

McGuire, Thomas
1986   *Politics and Ethnicity on the Rio Yaqui:
        Potam Revisited.* University of Arizona
        Press, Tucson.

McKern, William C.
1939   The Midwestern Taxonomic Method as an
        Aid to Archaeological Culture Study. *Ameri-
        can Antiquity* 4:301–313.

Merbs, Charles F.
1967   Cremated Human Remains from Point of
        Pines, Arizona: A New Approach. *American
        Antiquity* 32:498–506.

Meskell, Lynn
2002   The Intersections of Identity and Politics in
        Archaeology. *Annual Review of Anthropol-
        ogy* 31:279–301.

Mills, Barbara
1998   Migration and Pueblo IV Community
        Reorganization in the Silver Creek Area,
        East-Central Arizona. In *Migration and
        Reorganization: The Pueblo IV Period in the
        American Southwest*, edited by K. A. Spiel-
        mann, pp. 65–80. Anthropological Research
        Papers No. 51. Arizona State University
        Press, Tempe.
2005   Curricular Matters: The Impact of Field
        Schools on Southwest Archaeology. In
        *Southwest Archaeology in the Twentieth Cen-
        tury*, edited by Linda S. Cordell and Don D.
        Fowler, pp. 60–80. University of Utah Press,
        Salt Lake City.
2011   Themes and Models for Understanding
        Migration in the Southwest. In *Movement,
        Connectivity, and Landscape Change in the
        Ancient Southwest*, edited by Margaret C.
        Nelson and Colleen Strawhacker, pp. 345–
        362. University Press of Colorado, Boulder.

Montgomery, Barbara K.
1993   Ceramic Analysis as a Tool for Discovery
        Processes of Pueblo Abandonment. In
        Abandonment of Settlements and Regions,

REFERENCES CITED

edited by C. M. Cameron and S. A. Tomka, pp. 157–164. Cambridge University Press, Cambridge.

Montgomery, Barbara K., and J. Jefferson Reid
1990 An Instance of Rapid Ceramic Change in the American Southwest. *American Antiquity* 55:88–97.

Moore, Henrietta L.
1986 *Space, Text and Gender: An Anthropological Study of the Marakwet of Kenya.* Cambridge University Press, Cambridge.

Morris, Elizabeth A.
1957 Stratigraphic Evidence for a Cultural Continuum at Point of Pines Ruin. Unpublished MA thesis, Department of Anthropology, University of Arizona, Tucson.

Morss, Noel
1931 *Notes on the Archaeology of the Kaibito and Rainbow Plateaus in Arizona.* Papers of the Peabody Museum of American Archaeology and Ethnology Vol. 12(2). Harvard University, Cambridge, MA.

Nanoglou, Stratos
2011 Building Biographies and Households: Aspects of Community Life in Neolithic Northern Greece. *Journal of Social Archaeology* 8(1):139–160.

Naranjo, Tessie
1995 Thoughts on Migration by Santa Clara Pueblo. *Journal of Anthropological Archaeology* 14:247–250.
2008 Life as Movement: A Tewa View of Community and Identity. In *The Social Construction of Communities: Agency, Structure and Identity in the Prehispanic Southwest*, edited by Mark D. Varien and James M. Potter, pp. 251–262. Altamira, Lanham, MD.

Neely, James A.
1974 The Prehistoric Lunt and Stove Canyon Sites, Point of Pines, Arizona. Unpublished PhD dissertation, Department of Anthropology, University of Arizona, Tucson.

Neely, James A., and Alan P. Olson
1977 *Archaeological Reconnaissance of Monument Valley in Northeastern Arizona.* Anthropological Research Report No. 3. Museum of Northern Arizona, Flagstaff.

Nelson, Ben A., and Roger Anyon
1996 Fallow Valleys: Asynchronous Occupations in Southwestern New Mexico. *Kiva* 61:275–294.

Nelson, Margaret
1999 *Mimbres During the Twelfth Century: Abandonment, Continuity and Reorganization.* University of Arizona Press, Tucson.

Nelson, Margaret C., and Michelle Hegmon
2001 Abandonment Is Not As It Seems: An Approach to the Relationship Between Site and Regional Abandonment. *American Antiquity* 66:213–236.

Neuzil, Anna A.
2008 *In the Aftermath of Migration: Renegotiating Ancient Identity in Southeastern Arizona.* Anthropological Paper No. 73. University of Arizona Press, Tucson.

Nichols, Deborah, and F. E. Smiley
1984 *Excavations on Black Mesa.* Research Report 39. Center for Archaeological Investigations, Southern Illinois University, Carbondale.

Nielsen, Axel E.
1995 Architectural Performance and the Reproduction of Social Power. In *Expanding Archaeology*, edited by J. M. Skibo, W. H. Walker, and A. E. Nielsen, pp. 47–66. University of Utah Press, Salt Lake City.

O'Gorman, Jodie
2010 Exploring the Longhouse and Community in Tribal Society. *American Antiquity* 75:571–598.

Olson, Alan P.
1959 An Evaluation of the Phase Concept in Southwestern Archaeology as Applied to the Eleventh and Twelfth Century Occupations at Point of Pines, East-Central Arizona. Unpublished PhD dissertation, Department of Anthropology, University of Arizona, Tucson.
1960 The Dry Prong Site, East Central Arizona. *American Antiquity* 26:185–204.

Ortiz, Alfonso
1969 *The Tewa World: Space, Time, Being, and Becoming in a Pueblo Society.* University of Chicago Press.

Ortman, Scott G., and Catherine M. Cameron
2011 A Framework for Controlled Comparisons of Ancient Southwestern Movement. In *Movement, Connectivity, and Landscape Change in the Ancient Southwest*, edited by Margaret C. Nelson and Colleen Strawhacker, pp. 233–252. University Press of Colorado, Boulder.

Owen, Bruce D.
2005 Distant Colonies and Explosive Collapse: The Two Stages of the Tiwanaku Diaspora in the Osmore Drainage. *Latin American Antiquity* 16:45–80.

Parker, Marion L.
1967 Dendrochronology of Point of Pines. Unpublished MA thesis, Department of Anthropology, University of Arizona, Tucson.
Parker Pearson, Mike, Niall Sharples, and Jacqui
Mulville
1996 Brochs and Iron Age Society: A Reappraisal.
Antiquity 70:57–67.
Pauketat, Timothy R.
2000 The Tragedy of the Commoners. In *Agency
in Archaeology*, edited by Marcia-Anne
Dobres and John E. Robb, pp. 113–129. Rout-
ledge, London.
2001a Practice and History in Archaeology: An
Emerging Paradigm. *Anthropological
Theory* 1:73–98.
2001b *The Archaeology of Traditions: Agency and
History Before and After Columbus.* Univer-
sity Press of Florida, Gainesville.
2008 The Grounds for Agency in Southwest
Archaeology. In *The Social Construction of
Communities: Agency, Structure and Identity
in the Prehispanic Southwest*, edited by Mark
D. Varien and James M. Potter, pp. 233–250.
Altamira, Lanham, MD.
Pauketat, Timothy R., and Susan M. Alt
2003 Mounds, Memory, and Contested Mississip-
pian History. In *Archaeologies of Memory*,
edited by Ruth M. Van Dyke and Susan E.
Alcock, pp. 151–179. Blackwell, Malden, MA.
Powell, Shirley
1984 *Excavations on Black Mesa, 1971–1976: A De-
scriptive Report.* Research Paper 48. Center
for Archaeological Investigation, Southern
Illinois University, Carbondale.
Powell, Shirley, Robert W. Layhe, and Anthony L.
Klesert
1980 *Excavations on Black Mesa, 1979: A Descrip-
tive Report.* Research Paper 18. Center for
Archaeological Investigations, Southern
Illinois University, Carbondale.
Powell, Shirley, and Francis E. Smiley (editors)
2002 *Prehistoric Culture Change on the Colorado
Plateau: Ten Thousand Years on Black Mesa.*
University of Arizona Press, Tucson.
Preucel, Robert, Jr.
1990 *Seasonal Circulation and Dual Residence in
the Pueblo Southwest.* Garland Press, New
York.
Price, T. Douglas, Clark M. Johnson, Joseph A.
Ezzo, Jonathan Ericson, and James H. Burton
1994 Residential Mobility in the Prehistoric
Southwest United States: A Preliminary

Study Using Strontium Isotope Analysis.
Journal of Archaeological Science 21:315–330.
Rapoport, Amos
1990 Systems of Activities and Systems of Settings. In *Domestic Architecture and the Use
of Space: An Interdisciplinary Cross-Cultural
Study*, by Susan Kent, pp. 9–20. Cambridge
University Press, Cambridge.
Reid, J. Jefferson
1989 A Grasshopper Perspective on the Mogollon
of the Arizona Mountains. In *Dynamics of
Southwestern Prehistory*, edited by Linda S.
Cordell and George J. Gumerman, pp. 65–
98. Smithsonian Institution Press, Washington, DC.
1997 Return to Migration, Population Movement, and Ethic Identity in the American
Southwest. In *Vanishing River: Landscape
and Lives of the Lower Verde Valley*, edited
by S. M. Whittlesey, R. Ciolek-Torrello, and
J. H. Altshul, pp. 629–638. SRI Press, Tucson.
2013 Encounters with Kinishba: A Grasshopper
Perspective. In *Kinishba Lost and Found:
Mid-Century Excavations and Contemporary Perspectives*, edited by John R. Welch,
pp. 289–294. Archaeological Series 206. Arizona State Museum, University of Arizona,
Tucson.
Reid, J. Jefferson, and Stephanie M. Whittlesey
1982 Households at Grasshopper Pueblo. *American Behavioral Scientist* 25:687–704.
1999 *Grasshopper Pueblo: A Story of Archaeology
and Ancient Life.* University of Arizona
Press, Tucson.
2010 *Prehistory, Personality, and Place: Emil W.
Haury and the Mogollon Controversy.* University of Arizona Press, Tucson.
Reynolds, H. T.
1984 *Analysis of Nominal Data.* 2nd ed. Sage University Paper 7. Sage Publications, Newbury
Park, CA.
Reynolds, W.
1981 The Ethnoarchaeology of Puebloan Architecture. Unpublished PhD dissertation,
Department of Anthropology, Arizona State
University, Tempe.
Riggs, Charles R.
2001 *The Architecture of Grasshopper Pueblo.*
University of Utah Press, Salt Lake City.
2013 A Grasshopper Architectural Perspective
on Kinishba. In *Kinishba Lost and Found:
Mid-Century Excavations and Contemporary Perspectives*, edited by John R. Welch,

pp. 123–145. Archaeological Series 206. Arizona State Museum, University of Arizona, Tucson.

Rinaldo, John B.

1959 *Foote Canyon Pueblo, Eastern Arizona.* Fieldiana: Anthropology 49(2). Chicago Natural History Museum.

1964 Notes on the Origins of Historic Zuñi Culture. *Kiva* 29:86–98.

Rinaldo, John B., and Elaine A. Bluhm

1956 *Late Mogollon Pottery Types of the Reserve Area.* Fieldiana: Anthropology 36(7):149–187. Chicago Natural History Museum.

Robb, John E.

1998 The Archaeology of Symbols. *Annual Review of Anthropology* 27:329–346.

Robinson, William J.

1958 A New Type of Ceremonial Pottery Killing at Point of Pines. *Kiva* 23(3):12–14.

1959 Burial Customs at the Point of Pines Ruin. Unpublished MA thesis, Department of Anthropology, University of Arizona, Tucson.

Robinson, William J., and Roderick Sprague

1965 Disposal of the Dead at Point of Pines, Arizona. *American Antiquity* 30:442–453.

Rodman, Margaret

1992 Empowering Place: Multilocality and Multivocality. *American Anthropologist* 94:640–656.

Rodrigues, Teresa

2008 Social Change and Skeletal Trauma in the Point of Pines Region (~AD 400–1450) of the American Southwest. Unpublished PhD Dissertation, Department of Anthropology, Arizona State University, Tempe.

Rothenbuhler, Eric W.

1998 *Ritual Communication: From Everyday Conversation to Mediated Ceremony.* Sage, Thousand Oaks, CA.

Rothschild, Nan, and Susan Dublin

1994 Deep Trash: A Tale of Two Middens. In *Exploring Social, Political and Economic Organization in the Zuni Region*, edited by T. L. Howell and T. Stone, pp. 91–100. Anthropological Research Paper No. 46. Arizona State University, Tempe.

Rothschild, Nan, Barbara Mills, T. J. Ferguson, and Susan Dublin

1993 Abandonment at Zuñi Farming Villages. In *Abandonment of Settlements and Regions*, edited by C. M. Cameron and S. A. Tomka, pp. 123–137. Cambridge University, Cambridge.

Rouse, Irving B.

1958 The Inference of Migrations from Anthropological Evidence. In *Migrations in New World Culture History*, edited by Raymond H. Thompson, pp. 63–68. Social Science Bulletin 27. University of Arizona Press, Tucson.

1986 *Migrations in Prehistory: Inferring Population Movement from Cultural Remains.* Yale University, New Haven.

Saunders, Tom

1990 The Feudal Construction of Space: Power and Domination in the Nucleate Village. In *The Social Archaeology of Houses*, edited by Ross Samson, pp. 181–196. Edinburgh University Press, Edinburgh.

Schiffer, Michael B.

1975 *Behavioral Archaeology.* Academic Press, New York.

1987 *Formation Processes of the Archaeological Record.* University of New Mexico Press, Albuquerque.

Schroedl, Alan R.

1989 *Kayenta Anasazi Archaeology and Navajo Ethnohistory on the Northwestern Shonto Plateau: The N-16 Project.* P-III Associates, Salt Lake City.

Scott, Barbara

1994 The Viking Move West: Houses and Continuity in the Northern Isles. In *Meaningful Architecture: Social Interpretations of Buildings*, edited by M. Locock, pp. 132–146. Ashgate, Brookfield, VT.

Service, Elman R.

1985 *A Century of Controversy: Ethnological Issues from 1860 to 1960.* Academic Press, Orlando, FL.

Shafer, Harry

1995 Architecture and Symbolism in Transitional Pueblo Development in the Mimbres Valley, SW New Mexico. *Journal of Field Archaeology* 22:23–47.

Sharples, Niall, and Mike Parker Pearson

1999 Norse Settlement in the Outer Hebrides. *Norwegian Archaeological Review* 32:41–62.

Sheffer, Gabriel

2003 *Diaspora Politics at Home and Abroad.* Cambridge University Press, Cambridge.

Shortman, Edward M., and Patricia A. Urban

1998 Culture Contact, Structure, and Process. In *Studies in Culture Contact: Interaction, Culture Change and Archaeology*, edited by James G. Cusick, pp. 102–125. Occasional

Paper No. 25. Center for Archaeological Investigations, Southern Illinois University, Carbondale.

Silliman, Stephen

2001   Agency, Practical Politics and the Archaeology of Culture Contact. *Journal of Social Archaeology* 1:190–209.

2009   Change and Continuity, Practice and Memory: Native American Persistence in Colonial New England. *American Antiquity* 74:211–230.

Smiley, F. E., Deborah L. Nichols, and Peter P. Andrews

1983   *Excavations on Black Mesa, 1981: A Descriptive Report*. Research Paper 36. Center for Archaeological Investigations, Southern Illinois University, Carbondale.

Smiley, Terah L.

1949   Tree-Ring Dates from Point of Pines. *Tree-Ring Bulletin* 15(3):20–21.

1952   *Four Late Prehistoric Kivas at Point of Pines, Arizona*. University of Arizona Bulletin 23(3), Social Science Bulletin 21. University of Arizona Press, Tucson.

Smith, Adam T.

2003   *The Political Landscape*. University of California Press, Berkley.

Snow, Dean R.

1995   Migration in Prehistory: The Northern Iroquoian Case. *American Antiquity* 60:59–79.

1996   More on Migration in Prehistory: Accommodating New Evidence in the Northern Iroquoian Case. *American Antiquity* 61: 791–796.

Stanislawski, Michael B.

1979   Hopi-Tewa. In *Handbook of North American Indians*, Vol. 9: *Southwest*, edited by Alfonso Ortiz, pp. 587–702. Smithsonian Institution Press, Washington, DC.

Stark, Miriam T., Mark D. Elson, and Jeffery J. Clark

1998   Social Boundaries and Technical Choices in Tonto Basin Prehistory. In T*he Archaeology of Social Boundaries*, edited by Miriam T. Stark, pp. 208–231. Smithsonian Institution Press, Washington, DC.

Stein, Gil J.

2002   From Passive Periphery to Active Agents: Emerging Perspectives in the Archaeology of Interregional Interaction. *American Anthropologist* 104:903–916.

Stein, Mary Ann

1984   Pottery Pueblo: A Tsegi Phase Village on Paiute Mesa, Utah. Unpublished PhD dissertation, Department of Anthropology, Southern Methodist University, Dallas.

Stein, Walter F.

1962   Mammals from Archaeological Sites, Point of Pines, Arizona. Unpublished MA thesis, Department of Anthropology, University of Arizona, Tucson.

1963   Mammal Remains from Archaeological Sites in the Point of Pines Region, Arizona. *American Antiquity* 29:213–220.

Stevenson, Marc G.

1982   Toward an Understanding of Site Abandonment Behavior: Evidence from Historic Mining Camps in the Southwest Yukon. *Journal of Anthropological Archaeology* 1:237–265.

Stock, Femke

2010   Home and Memory. In *Diasporas: Concepts, Interactions, Identities*, edited by Kim Knott and Seán McLouflin, pp. 24–28. Zed Books, London, UK.

Stone, Tammy

1992   The Process of Aggregation in the American Southwest: A Case Study from Zuñi, New Mexico. Unpublished PhD dissertation, Department of Anthropology, Arizona State University, Tempe.

1999   The Chaos of Collapse. *Antiquity* 73:110–118.

2000   Prehistoric Community Integration in the Point of Pines Region of Arizona. *Journal of Field Archaeology* 27:187–208.

2002a   Kiva Diversity in the Point of Pines Region of Arizona. *Kiva* 67:385–411.

2002b   Settlement Patterns in the Point of Pines Region of Arizona. Manuscript on file in the Arizona State Museum Archives, University of Arizona, Tucson.

2003   Social Identity and Ethnic Interaction in the Western Pueblos of the American Southwest. *Journal of Archaeological Method and Theory* 10:31–67.

2005a   Factional Formation and Community Dynamics in Middle-Range Societies. In *Nonlinear Modeling for Archaeology and Anthropology: Continuing the Revolution*, edited by W. Baden and C. Beekman, pp. 79–93. Ashgate Press, London.

2005b   Late Period Pithouses in the Point of Pines Region of Arizona. *Kiva* 70:273–292.

2006   Politics and Architecture at a Southwestern Pueblo: The Architecture of W:10:50 (ASM) in the Point of Pines Region of Arizona. Unpublished report on file in the Archives

of the Arizona State Museum, University of
Arizona, Tucson.

2008 Social Innovation and Transformation
During the Process of Aggregation. In
*Cultural Transformation and Archaeology:
Issues and Case Studies*, edited by Michael
O'Brien and Todd Van Pool, pp. 168–163.
Society for American Archaeology, Washington, DC.

2009 Room Function and Room Suites in Late
Mogollon Pueblo Sites. *Kiva* 75:63–86.

2013 Kayenta Ritual Structures from AD 1100–
1300. *Kiva* 78:177–206.

2014 House Variability in the Kayenta Region.
Paper presented at the 2014 Southwest Symposium, Las Vegas, NV.

Stone, Tammy, and Todd L. Howell

1994 Contemporary Theory in the Study of Sociopolitical Organization. In *Exploring Social,
Political and Economic Organization in the
Zuni Region*, edited by Todd L. Howell and
Tammy Stone, pp. 103–110. Anthropological
Research Paper No. 46. Arizona State University, Tempe.

Stone, Tammy, and William D. Lipe

2011 Standing Out vs. Blending in: Pueblo Migrations and Ethnic Marking. In *Changing
Histories, Landscapes, and Perspectives: The
20th Anniversary Southwest Symposium*,
edited by Margaret Nelson, pp. 277–298.
University Press of Colorado, Boulder.

Swarthout, Jeanne K., Sara Stebbins, Pat Stein,
Bruce G. Harrill, and Peter Pilles

1986 *The Kayenta Anasazi: Archaeological Investigations along the Black Mesa Railroad
Corridor*. Research Paper 30, No. 2. Museum
of Northern Arizona, Flagstaff.

Thomas, Julian

1996 *Time, Culture and Identity*. Routledge,
London.

Thompson, Raymond H.

2000 A Sequence of Inter-bedded Cultural and
Natural Deposits at Point of Pines, Arizona.
Kiva 65:319–340.

Thurston, Tina

2009 Unity and Diversity in the European Iron
Age: Out of the Mists, Some Clarity? *Journal
of Archaeological Research* 17:347–423.

Tilley, Christopher

1994 *A Phenomenology of Landscape: Places,
Paths, and Monuments*. Berg, Oxford.

Titiev, Mishca

1944 *Old Oraibi: A Study of the Hopi Indians of
Third Mesa*. Papers of the Peabody Museum
of American Archaeology and Ethnology
Vol. 22, No. 1. Harvard University, Cambridge.

Tomka, Marybeth Sarah Ford

1988 The Social Implications of the Great Kiva
at the WS Ranch Site, Alma, New Mexico.
Unpublished MA thesis, Department of
Anthropology, University of Texas, Austin.

Tomka, Steve A., and Mark G. Stevenson

1993 Understanding Abandonment Processes:
Summary and Remaining Concerns. In
Abandonment of Settlements and Regions,
edited by C. M. Cameron and S. A. Tomka,
pp. 191–195. Cambridge University Press,
Cambridge.

Triadan, Daniela

2013 Compositional Analysis of Some Fourteenth
Century Ceramics from Kinishba Pueblo:
Implications for Pottery Production and
Migration. In *Kinishba Lost and Found:
Mid-Century Excavations and Contemporary Perspectives*, edited by John R. Walsh,
pp. 209–242. Archaeological Series 206. Arizona State Museum, University of Arizona
Press, Tucson.

Trigger, Bruce G.

1989 *A History of Archaeological Thought*. Cambridge University Press, Cambridge.

Van Dyke, Ruth M.

2004 Memory, Meaning, and Masonry: The Late
Bonito Chacoan Landscape. *American
Antiquity* 69:413–431.

Van Dyke, Ruth M., and Susan E. Alcock

2003a Archaeologies of Memory: An Introduction.
In *Archaeologies of Memory*, edited by R. M.
Van Dyke and S. E. Alcock, pp. 1–13. Blackwell, Malden, MA.

2003b Memory and Construction of Chacoan Society. In *Archaeologies of Memory*, edited by
R. M. Van Dyke and S. E. Alcock, pp. 180–
200. Blackwell, Malden, MA.

Varien, Mark D.

1999 *Sedentism and Mobility in a Social Landscape*. University of Arizona Press, Tucson.

Varien, Mark D., and Barbara Mills

1997 Accumulations Research: Problems and
Prospects for Estimating Site Occupation
Span. *Journal of Archaeological Method and
Theory* 4:141–191.

Walker, William

2002 Stratigraphy and Practical Reason. *American Anthropologist* 104:159–177.

Walsh, Michael R.

1997   Material Evidence for Social Boundaries on the Pajarito Plateau, New Mexico. *Kiva* 65:197–214.

Ward, Albert E.

1975   *Inscription House: Two Research Reports.* Technical Series No. 16. Museum of Northern Arizona, Flagstaff.

Ware, John A.

2002   Descent Group and Sodality: Alternative Pueblo Social Histories. In *Traditions, Transitions, and Technologies: Themes in Southwestern Archaeology*, edited by Sarah H. Schlanger, pp. 94–112. University Press of Colorado, Boulder, CO.

Wasley, William W.

1952   The Late Pueblo Occupation at Point of Pines, East-Central Arizona. Unpublished MA thesis, Department of Anthropology, University of Arizona, Tucson.

Waterson, Roxana

1995   Houses and Hierarchies in Island Southeast Asia. In *About the House: Lévi-Strauss and Beyond*, edited by Janet Carsten and Stephen Hugh-Jones, pp. 47–68. Cambridge University Press, Cambridge, UK.

2000   House, Place, and Memory in Tana Toraja (Indonesia). In *Beyond Kinship: Social and Material Reproduction in House Societies*, edited by Rosemary A. Joyce and Susan D. Gillespie, pp. 177–188. University of Pennsylvania Press, Philadelphia.

Welch, John R., and T. J. Ferguson

2013   Apache, Hopi and Zuni Perspectives on Kinishba History and Stewardship. In *Kinishba Lost and Found: Mid-Century Excavations and Contemporary Perspectives*, edited by John R. Welch, pp. 261–287. Archaeological Series 206. Arizona State Museum, University of Arizona Press, Tucson.

Wells, Peter S.

1998   Identity and Material Culture in the Later Prehistory of Central Europe. *Journal of Archaeological Research* 6:239–298.

Wendorf, Fred

1950   *A Report on the Excavations of a Small Ruin Near Point of Pines, East Central Arizona.* University of Arizona Bulletin 21(3), Social Science Bulletin 19. University of Arizona Press, Tucson.

Wheat, Joe Ben

1952   Prehistoric Water Resources of the Point of Pines Area. *American Antiquity* 17:185–194.

1954   *Crooked Ridge Village (Arizona W:10:15).* University of Arizona Bulletin 25(3), Social Science Bulletin 24. University of Arizona Press, Tucson.

Whiteley, Peter M.

1988a   *Deliberate Acts: Changing Hopi Culture through the Oraibi Split.* University of Arizona Press, Tucson.

1988b   *Bacavi: Journey to Reed Springs.* Northland Press, Flagstaff.

2002   Archaeology and Oral Tradition: The Scientific Importance of Dialogue. *American Antiquity* 67:405–416.

Whittlesey, Stephanie

1992   *Archaeological Investigations at Lee Canyon: Kayenta Anasazi Farmsteads in the Upper Basin, Coconino County, AZ.* Statistical Research, Tucson.

Whittlesey, Stephanie, and J. Jefferson Reid

2012   Behavioral Archaeology: Assessing the Impact of Michael Brian Schiffer. Paper presented at the 77th Annual Meeting of the Society for American Archaeology, Memphis, TN.

Wilk, Richard R.

1990   The Built Environment and Consumer Decisions. In *Domestic Architecture and the Use of Space: An Interdisciplinary Cross-Cultural Study*, edited by Susan Kent, pp. 32–42. Cambridge University Press, Cambridge.

Willey, Gordon R., Charles C. Di Peso, William A. Ritchie, Irving Rouse, John H. Rowe, and Donald W. Lathrap

1955   An Archaeological Classification of Culture Contact Situations. *Memoirs of the Society for American Archaeology* 11:1–30.

Willey, Gordon R., and Philip Phillips

1958   *Method and Theory in American Archaeology.* University of Chicago Press.

Wilshusen, Richard H.

1989   Architecture as Artifact, Part II: A Comment on Gilman. *American Antiquity* 54:826–933.

Wilshusen, Richard H., and Scott G. Ortman

1999   Rethinking the Pueblo I Period in the San Juan Drainage: Aggregation, Migration and Cultural Diversity. *Kiva* 64:369–400.

Wilson, Gregory D.

2010   Community, Identity, and Social Memory at Moundville. *American Antiquity* 75:3–18.

Woodbury, Richard B.

1961   *Prehistoric Agriculture at Point of Pines,*

Arizona. Memoirs of the Society for American Archaeology 17.

Woodson, M. Kyle

1999   Migrations in Late Anasazi Prehistory: The Evidence from the Goat Hill Site. *Kiva* 65: 63–84.

Yaeger, Jason, and Marcello A. Canuto

2000   Introducing an Archaeology of Communities. In *The Archaeology of Communities: A New World Perspective*, edited by Marcello A. Canuto and Jason Yaeger, pp. 1–15. Routledge, London.

Zedeño, Maria N.

1994   *Sourcing Prehistoric Ceramics at Chodistaas Pueblo, Arizona: The Circulation of People and Pots in the Grasshopper Region.* Anthropological Paper No. 58. University of Arizona Press, Tucson.

2002   Artifact Design, Composition, and Context: Updating the Analysis of Ceramic Circulation at Point of Pines, Arizona. In *Ceramic Production and Circulation in the Greater Southwest*, edited by D. M. Glowacki and H. Neff, pp. 74–84. The Cotsen Institute of Archaeology, University of California, Los Angeles.

Zedeño, Maria N., and Daniela Triadan

2000   Ceramic Evidence for Community Reorganization and Change in East Central Arizona. *Kiva* 65:215–234.

Index

Numbers in *italics* refer to figures and tables.

burning: and kiva abandonment at Point of Pines Pueblo, 90; and room abandonment patterns at Point of Pines Pueblo, 69, *86*; of room blocks and kivas at Point of Pines Pueblo at end of Pinedale/Maverick Mountain phase, 63, 101, 103
Butler, Kim D., 13, 14

Cameron, Catherine M., 58, 71
Canaan Highlands (Middle East), and case study of migration, 9, 99
Canyon Creek phase: and archaeological research in Point of Pines region, 46–47; and building phases at Point of Pines Pueblo, 64–66, 103, *106*; remnants of ethnic differentiation at Point of Pines Pueblo during, 96–98; strengthening of community ties at Point of Pines Pueblo during, 91–96
Carsten, Janet, 28
case studies: architectural analysis of Point of Pines Pueblo as, 1–2, 10–12, 32–34, 99–104; and diversity of migration in middle-range societies, 8–12
ceramics: abandonment and density of sherds in room fill, 68–69, *70*; and building phases at Point of Pines Pueblo, 63–64, 66; and communication between Kayenta diaspora at Point of Pines Pueblo and homeland, 16–18; and evidence for ethnic differentiation at Point of Pines Pueblo, 89–90; and relative dating methods at Point of Pines Pueblo, 52–53; and Tularosa phase at Point of Pines Pueblo, 61
Chichinbito site, *37*
Childe, V. Gordon, 4
Choodistas site, 20
chronology, and use of relative dating methods at Point of Pines Pueblo, 52–56. *See also* building phases; dendrochronological dates
Cienega Creek, 40, *41*, 42
Cienega Creek site, *47*
Ciolek-Torrello, Richard, 50
Circle Prairie Phase, and archaeological research in Point of Pines region, 43
clans, and Hopi oral history, 38
Clark, Jeffery J., 18, 19
climate. *See* drought; subsistence stress
Clover Creek, 40
Cohen, Robin, 13
Colorado River, 35
communication: between ethnic enclaves in diasporas, 15, 18–20; Kayenta diaspora and maintenance of connections with homeland, 16–18
community: and abandonment in understanding of dynamics, 49–50; and elimination of ethnicity as axis of identity at Point of Pines Pueblo, 89–91; and historical context of structures, 7–8; increase in scale of in middle-range societies, 28–29; limits to subgroup factionalism versus integration in aggre-

gated, 88–89; negotiation of power relationships in aggregated, 88; and remnants of ethnic differentiation during Canyon Creek and Point of Pines phases at Point of Pines Pueblo, 96–98; strengthening of ties at Point of Pines Pueblo during Canyon Creek phase, 91–96; viewing interactions of through architecture, 30–32. *See also* host-migrant interactions
compound walls: and construction methods, 64, *65*, 66; Mogollon community and construction of at Point of Pines Pueblo, 91, *92*, 93–94, 103; and Point of Pines building phase at Point of Pines Pueblo, *106*
conflict: and burning of room blocks and kivas at Point of Pines Pueblo at end of Pindale/Maverick Mountain phase, 101; evidence for along ethnic lines at Point of Pines Pueblo, 89; ritual as potential source of, 84, 87
construction: of houses at Point of Pines Pueblo, 74–75; methods of at Point of Pines Pueblo, 56–58. *See also* architecture; building phases
Coombs site, *37*
Cordell, Linda S., 5
Corduroy Black-on-White (ceramics), 19
coursed masonry, *57*, 64, 75
Cow Springs site, *36*, *37*
Creese, John L., 74
Crooked Ridge Village, 43, *47*
Crown, Patricia, 19–20, 21
cultural resource management (CRM) projects, in Kayenta region, 36
culture, concepts of and social scale of migration, 24
culture history, and models of migration, 3–5
Cummings Mesa, *36*, *37*

Davis site (Arizona), 16–21
Dean, Jeffrey S., 38, 39, 45
decision-making process, in architectural design, 32
dendrochronological dates, for Point of Pines Pueblo, 52, 63
diaspora, and Kayenta migrations to Mogollon Highlands, 13–21
Di Peso, Charles C., 47
domestic space, and host-migrant interactions at Point of Pines Pueblo, 73–76. *See also* room(s); room blocks
droughts, in Kayenta region during Transition phase, 39
Dry Prong site, 44–45, *47*

Eagle Creek, 40
ethnicity: and communication between enclaves, 18–20; diasporas and distinct communities of, 15; elimination of as axis of identity at Point of Pines Pueblo, 89–91; and evidence for conflict at Point of Pines Pueblo, 89; implications of Point of Pines

Pueblo as case study of migration in middle-range societies, 1–2, 10–12, 32–34, 99–104; as integral to understanding of migration, 1; and internal organization of domestic space at Point of Pines Pueblo, 75–76; and political dynamics at Point of Pines Pueblo, 84; public indicators of in domestic architecture at Point of Pines Pueblo, 76; public indicators of in ritual architecture at Point of Pines Pueblo, 76–84; remnants of differentiation by at Point of Pines Pueblo during Canyon Creek and Point of Pines phases, 96–98; role of ethnic identity in host-migrant interactions, 25–30; and strengthening of community ties at Point of Pines Pueblo during Canyon Creek phase, 91–96. *See also* identity; Kayenta region

ethnography, and theoretical debates on migration, 2–3

evolutionary models, of migration, 2, 3

excavation methods, at Point of Pines Pueblo, 50–52

Ezzo, Joseph A., 20

field notes, and excavation methods, 52

floors, and construction of Point of Pines Pueblo, 58

Foote Canyon Pueblo, 83

Forestdale Black-on-Red (ceramics), 19

Forestdale Valley, 42

foundation stones, and construction of Point of Pines Pueblo, 56

Geib, Phil R., 38

gender, and imbalance of migrant population at Grasshopper Pueblo, 20

Gerald, M. Virginia, 48, 60

Gillespie, Susan D., 32

Gladwin, Harold S., 4, 42

Goat Hill site (Arizona), 16–21

Grasshopper Plateau (Arizona), 10, 20

Grasshopper Pueblo: and Great Kiva, 83–84, 94; migrants in burial assemblage at, 10; and Roosevelt Red Wares, 20

Great Kiva: elaboration and remodeling of during Canyon Creek phase at Point of Pines Pueblo, 64, 66, 71, 91, 94–95, 103, *106*; and Pinedale/Maverick Mountain phase at Point of Pines Pueblo, *105–6*; and public indicators of ethnicity of Kayenta migrants at Point of Pines Pueblo, 79, 82–84, 88

Haas, Jonathan, 38, 40

Hano Pueblo (Tewa), 30

Hasting, Russell, 42

Haury, Emil W., 11, 33, 41, 42, 50

Hawikuh (Zuñi village), 43

Higgins Flat Pueblo, 83, 84

historical context: of community structure, 7–8; and

social scale of migration, 24–25. *See also* social memory

historically-based models, of migration, 2, 3

Holl, Agustin F. C., 9

homeostasis, and push-pull models of migration, 6

Hopi: and oral history on migrations, 13, 21, 24, 27, 38, 40; and participation of Tewa residents in rituals on First Mesa, 30; and use of pithouses on Third Mesa, 56

host-migrant interactions: architectural analysis of Point of Pines Pueblo as case study of, 1–2, 10–12, 32–34, 99–104; and domestic space at Point of Pines Pueblo, 73–76; and Kayenta abandonment patterns after first fifty years of occupation at Point of Pines Pueblo, 84–87; and political dynamics during first fifty years of occupation at Point of Pines Pueblo, 84; and public indicators of ethnicity in domestic and ritual architecture at Point of Pines Pueblo, 76–84; role of ethnic identity in, 25–30. *See also* community; ethnicity; Kayenta region; migration

house(s), construction of at Point of Pines Pueblo, 74–75

house compounds, in Outer Hebrides of Scotland, 9

house societies, 27–28, 100; core house of the lineage, 27, 34, 71, 73, 76, 102

Hugh-Jones, Stephen, 28

Human Area Relation Files (HARF), 78

identity: elimination of ethnicity as axis of at Point of Pines Pueblo, 89–91; Great Kiva as signal of Mogollon at Point of Pines Pueblo, 91; as integral to understanding of migration, 1; models of based in concepts of agency and active engagement of material culture, 7–8; role of ethnic in host-migrant interactions, 25–30. *See also* ethnicity

ideology: emphasis on in models of migration, 2, 3; return to homeland in diasporas, 15

Inscription House site, 37

interest groups, and alliances in aggregated communities, 29

internal organization, of domestic space at Point of Pines Pueblo, 75–76

Iroquois, migration of Northern in New York and Ontario, 10, 99

katchina dances, 30

Kayenta Black-on-Red ceramics, 89–90

Kayenta region: abandonment patterns at Point of Pines Pueblo after first fifty years of occupation by migrants from, 84–87; and architectural analysis of Point of Pines Pueblo as case study on migration and host-migrant interactions, 1–2; history of archaeological research in, 35–40; and host-migrant interactions at Point of Pines Pueblo, 11–12, 29–30,